JOHN BETJEMAN

John Betjeman was born in 1906 and educated at Marlborough and Magdalen College, Oxford. He gave his first radio talk in 1932; future appearances made him into a national celebrity. He was knighted in 1969 and appointed Poet Laureate in 1972. He died in 1984.

STEPHEN GAMES

Stephen Games writes on architecture and language. He was educated at Magdalene College, Cambridge. He has worked for the *Independent*, *Guardian* and *Los Angeles Times*, and was deputy editor of the RIBA Journal. He is the editor of *Trains and Buttered Toast*, a collection of John Betjeman's radio talks.

CONTENTS

PREFACE

Tennis Whites and Teacakes includes a wealth of examples of Betjeman's writing over half a century, from 1927 to 1979. To give this writing a structure that will help the reader make sense of it, the book has been broken down into themes that illustrate his deep engagement with England and also the way in which he uses events in his own life to explore aspects of Englishness. These themes are loosely chronological, though what they contain is only as chronological as sense would allow.

As always, space was the principal factor determining how much material went in, but there was also a strong editorial feeling that this should be an enjoyable book. For that reason a lot of his more serious writings have been omitted, as well as his more scornful, which necessarily includes many of his bitter humoresques from the 1950s, which can go on at some length to make points that we now regard as self-evident. The drudgework that he did by rote once, twice and three times a week has also been left out and I talk about this at greater length in the Introduction.

In editing the texts I have not felt that there was any definitive version that deserved to be replicated. Having examined many of Betjeman's earlier and later drafts, where they exist, I have noted extensive variations between what he first put down on paper and what was eventually published, whether because what he first wrote was hurried or because words were wrongly transcribed by his secretaries or because changes – for content or housestyle – were imposed on him after he had handed his copy in. He tended to write in long paragraphs which were regularly broken up into smaller paragraphs by newspaper sub-editors; and sometimes his most florid phrases – quite possibly written just to annoy the man on the desk with the green eye-shade and the stubby pencil – were hastily deleted, as he presumed they would be.* A recurring editorial task has been the question of what to reinstate. Since this is not an academic book, however, such decisions have not usually been footnoted.

Writing is not a precise science; nor does meaning stay the same. Occasionally, where there was good reason for doing so, I have made adjustments that help Betjeman's meaning and make it more immediate. In doing so I have acted as any editor would have done had he or she been working with a living author. In the same way I have tried to bring consistency to Betjeman's style of presentation, which itself changed during the course of his lifetime, and to iron out glitches where his punctuation grated with or fought against his meaning. I have also tried to bring consistency to writings culled from different publishing houses and edited in different ways: Batsford in the 1940s did not edit in the same way as Times Newspapers in 1970; Penguin Books in the late 1940s did not like full stops after 'Mr'; other publishers did. And then there is the different house style of John Murray. Had appropriate changes not been made, I would have done Betjeman a disservice by making his writing look incoherent.

Modes of writing and punctuation have changed. Commas were used liberally in the past; today, however, they can act as impediments. We no longer use them to chop sentences into phrases; nor do we any longer feel the need for what are known as Oxford commas, which American publishers still use quite liberally; nor do we add a comma after a phrase that locates what is to follow in time ('In 1876 the family moved to Clifton', not 'In 1876, the family moved to Clifton') even though a slight pause may be called for. Some changes have to do with meaning and the immediacy with which punctuation ought to serve meaning. Other changes are more stylistic: we no longer write 'to-day' or ''bus' or ''teens' or 'Oxford-street',

---

* For example, a book review dated 19 March 1950 – not included here – starts with one of his conventional apostrophes to nature and the landscape ('White violets and wood anemones were out, chestnut buds were sticky, bird-song had rinsed the air, stone cottages and church towers were gold against the blue skies, ploughs looked wet and brown and grass was emerald. Even in the towns we could not help knowing it was spring and things were coming to life . . .'). One quick stroke of the pencil shows that his sub-editor was less charmed by his lyrical diversions than we are.

as Betjeman or his copyeditors would have done. New compound words, once hyphenated or written as separate words, may have fused into single words. And because time has moved on, it may not help the reader to allow decades to appear as, say, 'the thirties' if there is any doubt about whether the writer means the 1830s or 1930s. Where these and other points may have led to questions, even momentarily, I have made changes. I have also adjusted colons and semi-colons where Betjeman's use of these has gone against the conventions of today.

At the same time I have tried to pay respect to what we would now regard as various archaisms of his such as a far more liberal approach to capital letters, especially in place names – 'Paddington Station' rather than 'Paddington station'.

In several letters Betjeman made it clear that he regarded his first drafts as imperfect and relied on professionals to put the appropriate amount of polish on them. I hope that, in all this, I have done what he would have expected any other editor or, at the BBC, producer to do. On the question of how to edit Betjeman's television scripts – a format not well received by the general reader and not easily replicated in a book such as this – I refer to the problems this gives rise to in my Introduction. Briefly, I have sought a compromise that distinguishes the metrical writing from the unmetred and that takes up less space on the page than the two-column convention in which TV scripts are usually written.

Material for this book has come from numerous sources but in particular from the Special Collections Library of the University of Victoria in British Columbia, which is where Betjeman's archive resides. I have received endless help from the staff there, most notably Terry Tuey who has worked conscientiously and promptly to help me find and identify material, both at long distance and during my visit to the library during 2006. I am grateful to Jeff Walden of the BBC Written Archives Centre in Caversham, Berkshire, who has assisted me with many inquiries. I should like to thank the staff at the British Library at King's Cross and at the BL's Newspaper Library in Colindale for their help. And I am endlessly indebted to Peter Gammond and John Heald of the John Betjeman Society, for their friendly encouragement and for their invaluable checklist of

Betjeman's writings, the 2005 version of which I made great use of along with Bill Peterson's bibliography.

As for individuals, I want to record my thanks to: Edward Mirzoeff, for making available the scripts of the BBC television programmes that he made with Betjeman and for providing me with information about the production process that I incorporated into my Introduction; Jonathan Stedall, who directed Betjeman in television programmes emanating from the West of England and who also discussed their making with me; Mark Tewdwr-Jones of University College London who provided me with a Betjeman script and helped me with other questions; Candida Lycett Green, Betjeman's daughter, for replying to points that I raised and for supporting this project; Colin Wright of the John Betjeman Society; John Fisher of Peretti Publishing in Devon; Angela Jones and Dennis Pratt, both of ITV West; the Reverend Stephen Skinner of Lydiard Tregoz; Terry Rogers of Marlborough College; Colin Wright on William Lisle Bowles; Tony Rouse of Exeter Local Studies Library; Dr Robin Darwall-Smith of Magdalen College, Oxford; Helen Rogers of Victoria Library, Westminster, and many others.

(Not everyone I spoke to was as informed as I would have liked, however. Someone I wrote to in Devon to check the spelling of Lew Trenchard said she didn't know Lew Trenchard and asked who he was.)

I am hugely grateful also to: Rowan Yapp, my editor at John Murray, who has exercised impeccable editorial judgement in reconciling difficult questions about the direction of the book; the rest of the John Murray team including Caroline Westmore, Peter James, my copyeditor, Nick de Somogyi who proofread, and Douglas Matthews who compiled the index; Clare Alexander of Gillon Aitken; and Bracha Nemeth for her certain touch as an agent and for providing me, during the editing of this book, with my first child.

Finally, every effort has been made to clear permissions. If permission has not been granted and is needed, please contact the publisher who will include a credit in subsequent printings and editions.

Stephen Games
Muswell Hill, 2007

INTRODUCTION

This new collection of John Betjeman's writings, *Tennis Whites and Teacakes*, can be regarded as the second in a series of three Betjeman anthologies, the first being *Trains and Buttered Toast* and the third, *Sweet Songs of Zion*. These books expand our appreciation of Betjeman by presenting the lay reader with texts that have never been readily accessible before. We already knew Betjeman as the most engaging poet of the twentieth century; we now start to rediscover that he was a captivating prose writer too and one of considerable energy.

Together, the three books give more emphasis to Betjeman's prose writings than he has received before but there are important differences. *Trains and Buttered Toast* looked specifically at the best of the radio talks that Betjeman gave on the BBC – essays that Betjeman developed in partnership with his BBC producers and that represent his most considered and sustained performances on air. The essays in that book span his various interests from church architecture to seaside topography as well as marvellously funny recreations of Victorians whose eccentricities he relished or whose writings made them, in his view, heroic as missionaries for Christianity or Englishness. *Tennis Whites and Teacakes* illustrates the wide range of media he wrote for – books, newspapers, journals and television as well as radio; it also tries to make the links between these writings and his poetry more explicit.

Do a poet's prose writings deserve the same attention as his poetry? Betjeman always insisted that he was a poet first and claimed to be indifferent to his prose, if not contemptuous of it. In his autobiographical poem *Summoned by Bells*, published in 1960, he wrote:

> I knew as soon as I could read and write
> That I must be a poet.

Six years earlier, when reviewing the reception given to his latest volume of poems, he insisted on the primacy of poetry over prose: 'As early as I can remember I have read and written verse. I have always preferred it to prose, known that its composition was my vocation and anything else I have written has been primarily a means of earning money in order to buy the free time in which to write poetry.' As for journalism, he openly despised both the hackwork of Fleet Street and its aura of glamour. Reviewing a biography of the popular novelist William Le Queux in 1939, he wrote:

> Every year young people who were 'good at school' or who learned Anglo-Saxon and Northumbrian, which is mostly taught in the name of English literature at Oxford – every year such literary aspirants come to London under the impression that they will do well in journalism. Poor innocents, they have no idea what journalism is. I would advise them to read this life of a successful journalist and then take to farming.

In spite of all he said, however, Betjeman was far from immune to the lure of the popular press. He had always found writing easy and was happy to accept a succession of high-profile positions with national newspapers, not least because such posts gave him status, an expense account and privileged access to celebrities. He landed his first column – that of film critic for the *Evening Standard* – at the age of twenty-seven and went on to become book critic for the *Daily Herald* and *Daily Telegraph*, diarist at the *Spectator* and *Daily Telegraph* and editor of *Decoration* (briefly) and *Time and Tide*. He wrote two series for the *Daily Express* and frequent ad-hoc articles for the *New Statesman and Nation*, *Punch* and other periodicals.

The quality of his journalism was patchy and reached a low point in his film and book reviews. In the case of his film writing, his contempt for the movie industry deterred him from finding a skilful way of writing about it. He was tortured by his moral objection to the commercialism and hyperbole of film-making and by his involuntary role as a cog in its publicity machine. He was also embarrassed that his readers were mostly women and that, in his own words, film writing was 'pandering to the box-office and to the lowest elements in a cinema audience'. Initially, and with only a slender knowledge of movies, he tried to write against the medium. He would under-play the stars he was sent to interview during breaks in filming at Elstree and other English studios and promote whatever alternatives he could find to Hollywood – notably shorts and documentaries – as long as they were natural rather than 'arty'. In a futile but characteristic campaign of resistance he would also doctor his articles with waggish untruths. He claimed, for example, in one piece that the American actresses Anna May Wong and Myrna Loy shared an interest in medieval ecclesiastical architecture and in another that 'the original Mr Metro' of Metro-Goldwyn-Mayer 'took his name from the Underground system in Paris, although he was an American'. Sometimes, he even got mileage out of those readers who thought he cared about what he wrote: 'Professor Julian Huxley, who is now secretary of the Zoological Society of London, writes to point out that I was inaccurate in stating that Claude Dampier, the wireless comedian and film actor, is a descendant of the famous biologist Professor Thomas Huxley, who was Professor Julian Huxley's grand-father.'

As he saw more films, he began to appreciate more the mechanics of film directing and editing and was more willing to admit to an enthusiasm for at least two of its genres: thrillers and comedies (but not musicals or historical romances). None of this translated into articles of greater sophistication. Instead, every Monday, Wednesday and Saturday, for a year and a half, he wrote the same schoolgirlish reviews, usually printed prominently across the top halves of a double-page spread. Here he listed the bits he liked and disliked in the latest films, peppering his notes with quirky snippets about stars and studio execu-tives:

> Jessie Matthews lying in bed in very elab-
> orate silk pyjamas. That was one glimpse I
> was allowed at Shepherd's Bush. George
> Arliss being hauled up before a French
> magistrate. That was the other. You will
> notice a slight change in Jessie Matthews's
> appearance in her new film, 'First a Girl',
> which is directed by Victor Savile. She is

3

> dressed as a boy. So her forehead has been
> lowered. This means the most skilful make-
> up; increasing the extent of her hair over
> her forehead by about an inch. 'Otherwise
> I look bald,' she told me.

So childish were these pieces, with their occasional sideswipes at the entire industry and his requirement to pander to it, that one marvels today at his capacity to survive in the job. (Who else, even then, could get away with sentences like 'I have not finished about short films yet' or 'This is quite a good film' or 'This film is certainly interesting'?) That he did survive, for nineteen months, says a lot for how popular he was with that group of aristocratic friends who held court at the *Standard* and who had brought him on to the paper in the first place. Whether Betjeman himself knew how deplorable his film reviewing was is unclear. In a farewell article he wrote in August 1935, after being sacked for insubordination,* he suggested that over-exposure to films had damaged his capacity to write intelligently; in reality, his earlier and later pieces are indistinguishable.

In the case of his book reviews some years later, it wasn't antipathy to the medium that he complained about but the treadmill nature of the job. Book reviewing kept him extraordinarily well informed and gave him a platform to flaunt his entrée with the writers he wrote about but meant having to deal with up to a dozen novels every week, most of them – in his view – worthless, and this he regarded as an intolerable chore. His technique was 'writing the reviews at length first, and then reducing them to little more than three or four sentences. This is heart-breaking work.'† In addition 'I have to plan my articles in such a way that they can be cut without being made to look more than usually ridiculous.'‡ What he ended up with looked very much like his film reviews: gossipy summaries

---

* Betjeman had refused to interview a film star who had just arrived by boat at Southampton from New York.
† Contribution to 'Rates for Reviewing', *Author, Playwright and Composer*, Summer 1947.
‡ Ibid.

fleshed out with odd observations about writers and their publishing background.

None of these articles, nor his diary pieces in the *Spectator* and *Daily Telegraph*, demands space in *Tennis Whites and Teacakes*, even for illustrational purposes, nor does any of them give any indication of how well he wrote for other publications and under other circumstances. They show, instead, a practical problem that Betjeman had with his writing. Throughout his life, he felt he lacked financial security and this made him take on long-term commitments that he resented doing and carried out grudgingly. He had a claustrophobic horror of enforced drudgery: quoting his friend Evelyn Waugh he habitually referred to the modern political system as the 'slave state'. He needed novelty and stimulation; when he didn't get it, he coasted. Repetitive exercises drained him and made him intellectually lazy and self-excusing. That is not to say that his hackwork necessarily lacked passion. His columns for the *Spectator* and *Daily Telegraph*, in the 1950s and 1960s, included crusading paragraphs on the horrors of modern planning but the writing for these publications was invariably thin and fragmentary, often substituting bitterness and sarcasm for wit.

This, no doubt, is what Betjeman was thinking of whenever he dismissed his own journalism and prose as secondary to his poetry. And yet in his more jaundiced moments he could mock all his pretensions – poetic as well as journalistic. Here, for example, is how he represented himself in the farewell article in the *Evening Standard* referred to above:

> Yesterday I wrote my last article as film critic in this paper. When I started off, a pale green bogus-intellectual, a year and a half ago, what a different man I was.
>
> A visit to some Continental films, a sarcastic sneer to any people who told me they were in love with Greta Garbo, and that was the sum of my cinematic experience. The word 'montage' was on my lips, 'art' was written in poker work across my heart, 'prose style' was

---

* Far from being an elderly man, Betjeman was eight days short of his twenty-ninth birthday.

embroidered with raffia on the reverse side of it.

I was as typical a middlebrow as ever thought he was highbrow and tried to write poetry in Hampstead.

And now what would you see, were these lines of type to fly about and form themselves into a portrait of the author as on some French surrealist short film? You would see a bald elderly man,* still pale green, but with a tough expression, grim business-like lips and a pair of unscrupulous eyes gleaming behind recently acquired horn-rimmed spectacles. In fact, you would see a typical member of the film business.

Betjeman's outing of himself as a fraud and a chameleon crops up throughout his life. So does his portrayal of himself as either the beneficiary of undeserved good fortune or, as below, the victim of undeserved lack of recognition. 'This week I celebrated my fiftieth birthday,' he wrote in the *Spectator* in August 1956.

I had felt it coming on for some time. Standing nude in the bathroom two months ago, I suddenly realised I could not see my toes any more because my stomach was in the way. I started reviewing my past life through a magnifying mist of self-pity – never quite made the grade, not taken seriously by the *Times Literary Supplement*, Penguin Books, the Courtauld, the Warburg, the *Listener*, the University Appointments Board, the Library Association, the Institute of Sanitary Engineers. I thought of the many people at school with me who were now knights and politicians. I wanted to cry.

This, and many other examples of either mournfulness or self-deprecation (the latter, especially, in the context of attractive young women now out of his reach), may reflect real pangs of existential anxiety but they are also a form of exhibitionism that Betjeman employed – with some success – to gain sympathy (especially from women still within his reach). Taking his public dismissals of himself and of his writing at face value is therefore not a reliable guide to what he really thought. In a private letter to John Sparrow, during Sparrow's editing of Betjeman's *Selected Poems* in 1947, Betjeman expressed much more confidence.

To describe me purely as a poet of place is to put me on the same level as Drinkwater's 'Mamble' (a place poem if ever there was one) and suchlike Georgians and to link me with Bloomfield than whom, I like to think, I am a better poet . . . I think I have something in common with Cowper (and Eliza Cooke, Jean Ingelow, Tom Hood) but nothing in common with Clare or Bloomfield. Those two last are poets of place only (Clare sometimes also of nature). Also my view of the world is that man is born to fulfil the purposes of his Creator, i.e. to Praise his Creator, to stand in awe of Him and to dread Him. In this way I differ from most modern poets, who are agnostics.

Betjeman did not write in the same confident way about his prose but he did address the general principle of prose's relationship with poetry. In the introduction to an anthology of prose and poetry about the Home Counties in 1947,* he scotched the notion of poetry's innate superiority, commenting that he found 'Miss Mitford's description of Richmond, for instance . . . infinitely better than the tedious poem by Maurice called *Richmond Hill*, which uses as many pages as Miss Mitford uses words to convey half the effect of that luxuriant landscape'. He went on to quote three paragraphs from a mid-nineteenth-century writer whose description of the Vale of the White Horse and of coursing on the Berkshire Downs – where Betjeman lived and which he himself wrote poems about – was 'one more example of prose that is topographical poetry'.

The attentive reader is struck by a similar equivalence of poetry and prose in areas of Betjeman's own work. Betjeman was a natural storyteller and consequently, perhaps, the best narrative poet of the twentieth century. He had several subjects that he went back to again and again – childhood, Oxford, the railways, landscape – and he used the same techniques to explore these subjects, whatever medium he was writing in. Sometimes his language and phrasing were interchangeable; sometimes what he said in one medium was a variant of what he had already said in another. *Tennis Whites and Teacakes*

---

* Introduction to *An Anthology of the Home Counties*, edited by John D. Mortimer (Methuen, 1947).

includes three versions – two in poetry, one in prose – of what was obviously a painful memory from his childhood, that of being thought a 'common little boy' by an adult whom he liked and wanted to be liked by. Each version has its differences – different names, different locations – and these differences, illustrating how much Betjeman's autobiographical 'facts' were subject to creative manipulation, only become fully apparent when seen together, as here.

Tennis Whites and Teacakes also makes the interplay of Betjeman's poetry and prose explicit by taking four of his longer essays – 'Childhood Days' (1950), 'Upper School' (1932). 'My Oxford' (1977) and 'The Great Western' (1970) – as well as the shorter fragment 'Tea Dances and Nightclubs' (1954) and interleaving poems into them. The point of this is to highlight the extent to which Betjeman's poetry and verse overlap and borrow from each other and to raise the question of where the dividing line comes between the two forms. If such editorialising seems over-interventionist, one need only look at Betjeman's own television scripts to see that he did exactly the same thing himself, oscillating

> from verse to prose to verse and back again,
> or sometimes hovering somewhere in between,

or breaking up his own newly minted narrative

> with fragments of his own and others' poems.★

Here, for example, is a simple rendering of what a television viewer would have heard him say in 'The Englishman's Home', the first of three programmes that he made as part of a thirteen-part BBC series called *Bird's-Eye View* that was broadcast on bank holidays between April 1969 and April 1971:

Seaside brings out the best in all of us. When England left her inland spas for sea, following royal fashion (not able to travel to Europe because of the wars with Napoleon), Brighton became what still it is: the best-looking seaside resort we've got. Those cheerful stucco squares and promenades, those winding paths, romantic clumps of

---

★ These are Stephen Games's lines, not Betjeman's.

shrub, all in the curving Georgian landscape style, an intended contrast with straight seaside fronts, they were all the work of speculative
builders before spec. building got its dirty name. Spec. building of the
Thirties – 1830s.

What his words actually looked like laid out on the page of the script
was this:

> Seaside brings out the best in all of us
> When England left her inland spas for sea
> Following royal fashion
> (not able to travel to Europe because of the
>   wars with Napoleon)
> Brighton became what still it is:
> The best-looking seaside resort we've got.
>
> Those cheerful stucco squares and promenades
> Those winding paths, romantic clumps of shrub
> All in the curving Georgian landscape style
> An intended contrast with straight seaside fronts,
> They were all the work of speculative builders
> Before spec. building got its dirty name.
> Spec. building of the Thirties – 1830s.

Is this prose? Is it poetry? Is it partly one and partly the other?
In this case, normal textual analysis – asking whether his lines are
short, for example, because they are poetic or because this is how
all speech is formatted in the narrow right-hand column of a television script – misses the point that the words themselves were not
the finished product. As Edward Mirzoeff, the producer and editor
of the *Bird's-Eye View* series, observes, 'Betjeman's delivery was
always poetic in my films, with occasional, and deliberate, excur-
sions into conversational speech. It is important to remember that
in these films Betjeman was writing words to be spoken, not read.
They counterpointed the pictures. The films *as a whole* he saw as
poems, not the words alone. (That was why he did not believe they
should be printed.)' As for the appearance of Betjeman's words on
the page, 'His texts have nothing to do with the way TV scripts
were typed. He wrote the lines, by hand, in that poetic way, with

capitalisation and line breaks, partly because that was how he wrote poetic prose, to get the rhythms and pacing – rhythm was everything – and partly of course to match the pictures. It was all about how he heard the rhythms in his inner ear and how he was to speak it when we recorded the commentary.'*

While all Betjeman's television scripts may be poetic, not all depend on blank verse (unrhymed lines of five iambs), although 'iambic pentameter was the rule, often varied and broken' as Mirzoeff adds, because 'Betjeman believed that people often spoke in this rhythm without realising it.' Sometimes he rhymes, in couplets, triplets or alternate lines; and sometimes the metre changes from pentameter (five feet) to heptameter (seven feet).

Betjeman was in his early sixties when he participated in Mirzoeff's *Bird's-Eye View* programmes. In a series of fifteen-minute films that he made in his late fifties for TWW,† his approach to the writing had been more spontaneous and there was no assumption that the scripts would be poetic. For a programme about Clevedon, which the film crew visited in winter, 'Betjeman imagined what the elderly residents of a hotel were thinking and feeling and saying to each other,' recalls the director of these films, Jonathan Stedall; 'in Bath, he carried on an imaginary dialogue with a property developer: he was a wonderful mimic. In Sidmouth he wrote in verse but there was no conscious policy about him doing this: it just evolved as we went along.'‡

Betjeman's most highly crafted programmes (which therefore excludes his unscripted appearances in television panel games and quizzes) prior to the 1960s were his radio talks for the BBC, from the 1930s to the 1950s. Here, where he was carrying the entire burden of the broadcast rather than complementing a televisual image, any poetry that there might have been in his writing depended on the subject. The introduction to *Trains and Buttered Toast* quotes two of his radio talks from the first series of *Coast and Country* (1949), both of which begin

---

* Correspondence with Stephen Games, 27 February 2007.
† Television Wales and the West, the ITV broadcaster in Wales and the West of England from 1958 until 1968 when it lost its ten-year broadcasting franchise to HTV (Harlech Television).
‡ Conversation with Stephen Games, 28 February 2007.

with prose sentences written in blank verse: 'We came to Looe by unimportant lanes' and 'Safe and wide and sheltered Weymouth Bay!' What follows are pictorial descriptions of static scenes that rival classic English watercolours in their impact. The talk about Looe, for example, continues with three sentences, all of similar form:

> Burnt brown August hedges were high as houses either side of narrow lanes. Grey slate farms with granite round their windows hung on hill slopes. Little fields descended in steps of grass below them, to deserted mines, to meadows heavy with the smell of mint.

This clustering of detail into sequences of two and three sentences is typical of Betjeman's prose and his layering of information – here, in bands of colour. A few sentences later, he changes technique:

> I must confess to you here that when we first came into Looe by road, I was disappointed. I could hardly see the two old towns and the long Victorian stone bridge that joins them. I could hardly see the houses for motorcars. Motor coaches from Manchester, new private cars like sleek sausages belonging to Government officials and black-market men, battered pre-war motors belonging to failed literary men like me – there they stretched along the quays in thousands.

In this section poetic effect is achieved through delay and repetition ('I could hardly see the two old towns . . . I could hardly see the houses . . .'; 'Motor coaches from Manchester . . . new private cars like sausages . . . battered pre-war motors . . .'). When he finally explains his thought, he delivers it in pentameter ('there they stretched along the quays in thousands'), just as he had in the previous extract ('to meadows heavy with the smell of mint'). 'Sense matters less than the music the words make when they are spoken,' Betjeman wrote in his foreword to a book of children's nursery rhymes in 1975.* 'Nursery rhymes sing in the head before we ever learn to read. And if we don't quite know what they mean it doesn't matter: the rhythm and the jingle stay for life.'

---

* *Mother Goose: The Classic Purnell Edition.* Rearranged and edited by Eulalie Osgood Grover. Illustrated by Frederick Richardson. Purnell (Maidenhead, 1975).

One other lyrical quality that Betjeman brought to his prose was that of wistfulness or sentimentality, ornamented with Victorian apostrophes: 'Ah!', 'O!', 'Farewell!' and other exclamations. Sometimes the wistfulness relates to a personal regret:

Ah, with what longing did the girls of Weymouth, Wyke and Rodwell, lean from upstairs windows and look across to those twinkling lights and whisper the magic words 'The Fleet is in'! What dances! What parties! And do I not remember myself how, far too many years ago, I fell desperately in love with a Weymouth girl, the most beautiful girl I have ever seen in my life. I never declared my affection then. It is too late to declare it now for I am married and she may be dead or married too. But her surname was Streetfield and her Christian name, I think, Diana. A dance at the Gloucester Hotel was it – and something to do with the Yacht Club? I do not think I even had a dance with her. I just looked and loved while the moon shimmered in Weymouth Bay and the fleet twinkled in Portland Harbour and the band played 'My Sweet Hortense'. Weymouth of the Fleet, farewell!

Sometimes the wistfulness relates to a threatened world:

When I am abroad and I want to remember what is the most typically English town – if anything is typically English – then I think of Highworth. It is the sort of town read about in novels from *Cranford* to Miss Macnaughten. Ah, Highworth as a whole! Churches and chapels; doctors' houses; the vicarage; walled gardens with pears and plums; the railway station; inns; the distant cemetery; old shops and winding streets.*

The poetic voice that Betjeman employed in writing and narrating these radio talks of 1949 and 1950 was partly natural and partly acquired. The acquired part went back a decade and a half earlier to his befriending and writing about a number of architects of his grandfather's generation (in his words, 'with the stimulus of hospitality and a sympathetic ear') whose elderly manners he started to affect along with his fondness for their now unfashionable Arts and

---

* From the second series of *Coast and Country*, 1950.

Crafts architecture. This self-conscious ageing was fostered by a young BBC producer from the year below him at Oxford, J. C. Pennethorne Hughes. Betjeman had come down from Oxford without a degree and with no idea of what he wanted to do. Friends encouraged him to give talks on the radio but most of his contacts at the BBC found him too juvenile to risk putting on air, a rejection that made him feel increasingly at odds with London, authority and the modern world, all of which he identified the BBC with. As *Trains and Buttered Toast* reveals at greater length, it was only as a result of moving out of London in early 1934 – a move intended as a counter-rebuff – that his fortunes as a radio broadcaster started to improve. He chose Uffington, on the edge of Oxfordshire and Berkshire, as his new home because it was the farthest country station on any line from London that had trains to fit in with his work hours. By chance this brought him within range of the BBC's new West of England studios in Bristol, where Pennethorne Hughes got him to calm down, drop his shrill manner and use the more elderly persona that would become his hallmark. In his new identity, Betjeman presented a series of talks in 1937 that attacked what he regarded as the corrosive cosmopolitanism of modern town planning. The talks were extremely successful, forcing the BBC in London to reappraise him and to start giving him the opportunities that would turn him into a minor celebrity after the war broke out. It was through this chain of events that we start hearing his slower speaking voice and the poetry that came with it – a voice marvellously represented by those wartime talks in which he muses on the emotions triggered by distant thoughts of the English landscape and by the musicality of English place names: Huish Episcopi, Whitchurch Canicorum, Willingale Spain, Tickencote, Bourton-on-the-Hill.

Betjeman's sentimentality about the country and his opposition to the encroachment of London made him the trademark figure we now always visualise him as. We can barely imagine him except as he appeared on television in later life: a plump, elderly uncle in a battered felt hat, peering into churches and lamenting the building of pylons and motorways. But before the old Betjeman there was a young Betjeman who, in his earliest days as a journalist – before his ideas had started to coalesce – was surprisingly open about the world that he had been let loose into. There is very little poetry in his prose writings of this period but this is more than compensated for by his sheer vitality as a fledgling writer just starting to look around and get the measure of himself and his surroundings.

What brought Betjeman's early prose to life was its energy. At the same time as he was writing his grumbly film reviews for the *Evening Standard* he was also writing the *Standard* busy pieces on subjects other than film: articles on eccentric peers (December 1933), the new Empire Swimming Pool in Wembley (July 1934), bullying at public school (August 1934), hardship among the clergy (November 1934), varieties of teashop (June 1935), May Day celebrations (May 1936), railway branch lines (August 1936) and London sightseeing tours (September 1936) – all of which can be found in the pages that follow. As one of his radio producers, David Winter, said of him forty years later, 'What I came to learn was that he did everything with enthusiasm, mainly because if it didn't enthuse him he simply didn't do it at all.'

Betjeman's early prose shows him exploring a far greater range of ideas than is usually acknowledged. Alongside a treasury of articles about the joys of English railways or the effect of light on the Cornish coast, we find him, for example, welcoming in 1935 the architecture of Gropius and in 1938 American prefabrication – astonishing, now, for the man who has become the patron saint of the heritage industry. The common response to this is to dismiss it as a youthful aberration – a self-deluding attempt to fit in with the smart set at the *Architectural Review*, where he worked between 1930 and 1935. His own writings provide a better explanation – and one that has been played down: that he gravitated towards Gropius not so much because he was in love with Bauhaus minimalism as because he saw it as a purgative to something he disliked much more – the mainstream architecture of the day. Years later, as an old man who liked to please, he welcomed initiatives from young historians to preserve buildings from the 1930s but during the 1930s and for most of his life he deplored these buildings as much as he deplored the rash of mock-Tudor bungalows then spreading across the country. This was not just because he preferred what was there before but because he regarded the new architecture, with its gigantism, its uplighting, its Classical and Spanish and Mayan and Egyptian themes, its streamlining, its zigzagging, its urns, its friezes, its scallops and its swags, as phoney. 'The most modern flats and houses in Germany have nothing so repulsively pretentious to show as the various modernistic designs that glisten in many a British parlour, the smartistic inspiration of some purely commercial workshop,' he told readers of the *New Statesman and Nation* in 1935 – not because he admired German discipline but because he was sickened by British vulgarity. Not until 1979, five years before his death, did he volunteer that in the case of Giles Gilbert Scott, the architect of Battersea Power Station (1929–35), he might be prepared to make an exception. (His early prose also lays the ghost that he was coerced into writing favourably about modern architecture while working at the *Architectural Review*. His writing was always his own and he was always able and allowed to show dissent.)

Betjeman's private letters show that in his early days, during England's last romp as an imperial power, he was indisputably a child of his times. In a radio talk about Evelyn Waugh in 1946, he remarked that 'we have both known Oxford of the twenties, schoolmastering, country house life in England and Ireland, chattering parties with the Bright Young Things in chromium flats and then piling into open cars to drive through midnight London and bathe by the moon in a Middlesex pond.' A particularly enjoyable read is his account of his first, excitable love affair. 'I ought to tell you that I proposed marriage to a jolly girl last weekend and got accepted,' he wrote in 1931 to his famously homosexual Oxford friend Patrick Balfour, Lord Kinross.

> I kissed first the tip of the nose and then the neck and then the forehead and we took off our shoes in order to go upstairs quietly and we turned off the lights and stood on the stone floor of the hall and suddenly two cool little hands were in mine and then a subtly unresisting body pressed against me and I kissed her full on the lips for the first time.

This was spiced with the revelation that, at twenty-five, he already had enough of a reputation to have to take steps to have the liaison hushed up. This was something of a shift for a man who had written to Balfour three years earlier 'I have got to go out with a lot of jolly girls now – oh God I wish I were dead.'

His writings show that he was equally at odds with his times. In a radio talk in August 1940, he admitted that he used to wish he had been born about 120 years earlier.

> I should have liked a childhood in the days of the Prince Regent. I should have liked to have woken up in the early morning to the sound of rumbling drays and rolling coaches and to have gone snipe shooting as a youth among the battalions of reeds and rushes that grew in London where Victoria Station stands today.

Alienation from the modern world was something he explored on many occasions, soliciting our pity but also courting our admiration. In his autobiographical poem *Summoned by Bells* (1960), he wrote of himself as:

> An only child, *deliciously* apart,
> Misunderstood and not like other boys.

Physically he thought himself ugly – 'There wasn't any reason for people to be kind to me. I wasn't attractive. I was a toothy yellow-faced little boy with a strong tendency to show off'* – but his low self-esteem was counterbalanced by a powerful sense of himself as a romantic rebel. In that guise his boy-self imagined that he had acquired a dramatic status in the world:

> Deep, dark and pitiful I saw myself
> In my mind's mirror, every step I took,
> A fascinating study to the world.

To be at odds with others, Betjeman's prose makes clear, was therefore not a tragedy but a triumph for him. It meant being special and superior and was thus a condition that he sought out rather than one he tried to avoid. His attraction to homosexual friends at Oxford was, similarly, for him, a positive expression of his revolt against the normal. And he was not alone, after the national trauma of the First World War, in finding a home for his alienation inside homosexuality. Where Betjeman went further was in revolting against his own revolt. He warmed to the older generation – the generation of Field

---

* From *Childhood Days*, BBC Home Service, 16 July 1950.

Marshal Douglas Haig – that his own generation felt had betrayed it and he championed individuals such as Henry Newbolt whose poetic and sentimental depictions of war had made him into a figure of ridicule and loathing for the young.

His letters show his contrarianism surfacing in a different way during the Second World War, when he challenged the Government's case for war and mocked the clichés of official propaganda:

> We are fighting for LIBERTY to make the world fit to live in for Democracy, to keep our splendid system of Local Government going, to make the world safe for Slough to go on and to see that every John Citizen gets a square deal so he can pay up his instalments into the Building Society without having to go without his Ovaltine . . . I enclose a poem, to hearten our lads 'somewhere in France'. Of course none of us wanted a scrap, but now it's here let's keep smilin' through. *There's a war on, you know* . . . Jolly, all this, isn't it?

'At present fighting in a war seems to me to be committing a new sin in defence of an old one,' Betjeman wrote to the church architect Ninian Comper more gravely in October 1939 and he told his friend the artist John Piper wearily in 1941, 'I wish I cared more about the war.' The man who fought tirelessly in his own war for the survival of Englishness was lukewarm when it came to taking up arms in other people's. *Tennis Whites and Teacakes* records his disenchantment.

We learn so much about Betjeman – and about his particular view of England and of poetry – from his prose that we have to give more weight to it than he did. Admittedly he loved his poetry more: 'I've shouted it out to myself time and time over, every line, hundreds of times over. I've shouted when driving motor cars, when walking in the streets or when I find myself in an empty railway carriage, and in this way I've polished and repolished stanzas and added internal rhymes to them.' He also practised his poetry on his friends. His prose was nothing like so burnished: it was written fast, alone – though with varying amounts of input from producers and commissioning editors – and to deadline. It was also routinely cut and pruned.* But it provides an essential context for understanding him better.

---

* See Preface.

Most obviously missing from this collection – apart from Betjeman's film writings and book reviews, already mentioned – are his more serious and didactic writings, especially on architecture. Also missing is much of his comic writing – for *Punch*, for example – usually because it lacks the freshness and insight that made him amusing in person. We are left with a boisterous, ambitious pre-war Betjeman who thinks he has the strength to save the world and a post-war Betjeman who, like Waugh, exists in a world that he has lost faith in and largely written off.

One other conspicuous absence is the writing he did not do. It turns out that he wrote no prose about beautiful women, only verse; and he wrote no verse about beautiful steam trains, only prose.* And then there is the mythology of what he wrote. The popular image of John Betjeman – popularised by his appearances on television, accompanied perhaps by the music of Walton's *Façade* – is that of an iconic Englishman, forever celebrating the Englishness of cricket on the village green, vicarage tea parties and morris dancing in the cathedral close. As *Tennis Whites and Teacakes* shows, this image is wholly false. Betjeman's view of England was always sceptical. The Victorian Sunday, so peaceful that you can hear the sheep grazing, is also the day when children are tyrannised by Papa for forgetting the catechism and the genteel classes look the other way when tradesmen pass. An Edwardian dinner party is overshadowed by the insensitivity of the guests and by our knowledge of their future deaths in the Great War. The thrill of thundering steam railways and remote branch lines is eclipsed by their future amalgamation into British Railways in 1947 and subsequent closure by Beeching. A cloud hangs over almost everything he cherishes. In Betjeman's writings about his childhood, both in prose and verse, he has a metaphor for this spoiling of longed-for delights: 'sand in the sandwiches'. The wonder of Betjeman, however, is that even as we read these refractory texts, what we come away with is the memory of tennis whites and teacakes.

---

* He has poems about the landscape that steam trains go through and about his experience of being ill on a train but not about his favourite prose theme, the majesty of the railways.

I

CHILDHOOD

Bullies and Beauties

Childhood Days (1950)
N.W.5 & N.6 (1957–8)
Narcissus (1965)
The Need to be a Poet (1960)
Peggy Purey-Cust (1960)
Miss Usher (1960)
False Security (1955)
Rivals (1960)
A German Spy (1960)
Highgate Junior School (1960)

CHILDHOOD DAYS

BBC Home Service
16 July 1950
Producer: Eileen Molony

• • •

Outside life was a see-saw when I was young. I expect it was the same with you. One moment ecstatic, rested, friendly, warm, unafraid. The next terrified, alone, ready to be hurt, secrets likely to be extracted by physical force. And over all there brooded the loneliness of Eternity. 'World without end, Amen.' That was the first phrase I can remember that really struck amazed terror to my heart. Something without an end. It was an appalling idea. And stars going on without stopping for millions of miles behind one another.

Lying in bed of a late summer evening I remember hearing the bells ring out from St Anne's Highgate Rise – the church where I was christened. They poured their sound, deep and sorrowful, over the chestnuts of the Burdett-Coutts estate, through the hornbeam leaves I could see from bed. Maud, the nurse, was looking out of the open window. Crossed in love, I suppose, and for once fairly gentle with me. I remember asking her if I should go to Heaven. 'You will, but I won't,' she said. I remember recognising even then that she spoke from her heart about herself. I did not recognise this, at the time, as any sign of grace in Maud. Nor did I really believe I would go to Heaven. Still less do I think so now.

N.W.5 & N.6

The Cornhill Magazine
Winter 1957–8

Red cliffs arise. And up them service lifts
Soar with the groceries to silver heights.
Lissenden Mansions. And memory sifts
Lilies from lily-like electric lights
And Irish stew smells from the smell of prams★
And roar of seas from roar of London trams.

Out of it all my memory carves the quiet
Of that dark privet hedge where pleasures breed,
There first, intent upon its leafy diet,
I watched the looping caterpillar feed
And saw it hanging in a gummy froth
Till, weeks on, from the chrysalis burst the moth.

I see black oak twigs outlined on the sky,
Red squirrels on the Burdett-Coutts estate.
I ask my nurse the question 'Will I die?'
As bells from sad St Anne's ring out so late,
'And if I do die, will I go to Heaven?'
Highgate at eventide. Nineteen-eleven.

'You will. I won't.' From that cheap nursery-maid,
Sadist and puritan as now I see,
I first learned what it was to be afraid,
Forcibly fed when sprawled across her knee
Lock'd into cupboards, left alone all day,
'World without end.' What fearsome words to pray.

'World without end.' It was not what she'd do
That frightened me so much as did her fear
And guilt at endlessness. I caught them too,

★ 'Prams', here, is a colloquialism for cars.

Hating to think of sphere succeeding sphere
Into eternity and God's dread will.
I caught her terror then. I have it still.

Then I had a clear vision of the Devil. I used to go up in a black lift made of wood. We would arrive at the top where it was blindingly white and I would be in this little wooden lift one side of which was open and showed that we were floating on a limitless white sea. But I was not alone in the lift. Oh no! There rose up from the corner a tall thin-faced man with ram's horns springing out of his forehead. He was the Devil. His horns were outlined black against the sky. He was coming nearer. There was no escape.

As dreams became less real, people became more so. Friends were important. Bill, Mary and Betty lived next door. They were my chief friends. Bill was, my mother told me, 'easily led'. Perhaps this was why I liked him so much. Mary had freckles and blue eyes. I have always loved people with freckles and blue eyes since. I think the saddest moment of my life, as numbing as any subsequent loss, was the time when Bill, Mary and Betty left the district. I was about seven years old. The pavements outside our houses on West Hill, the Heath, our little gardens, seemed empty for ever.

NARCISSUS

London Magazine
June 1965

Yes, it was Bedford Park the vision came from –
    de Morgan lustre glowing round the hearth,
And that sweet flower which self-love takes its name from
    Nodding among the lilies in the garth,
And Arnold Dolmetsch touching the spinet,
And Mother, Chiswick's earliest suffragette.

I was a delicate boy – my parents' only –
    And highly strung. My father was in trade.

And how I loved, when Mother left me lonely,
   To watch old Martha spice the marmalade.
Or help with flower arrangements in the lobby
Before I went to find my playmate Bobby.

We'd go for walks, we bosom boyfriends would
   (For Bobby's watching sisters drove us mad),
And when we just did nothing we were good,
   But when we touched each other we were bad.
I found this out when Mother said one day
She thought we were unwholesome in our play.

So Bobby and I were parted. Bobby dear,
   I didn't want my tea. I heard your sisters
Playing at hide-and-seek with you quite near.
   As off the garden gate I picked the blisters.
Oh tell me, Mother, what I mustn't do –
Then, Bobby, I can play with you again.

For I know hide-and-seek's most secret places
   More than your sisters do. And you and I
Can scramble into them and leave no traces,
   Nothing above us but the twigs and sky,
Nothing below us but the leaf-mould chilly
Where we can warm and hug each other silly.

My Mother wouldn't tell me why she hated
   The things we did, and why they pained her so.
She said a fate far worse than death awaited
   People who did the things we didn't know,
And then she said I was her precious child,
And once there was a man called Oscar Wilde.

'Open your story book and find a tale
   Of ladyes fayre and deeds of derring-do,
Or good Sir Gawaine and the Holy Grail,
   Mother will read her boy a page or two
Before she goes, this Women's Suffrage Week,
To hear that clever Mrs Pankhurst speak.

Sleep with your hands above your head. That's right –
   And let no evil thoughts pollute the dark.'
She rose, and lowered the incandescent light.
   I heard her footsteps die down Bedford Park.
Mother where are you? Bobby, Bobby, where?
I clung for safety to my teddy bear.

As early as I can remember I wanted to be a poet. Even today
when I am not writing poetry, I feel I am not fully justifying my
existence. I used to take Bill out on to Parliament Hill Fields and say
'We will write poetry.' I would sit on a seat on top of one of those
two little hills above Highgate Ponds and wait for inspiration, pencil
and paper on my knees. What he did I can't remember, except that
I made him bring pencil and paper too.

THE NEED TO BE A POET★

1960

I knew as soon as I could read and write
That I must be a poet. Even today,
When all the way from Cambridge comes a wind
To blow the lamps out every time they're lit,[†]
I know that I must light mine up again.
   My first attraction was to tripping lines;
Internal rhyming, as in Shelley's 'Cloud',
Seemed then perfection. 'O'er' and 'ere' and 'e'en'
Were words I liked to use. My father smiled:
'And how's our budding bard? Let what you write
Be funny, John, and be original.'
Secretly proud, I showed off merrily.
But certain as the stars above the twigs

★ Extract from Chapter 2, 'The Dawn of Guilt', of Betjeman's autobiographical
poem *Summoned by Bells*.
† A reference to the new 'modern' literary criticism being developed at Cambridge
under F. R. Leavis.

And deeply fearful as the pealing bells
And everlasting as the racing surf
Blown back upon itself in Polzeath Bay,
My urge was to encase in rhythm and rhyme
The things I saw and felt (I could not *think*).

    And so, at sunset, off to Hampstead Heath,
I went with pencil and with writing-pad
And stood tip-toe upon a little hill,
Awaiting inspiration from the sky.
'Look, there's a poet!', people might exclaim
On footpaths near. The muse inspired my pen:
The sunset tipped with gold St Michael's church,
Shouts of boys bathing came from Highgate Ponds,
The elms that hid the houses of the great
Rustled with mystery, and dirt-grey sheep
Grazed in the foreground; but the lines of verse
Came out like parodies of *A* & *M*.★

    The gap between my feelings and my skill
Was so immense, I wonder I went on.
A stretch of heather seen at Haslemere
And 'Up the airy mountain' (Allingham)
Merged in the magic of my Highgate pen:

> When the moors are pink with heather
>   When the sky's as blue as the sea
> Marching all together
>   Come fairy folk so wee.

My goodness me! It seemed perfection then –
The brilliance of the rhymes, A B, A B!
The vastness and the daintiness combined!
The second verse was rather less inspired:

> Some in green and some in red
>   And some with a violet plume,
> And a little cap on each tiny head
>   Watching the bright white moon.

★ *Hymns Ancient and Modern.*

I copied out the lines into a book,
A leather-bound one given me for verse
And stamped with my initials. There it stood
On the first page, that poem – a reproach.
In later years I falsified the date
To make it seem that I was only seven,
Not eight, when these weak stanzas were composed.
　　The gap from feeling to accomplishment!
In Highgate days that gap was yawning wide.

My father used to talk to me about the 'muse' and told me always to be original. And, of course, like all precocious children, I was derivative without realising it. Only healthy, normal children not afraid to be themselves are truly original. I wasn't at all healthy. Always in love. I mean even when I was seven and eight. Generally girls with red or gold hair and always with blue eyes.

PEGGY PUREY-CUST*

1960

O Peggy Purey-Cust, how pure you were:
My first and purest love, Miss Purey-Cust!
Satchel on back I hurried up West Hill
To catch you on your morning walk to school,
Your nanny with you and your golden hair
Streaming like sunlight. Strict deportment made
You hold yourself erect and every step
Bounced up and down as though you walked on springs.
Your ice-blue eyes, your lashes long and light,
Your sweetly freckled face and turned-up nose
So haunted me that all my loves since then
Have had a look of Peggy Purey-Cust.
Along the Grove, what happy, happy steps

---

* Extract from Chapter 3, 'Highgate', of *Summoned by Bells*.

Under the limes I took to Byron House,
And blob-work, weaving, carpentry and art,
Walking with you; and with what joy returned.
Wendy you were to me in *Peter Pan*,
The Little Match Girl in Hans Andersen –
But I would rescue you before you died.
And once you asked me to your house to tea:
It seemed a palace after 31* –
The lofty entrance hall, the flights of stairs,
The huge expanse of sunny drawing-room,
Looking for miles across the chimney-pots
To spired St Pancras and the dome of Paul's;
And there your mother from a sofa smiled.
After that tea I called and called again,
But Peggy was not in. She was away;
She wasn't well. *House of the Sleeping Winds*,
My favourite book with whirling art-nouveau
And Walter Crane-ish colour plates, I brought
To cheer her sick-bed. It was taken in.
Weeks passed and passed . . . and then it was returned.
Oh gone for ever, Peggy Purey-Cust!

The enjoyable things of childhood one takes for granted. My mother making my old teddy bear Archie talk, my father taking me for silent, deeply contented walks, old Mrs Wallis letting me read poetry to her while we ate slices of hot buttered toast. And now while I'm on them, those enjoyable things, let me remember them while you remember people who were kind to you when you were a child.

There wasn't any reason for people to be kind to me. I wasn't attractive. I was a toothy yellow-faced little boy with a strong tendency to show off. Yet lots of people were – always. It is so hard to be kind to children without being frightening (as I am) or unconsciously cruel. For I now recollect the shameful and cruel incident of Miss Tunstead. She was a governess down in Cornwall. Whatever she

---

* 31 West Hill, Highgate – the Betjeman family home. The Purey-Custs lived at No. 82.

said was right. And she said Miss Fisher was coming to stay. All of us
children must try to please Miss Fisher. Miss Fisher was very nice
indeed. Well, I went hell for leather to please Miss Fisher. I had something to say all the time. 'Did Miss Fisher like me?' I asked after she
had gone. 'Shall I tell you what Miss Fisher said, John? – *pause* – she
said she thought you were rather a common little boy.'

MISS USHER *

1960

Do you remember, Joan, the awkward time
When we were non-co-operative at sports,
Refusing to be organised in heats?
And when at last we were, and had to race
Out to low-tide line and then back again,
A chocolate biscuit was the only prize?
I laughed. Miss Tunstall sent me home to bed.
You laughed, but not so loudly, and escaped.
   That was the summer Audrey, Joc and I
And all the rest of us were full of hope:
'Miss Usher's coming.' Who Miss Usher was,
And why she should be coming, no one asked.
She came, a woman of the open air,
Swarthy and in Girl Guide-y sort of clothes:
How nice she was to Audrey and to Joc,
How *very* nice to Biddy and to Joan . . .
But somehow, somehow, not so nice to me.
'I *love* Miss Usher,' Audrey said. 'Don't you?'
'Oh yes,' I answered. 'So do I,' said Joc
'We vote Miss Usher topping. Itchicoo!'
What was it I had done? Made too much noise?
Increased Miss Tunstall's headache? Disobeyed?
After Miss Usher had gone home to Frant,

---

* Extract from Chapter 4, 'Cornwall in Childhood', of *Summoned by Bells*.

Miss Tunstall took me quietly to the hedge:
'Now shall I tell you what Miss Usher said
About you, John?' 'Oh please, Miss Tunstall, do!'
'She said you were a common little boy.'

Why did I mind? Heaven knows. But I still do and I bet you would
too. Silly Miss Tunstead, that wasn't the way to make me improve my
manners! The enjoyable things I took for granted – it's the first signs
that people aren't perfect that stick in my memory. They come as
such a shock.

FALSE SECURITY

London Magazine
May 1955

I remember the dread with which I at a quarter past four
Let go with a bang behind me our house front door
And, clutching a present for my dear little hostess tight,
Sailed out for the children's party into the night
Or rather the gathering night. For still some boys
In the near municipal acres were making a noise
Shuffling in fallen leaves and shouting and whistling
And running past hedges of hawthorn, spikey and bristling.
And black in the oncoming darkness stood out the trees
And pink shone the ponds in the sunset ready to freeze
And all was still and ominous waiting for dark
And the keeper was ringing his closing bell in the park
And the arc lights started to fizzle and burst into mauve
As I climbed West Hill to the great big house in The Grove,
Where the children's party was and the dear little hostess.
But halfway up stood the empty house where the ghost is
I crossed to the other side and under the arc
Made a rush for the next kind lamp-post out of the dark
And so to the next and the next till I reached the top
Where the Grove branched off to the left. Then ready to drop

I ran to the ironwork gateway of number seven
Secure at last on the lamplit fringe of Heaven.
Oh who can say how subtle and safe one feels
Shod in one's children's sandals from Daniel Neal's,
Clad in one's party clothes made of stuff from Heal's?
And who can still one's thrill at the candle shine
On cakes and ices and jelly and blackcurrant wine,
And the warm little feel of my hostess's hand in mine ?
Can I forget my delight at the conjuring show?
And wasn't I proud that I was the last to go?
Too overexcited and pleased with myself to know
That the words I heard my hostess's mother employ
To a guest departing, would ever diminish my joy,
I WONDER WHERE JULIA FOUND THAT STRANGE, RATHER
    COMMON LITTLE BOY?

I knew I wasn't perfect myself. But I had always assumed that
everyone else was and that there was something wrong with me. I
mean, that strong desire to smash the faces of china dolls, locking a
little girl into the lavatory and waiting outside until she cried – things
of a sort I thought were peculiar to me. Being an only child I didn't
compare notes. I preferred my own company to that of other children always. I preferred electric trains and maps of the underground
railways to people any day. I believed inanimate objects could feel and
think. I felt very sorry for horse chestnuts if they were left on the
road. I picked them up and took them home. A wooden train I had
gave me a lot of trouble. It was badly smashed but I thought it would
be offended if I threw it away. I kissed it good night every night so
that it should not be offended. If you are a psychoanalyst listening
you can probably explain all this. But I've since discovered that most
young children are animists so it's not so unusual after all.

Growing out of this private world of trains, maps, flags of nations,
poems and church bells was painful. I recollect Jack Drayton, a dis-
senting minister's son. He asked me to tea. He was very nice to me.
He showed off at tea and made me laugh. Then he grew thick with
Willie Dunlop, a fat little boy who even when he was seven looked
like the beefy business man he probably now is. Together they waited

for me after school one afternoon. 'You come down Fitzroy Avenue,' they said. I did. But they seemed a bit strange. 'Stand here,' said Drayton and stood me against a wall. 'You're not to speak to us, see?' 'Yes.' 'Promise.' 'Yes.' 'Punch him, Willie.' Willie punched. It winded me a bit. I started to blub. They ran away. I had no idea why they had suddenly turned nasty. I don't know to this day. Perhaps one of their parents had said, 'You're not to know that horrid little Betjeman boy.' That happened going home from a kindergarten – Byron House, Highgate. It was an enlightened, happy place. Jack and Willie were its only blots.

RIVALS★

1960

And at that happy school in Byron House
Only one harbinger of future woe
Came to me in those far, sun-gilded days –
Gold with the hair of Peggy Purey-Cust –
Two other boys (my rivals, I suppose)
Came suddenly round a corner, caught my arms
And one, a treacherous, stocky little Scot,
Winded me with a punch and 'Want some more?'
He grunted when I couldn't speak for pain.
Why did he do it? Why that other boy,
Who hitherto had been a friend of mine,
Was his accomplice I could not divine,
Nor ever have done.

When I went on to another day school, this detestable couple had got there first. The 1914 war had just broken out. I was eight. One of the most hellish things then was having a foreign name. Though any educated person knows that a name with 'etje' must be Dutch or Flemish, all foreign names were German in those days. So I was

---

★ Extract from Chapter 3, 'Highgate', of *Summoned by Bells*.

greeted by Jack Drayton and Willie Dunlop, and some others they had gathered round, with 'Betjeman's a German spy! Betjeman's a Geman spy!' They shouted and danced round me in rings. Oh, would to God I were called Smith or Brown! I blubbed until the bell rang for school.

A GERMAN SPY*

1960

In late September, in the conker time,
When Poperinghe and Zillebeke and Mons
Boomed with five-nines, large sepia gravures
Of French, Smith-Dorrien and Hague were given
Gratis with each half-pound of Brooke Bond tea.
A neighbour's son had just been killed at Ypres;
Another had been wounded. *Rainbow* came
On Wednesdays – with the pranks of Tiger Tim,
And Bonnie Bluebell and her magic gloves.
'Your country needs you!' serious Kitchener
Commanded from the posters. Up West Hill
I walked red-capped and jacketed to school,
A new boy much too early: school at nine,
And here I was outside at half-past eight.
I see the asphalt slope and smell again
The sluggish, sour, inadequate latrines.
I watch the shrubbery shake as, leaping out,
Come my two enemies of Byron House,
But now red-capped and jacketed like me:

> 'Betjeman's a German spy –
> Shoot him down and let him die:
> Betjeman's a German spy,
> A German spy, a German spy.'

---

* Extract from Chapter 3, 'Highgate', of *Summoned by Bells*.

They danced around me and their merry shouts
Brought other merry newcomers to see.

Merciful school bell. The dullest lessons were preferable to the
company of the boys in the breaks. 'Booting' was the great thing at
that school. Two boys held you and another took a running kick at
your bottom to see how far he could boot you down an asphalt
slope.

The school was so bad that when a boy with a withered arm
was admitted, the headmaster had to come round and tell us not to
laugh at him for it. All boys are self-righteous prigs, so of course we
didn't – once we were told. And the headmaster of this London day
school terrified us. He used to stand us round in a ring in class and
ask us questions. When we couldn't answer he shook us till we cried.
One good thing he did was to stop the throwing of steel-pointed
darts dipped in ink. One stuck in my head and raised a lump.

HIGHGATE JUNIOR SCHOOL*

1960

Let those who have such memories recollect
Their sinking dread of going back to school.
I well remember mine. I see again
The great headmaster's study lined with books
Where somewhere, in a corner, there were canes.
He wrapped his gown, the great headmaster did,
About himself, chucked off his mortar-board
And, leaning back, said: 'Let's see what you know,
How many half-crowns are there in a pound?'
I didn't know. I couldn't even guess.
My poor fond father, hearing nothing, smiled;
The gold clock ticked; the waiting furniture
Shone like a colour plate by H. M. Brock . . .

---

* Extract from Chapter 3, 'Highgate', of *Summoned by Bells*.

No answer – and the great headmaster frown'd;
But let me in to Highgate Junior School.
. . .

    See the rich elms careering down the hill –
Full billows rolling into Holloway;
In the tall classroom hear again the drone
Of multiplication tables chanted out;
Recall how Kelly stood us in a ring:
'Three sevens, then add eight, and take away
Twelve; what's the answer?' Hesitation then
Meant shaking by the shoulders till we cried.

Worst of all was returning from that day school in the afternoon. I used to be set on by another, even nastier, pair than Drayton and Dunlop. 'Come with us down Swain's Lane,' they used to say. It was a mile out of my way. 'We won't do anything to you – honestly we won't.' 'Cross my heart.' 'Honestly.' 'Oh why d'you want me then?' 'We like you. We want you to come with us.' Always the same thing happened. There was a hole in the fence of either Waterlow Park or Highgate Cemetery in a deserted part of that lane – it was unmetalled and tree-hung then. They dragged me through it, took off most of my clothes and threw me into a holly bush. I can't think why I went with them. I think it was a deep-seated terror of having to fight if I didn't go with them.

I am eternally grateful to my parents for taking me away from the place to Hum Lynam and his preparatory school at Oxford where I found refuge. But I learned a lot at that tough London boys' school. I learned how to get round people, how to lie, how to show off just enough to attract attention but not so much as to attract unwelcome attention, how to bribe bullies with sweets (four ounces a penny in those days) – and I learned my first lessons in mistrusting my fellow beings.

People tell me schools are happier places now and boys are much kinder to one another. I used to hear old people talking like that too. I knew it wasn't true then. I don't believe it now. Has sin suddenly stopped then and is no one ever unkind to anyone else? Has evil been charmed or psychoanalysed out of all children? I don't believe it.

Childhood days! They aren't all sunny smiles on the municipal swing as shown in the education officer's brochure. There's the dark corner in the locker room, the yard at the back of the coal shed – they're still there too. If bullying doesn't take one form, it'll take another. You can't stamp it out in a generation.

2

SCHOOL

Fags and Fires

LITTLE HELLS LET LOOSE

Evening Standard
1 August 1934

• • •

This week children of the upper and upper-middle classes are flooding home with unbrushed hair and uncut nails from private schools. As almost any prospectus will tell you, a private school is an establishment for preparing the sons of gentlemen for entry into public schools and the Navy. That is to say, it caters for the children (under fourteen years of age) of a rapidly diminishing class that can afford an education that is not by any means free of charge.

A private school can be a paradise or a hell. Saved from the conformities and constant inspections imposed on elementary school teachers, the headmaster of a private school is an absolute monarch in his little kingdom. No complaints need leak out to parents (all little boys are snobs and affect to despise 'sneaking') because letters home can be read to see what is written and unless a boy actually dies or shows signs of starvation or ill-treatment, a bad headmaster may become an indulged egomaniac recognisable as such only to those who have the misfortune to meet him unprofessionally during the holidays.

In fact, a private – otherwise called a 'preparatory' – school entirely depends on the headmaster. The one to which I was sent was one of the happiest places in the world and made all subsequent education seem repulsive. The school was happy because it was run not as a money-making concern but as a place of education.

That is the bright side of the picture. But to this day there are preparatory schools run purely as sources of profit to their headmasters. They are the dark side of the picture, darker than you cocksure parents

39

at present sitting in comfortable armchairs and reading this article can imagine. Unless you know your children very well you will never find out how bad they are for no amount of questioning will tell you.

All private schools are subject to two dangers: incompetent masters and overdeveloped boys. You will rarely find a school that does not suffer from one or the other. Let us take the headmaster and his assist-ants first of all. This is how a preparatory school is often founded: a clergymen without a benefice but with a little capital, or a young man with an honest fourth-class degree at the university, decides to run a school. With a 'Reverend' before or with letters after his name, he is entitled to call himself Doctor or Principal or merely headmaster. He buys a detached house originally intended for a Victorian family of eight or nine. By installing a new bathroom and an unmarried sister as matron, by erecting an army hut in the garden, by calling the croquet lawn a cricket field and by filling all those rooms that he has not appro-priated to himself with desks on the ground floor and beds on the upper storeys, the house – originally built to hold eight or nine – is ready for thirty or forty inhabitants. Only the staff and the boys are wanted to make it a thoroughly profitable school.

Next the headmaster has to choose his 'fully qualified staff'. A variety of types arrive from the agencies and elsewhere: young men doing a correspondence course to get a degree, old men who have their degrees but who have lost everything else, drunkards, sleek bounders with low rakish cars, loud school ties and violent plus-fours, emaciated aesthetes, tough men-of-the-world with square and hairy chins and a mental age of fifteen. All these apply for a post at £80 a year, including board and lodging. They are not sharp enough for banks or stockbroking, too lazy or inefficient for the colonies. What alternative to manual labour does England offer them beyond private schoolmastering? These men are not interested in education. If they can keep order and can play hymn tunes, if they are good at games or of presentable appearance, little else is demanded of them for securing the most responsible position a man can occupy in the world today – the care and instruction of young children. For this they hardly seem qualified.

The general methods of some masters defy description. And it is not only a matter of beating. I have seen more repulsive methods of coercion resorted to. Here is a sample. 'Well, Smith, I am not going to ask you to translate this again. I put you boys on your honour to do your preparation. I expect to be able to trust you. I know I can trust *you*, Greene' (leering at a favourite) 'and, indeed, most of you here – all of you, in fact, except Smith. What am I to do with a boy who has no sense of honour? Who refuses to do the work he has promised to do?' (Smith, aged nine, begins to weep.) 'Well, I shall do nothing.' (Murmurs of 'Swine, Smith,' 'You wait till after,' 'Little beast,' 'Rotter.') 'I leave it to the form to deal with him. Go on translating, Greene.' And afterwards the boys, hot with a moral indignation that is purely hypocritical, will be glad of a legal opportunity of sitting on Smith, stealing his model airplane, smashing his photographs and tearing up his stamp collection. And Smith will uncomplainingly receive his punishment; nor will it occur to him until perhaps twenty years after that there was any possibility of his not having deserved it.

For before puberty boys are devoid of all moral sense. They are snobbish and they are cruel, having no idea of what pain they inflict. That is why bullying in private schools is so much worse than in public schools, where the boys are older. There was one delightful practice at a private school on the South Coast recently – that of putting wire down boys' ears to see how far it would go. I have known of boys who have made others eat toothpaste, who have filed nails so far down that they bled, who have inflicted tortures rivalling Nazi terrorism with hairbrushes, toothbrushes, cricket stumps, spiked football boots, ropes and string.

Nor will supervision stop the rot, though it may detect it. The only way to quell the natural inhumanity of small boys is to interest them in things rather than in each other. This is the secret of the successful school. The natural gaiety of the place will overcome even those boys who are sexually developed too early and who are the greatest menace in a bad preparatory school. They will forget about bullying.

But how can they do this when the masters are bullies themselves? The only way you will find out whether your boy is at a bad preparatory school is by being a good parent. As yet I have never heard a parent who has been able to find out whether his boy is happy or not.

Mothers are subject to 'vain imaginings' and fathers to unwonted scepticism.

SHIVERING DOOM

Extract from Chapter 7, 'Marlborough'
Summoned by Bells
1960

• • •

Those few who read Dean Farrar's *Eric* now
    Read merely for a laugh; yet still for me
That mawkish and oh-so-melodious book
Holds one great truth – through every page there runs
The schoolboy sense of an impending doom
Which goes with rows of desks and clanging bells.
It filters down from God, to Master's Lodge,
Through housemasters and prefects to the fags.
    Doom! Shivering doom! Inexorable bells
To early school, to chapel, school again:
Compulsory constipation, hurried meals
Bulked out with Whipped Cream Walnuts from the town.
At first there was the dread of breaking rules –
'Betjeman, you know that new boys mustn't show
Their hair below the peak of college caps:
Stand still and have your face slapped.' 'Sorry, Jones.'
The dread of beating! Dread of being late!
And, greatest dread of all, the dread of games!
    'The centre and the mainspring of your lives,
The inspiration for your work and sport,
The corporate life of this great public school

Spring from its glorious chapel. Day by day
You come to worship in its noble walls,
Hallowed by half a century of prayer.'
The Old Marlburian bishop thundered on
When all I worshipped were the athletes, ranged
In the pews opposite. 'Be pure,' he cried,
And, for a moment, stilled the sea of coughs.
'Do nothing that would make your mother blush
If she could see you. When the Tempter comes
Spurn him and God will lift you from the mire.'

UPPER SCHOOL

From *Little Innocents*
Edited by Alan Pryce-Jones
Cobden-Sanderson, 1932

• • •

For this incident of my early youth I will probably be accused of disloyalty to my old school. If such a true account is disloyalty, then I am guilty. But I ought in justice to Marlborough to say that the custom I have here described has now been abolished. Although Upper School, with its many inhabitants, still exists, I believe that its autocracy is altogether altered for the better. This account may seem to my contemporaries highly coloured. I merely describe it as it struck me. But then I was an unpleasant little boy, morbidly sensitive in some matters and 'highly strung'.

I never liked Crossman and I am sure I should not like him if I were to meet him now. He oiled up to the Bishop, who was the school Visitor. He did his prep without the aid of a translation. He was a great pet with some of the masters. When he left school and went to

Cambridge he was a great lad at the Palais de Danse and had a topping little two-stroke motorbike. The money that was supposed to be training him for Holy Orders he spent on morning coffee at a dashing Cambridge café. Somehow his was always the jolly face that greeted me when first I returned from the holidays. 'Bad luck, Betjeman, you're still in Boggins's form.' And he, knowing Boggins, knew what awful bad luck it was, and grinned. Characteristically he was the first person to bring me the most terrifying piece of news I have ever had in my life. 'They're going to put you in the basket tonight, Betjeman.'

For those who have not been through 'in-college' life at Marlborough shortly after the war, I must explain what putting in the basket means. There are six senior in-college houses and thirty-five boys from each, the toughest and the youngest, live during the day in an enormous barn-like structure called Upper School. It is about as large as the Horticultural Hall. It smells of old biscuits and bat oil and is lined with desks, save at one end, where there is a clearing so that the bloods may play indoor hockey. The bloods have double desks, chaps like me have small ones. If your desk is 'unflush' during prep, that is to say, so full of books that it will not close down properly, you are publicly beaten by a boy, known as a captain, when prep is over.

FOUR CAPTAINS*

1960

There was a building known as Upper School
(Abolished now, thank God, and all its ways),
An eighteen-fifty warehouse smelling strong
Of bat-oil, biscuits, sweat and rotten fruit.
The corporate life of which the bishop spoke
Went on within its echoing whitewashed walls.
    Great were the ranks and privileges there:
Four captains ruled, selected for their brawn
And skill at games; and how we reverenced them!

---

* Extract from Chapter 7, 'Marlborough', of *Summoned by Bells*.

Marlborough is a cold place, hundreds of feet above sea level and in beautiful downland country. In Upper School there are two fires. One is known as Big Fire. Four captains, chosen entirely because they are good at games, are allowed to sit here and the four captains choose about a dozen other boys, also good at games, to sit with them. The other 170 boys crowd around the other fire, known as Little Fire, or sit on hot-water pipes in those parts of the school to which they are allowed access.

Big Fire rules Upper School. It is true that a master comes in twice a day to take prep but otherwise no person in authority enters the place. 'By the boys for the boys' – that's the rule and with it all the advantages of communal life. Sometimes one house is not represented at Big Fire and suffers accordingly. My house was bad at work, bad at games and not keen on the OTC (Officer Training Corps). It was not represented at Big Fire and not very keen on it.

SCHOOL BEATINGS*

1960

Upper School captains had the power to beat,
Maximum six strokes, usually three.
My frequent crime was far too many books,
So that my desk lid would not shut at all:
'Come to Big Fire then, Betjeman, after prep.'
I tried to concentrate on delicate points –
Ut, whether final or consecutive?†
(Oh happy private-school days when I knew!) –
While all the time I thought of pain to come.
Swift after prep all raced towards 'Big Fire',
Giving the captain space to swing his cane:

---

* Extract from Chapter 7, 'Marlborough', of *Summoned by Bells*.
† 'Ut', in Latin final clauses, introduces the purpose of an action: 'so that' in English. In consecutive clauses, it introduces the consequence, usually of some exceptional condition: 'that' in English.

'*One*,' they would shout and downward came the blow;
'*Two*' (rather louder); then, exultant, '*Three!*'
And some in ecstasy would bellow '*Four.*'
These casual beatings brought us no disgrace,
Rather a kind of glory. In the dorm,
Comparing bruises, other boys could show
Far worse ones that the beaks and prefects made.

The most fearful disgrace that Marlborough can thrust you into is the basket. Your friends desert you. It only happens a few times a year but it is as bad as expulsion. In afterlife, Marlburians chatting about old times in the bars of local golf clubs will say: 'Oh – Betjeman! – not much of a chap. He was put in the basket, wasn't he?' It is in the power of that tough autocracy, Big Fire, to put you in the basket.

This is the process. There are two large wastepaper baskets in the Upper School. During the half-hour after 6.30 tea, before prep begins, Big Fire (with the captains watching at the door) comes in and seizes the victim. His clothes are taken off save his shirt and he is thrust into one of the baskets, filled with apple cores and wastepaper, by the fags. Sometimes ink, sometimes paper and sometimes only obloquy is poured on his head. He is allowed to remain on exhibition until just before prep begins when he is allowed to go and 'stamped out' of the building. When he returns to prep, the master in charge asks why he is late. 'Put in the basket, sir.' The master nods. It does a fellow good. He has probably been suspected of thieving or worn coloured socks before he had been in Upper School three times or . . . never mind. Boys know each other best. There is nothing like the moral indignation of someone who is fifteen or sixteen. Besides the fellow was unpopular.

I disliked Upper School so much that I used to keep my books in a basement where they cleaned the boots. When Crossman told me that I was to be put in the basket, I felt too sick to make a gay retort. I can see his smug figure now, as he went off to morning work, his preparation done, his clothes shiny and patched by some loving mother in a rectory. All that day I could do no work. Put in the basket. I tried to think of what I had done wrong and remembered too much. I tried to be cheerful. I distinctly saw two boys in my house standing talking and looking at me. When I passed a group I thought I heard my name mentioned. In the hall I could eat nothing. The afternoon came and evening prep was nearer. Then came 6.30 hall. No one ate much. There was a lot of talking. 'Someone's going to be basketed . . . I say, Betjeman, someone's going to be put in the basket.' When the master in charge of the hall let us go, there was a rush to the doors and across the court to Upper School. Even the greediest left his eating. There was no escape. If Big Fire did not catch me today, it would tomorrow. I got up and walked slowly across the dark gravel to Upper School. The same smell of old biscuits and bat oil was there. The gaslights were on. But there was a listlessness and excitement everywhere.

Inside, boys were walking down the alleyway between the desks. At one of them someone was sitting and pretending to read *The Autocar*. People passed by, as if by accident, just to catch a glimpse of his face. But no one came near him.

'It's Pringle.' So it wasn't me after all. I felt I had better wait to see if the glorious news were true. They might be going to put two of us in. At five to seven, Big Fire came in. Popington, an enormous fellow, as red as beef with a tiny head, and Spewett, a boy like a cod, and a cert for a forty-cap★ next year, whom I never wish to see again, were followed by six or eight satellites. They walked straight up to Pringle and took hold of him. He offered feeble resistance. They took off nearly all his clothes. Then a pot was fetched and he was smeared all over with red paint. We stood on desks and in clearings craning over each other's shoulders, watching in silence. An infant prodigy near me who was always a good little boy gave a skip of self-righteous delight because he was not being put in himself. There was no noise now except the creak of the basket. Big Fire hoisted it with Pringle in it on to a table that had been placed on a desk. We could just see Pringle's brown eyes through the slats. Big Fire stood around, smiling knowingly or looking official, ready to give the basket a stir if it were needed. Just before prep started, and the captains came in beating their canes on the desks for the fags to start cleaning up the

_____

★ 2nd XV colours. Until 1876 Marlborough played rugby with twenty players, so the 2nd XV were – and still are – known as 'The XL' or 'The Forty'.

floor, Pringle emerged. We stamped as he walked out, a bedraggled figure, carrying his trousers on one arm, and in his hand a pair of very pointed black shoes.

YOU'RE NEXT*

1960

'You're for it next,' said H. J. Anderson.
'I'm not.' 'You are. I've heard.' So all that term
And three terms afterwards I crept about,
Avoiding public gaze.

---

* Extract from Chapter 7, 'Marlborough', of *Summoned by Bells*.

3

OXFORD

Hearties and Aesthetes

My Oxford (1977)
Cycling (1960)
North Oxford (1960)
Oxford Churches (1960)
Magdalen (1960)
Aesthetes (1960)
Colonel Kolkhorst (1960)
Sezincote (1960)
Pembroke (1960)

MY OXFORD

Contribution to *My Oxford*
Edited by Ann Thwaite
Robson Books, 1977

• • •

For me, there were two Oxfords. There was the Oxford of 1916 when I was a boarder at the Oxford Preparatory School (as the Dragon School was still called by old folk) and there was the Oxford of 1925–8 when I was up at Magdalen College.

There was hardly anyone about in my first Oxford. Everyone was away at the Front. We were sent to visit the wounded soldiers who were occupying Somerville and the other women's colleges in bright blue flannel and we knitted gloves out of string for the sailors on the minesweepers. At that time, the school seemed almost in the country: north of Linton Road there were manifold allotments; east of us, across the narrow Cherwell, were misty meadows and distant elms. To the south, hawthorn hedges made fields between us and Lady Margaret Hall. The way into the shops was westwards. The city was further than we went on foot. The nearest shops were in North Parade ('NP', we called it), Gee's and Twinings the grocers and Ora Brown, the cheerful lady who sold us sweets.

There was very little traffic then. The infrequent wartime buses down the Banbury Road were worked by gas, housed in a balloon over the top deck. We went everywhere, when we were free, on bicycles and I spent many a summer evening bicycling round 'the square', as Bardwell Road, Charlbury Road, Linton Road and Northmoor Road were then called. Most of us could bicycle with our hands in our pockets, slowly zigzagging past the railed-in gardens where tamarisk and forsythia grew; or we would lean against the cream-coloured lamp-posts with their terracotta coloured gas-lamps that were placed at infrequent intervals down all the leafy North Oxford roads.

CYCLING★

1960

Take me, my Centaur bike, down Linton Road,
Gliding by newly planted almond trees
Where the young dons with wives in tussore clad
Were building in the morning of their lives
Houses for future Dragons. Rest an arm
Upon the post of the allotment path,
Then dare the slope! We choked in our own dust,
The narrowness of the footpath made our speed
Seem swift as light. May-bush and elm flashed by,
Allotment holders turning round to stare,
Potatoes in their hands. Speed-wobble! Help!
And, with the Sturmey-Archer three-speed gear
Safely in bottom, resting from the race
We pedalled round the new-mown meadow-grass
By Marston Ferry with its punt and chain.

The school was in the red-brick Anglo-Jackson part of North Oxford, which only burst into full beauty when the hawthorn and pink may was in flower. The inner North Oxford – Crick Road, Norham Gardens, Norham Road and the magic, winding Canterbury Road, the cottages and stables by North Parade and those ecclesiastical-looking houses gathered round the motherly spire of St Philip and St James ('Phil-Jim') – was more haunting and more daunting. Bicycling down those 'Phil-Jim' roads whose fenced-in gardens had speckled laurels and 'Beware of the Dog' and 'No

---

★ Extract from Chapter 5, 'Private School', of *Summoned by Bells*.

Hawkers' on their gates, one could glimpse the front-room windows where the widows of Heads of Houses and famous professors sat writing letters in crowded, gaslit rooms. Flowered-papers were on the walls and served as backgrounds to photographs in Oxford frames. Hansom cabs still trotted down these roads, taking the aged inhabitants to the dentist in Beaumont Street or to one of the two railway stations or shopping at Elliston & Cavell.

NORTH OXFORD★

1960

Show me thy road, Crick, in the early spring:
Laurel and privet and laburnum ropes
And gabled-gothic houses gathered round
Thy mothering spire, St Philip and St James.
Here by the low brick semi-private walls
Bicycling past a trotting butcher's-cart,
I glimpsed, behind lace curtains, silver hair
Of sundry old Professors. Here were friends
Of Ruskin, Newman, Pattison and Froude
Among their books and plants and photographs
In comfortable twilight. But for me,
Less academic, red-brick Chalfont Road
Meant great-aunt Wilkins, tea and buttered toast.

In all the wide-roaded silence, the deepest quiet was on Sunday afternoons when I would bicycle to No. 4 Chalfont Road. There my father's Aunt Lizzie and her husband, John R. Wilkins, ever generous with tea and rock cakes and jam puffs, lived a life entirely unconnected with the university or the school but closely bound up with the town. My great-uncle was architect to one of the breweries and did some nice little public houses in a free Tudor style. He also restored the Clarendon building and supervised the construction of Professor

---

★ Extract from Chapter 5, 'Private School', of *Summoned by Bells*.

Dicey's house on the corner of Bardwell and Banbury Roads on behalf of Colonel Edis.

The OPS, or Lynam's as we called the school, prided itself on its freedom. The boys did not have to wear Eton suits on Sundays and walk in a crocodile, as did the benighted pupils of Summerfields, further up Banbury Road. We could bicycle into the city and look at colleges. Together with my friend Ronnie Wright, the son of a barrister of Tractarian opinions and of a mother who had recently been converted to Rome, we bicycled off to Oxford churches, noticing their liturgical differences. My favourite was St Peter-le-Bailey, which was always empty and always open. I preferred it to the arid Norman revival of St Andrew's Church, which was also very evangelical. We usually ended our explorations at St Aloysius, the Roman Catholic church, where in a side chapel there was a relic of the True Cross, surrounded by candles, polished brass and jewels, which seemed to me very sacred and alarming, as, indeed, did the whole church with its apse of coloured saints and its smell of incense and many *dévoués* crossing themselves and looking back at us while on their knees. One of our schoolmasters, Gerald Haynes, who had a passion for church architecture – if it was medieval – took us bicycling round the village churches near Oxford and listened to our accounts of colleges we had explored and chapels we had visited in the university. He liked to take photographs of Norman features in churches and it was from him that I learned to think that Norman was the only style that mattered and that Iffley Church was far the most interesting building in Oxford or its vicinity.

OXFORD CHURCHES*

1960

Ronald Hughes Wright, come with me once again
Bicycling off to churches in the town:

---

* Extract from Chapter 5, 'Private School', of *Summoned by Bells*.

St Andrew's first, with neo-Norman apse,
St Old's – distinctly Evangelical –
And, Lower still, St Ebbe's, which smelt of gas.
In New Inn Hall Street dare the double doors,
Partitions and red baize till stands revealed
Peter-le-Bailey Irish gothic nave.
   St Giles' had still a proper fairground air,
For Oxford once had been a Cotswold town
Standing in water meadows of the Thames:
The cattle moaned in pens on Gloucester Green;
In George Street there were country cottages;
And thy weak Dec., St George-the-Martyr's church,
Prepared us for our final port of call –
St Aloysius of the Church of Rome.
Its incense, reliquaries, brass and lights
Made all seem plain and trivial back at school.

Five years later, Oxford – outwardly very little changed, except
for an increase in the number of motorcars so that one had to look
to right and left before crossing the Banbury Road or Magdalen
Bridge – was a city of pleasure. Schoolfriends from Marlborough
had gone to Oxford ahead of me, among them John Edward Bowle,
the historian, who had won a Brackenbury Scholarship to Balliol. I
was much affected by his outlook on Oxford. He regarded it as an
infinitely superior place to Marlborough – and so did I. Dons were
to him – as to me – cleverer and more learned than schoolmasters.
He thought Balliol the cleverest college and the Balliol dons therefore the cleverest in the world. I did, too.

I was at Magdalen and had beautiful panelled eighteenth-century
rooms on the second floor of New Buildings. From my bed I would
hear the Magdalen bells 'sprinkle the quarters on the morning
town'. They led the chorus of quarters chiming from Merton and
New College. I would wait until the fourth quarter had struck
and the bell announced the hour before getting up. This was usually
ten o'clock and so I was too late for breakfast. That did not matter
at all.

MAGDALEN*

1960

Balkan Sobranies in a wooden box,
The college arms upon the lid; Tokay
And sherry in the cupboard; on the shelves
The University Statutes bound in blue,
Crome Yellow, *Prancing Nigger*, Blunden, Keats.
My walls were painted Bursar's apple-green;
My wide-sashed windows looked across the grass
To tower and hall and lines of pinnacles.
The wind among the elms, the echoing stairs,
The quarters, chimed across the quiet quad
From Magdalen tower and neighbouring turret-clocks,
Gave eighteenth-century splendour to my state.
Privacy after years of public school;
Dignity after years of none at all –
First college rooms, a kingdom of my own:
What words of mine can tell my gratitude?

My tutor was the Reverend J. M. Thompson, a shy, kind, amusing man and a distinguished authority on French history. Rumour had it that he had been defrocked for preaching in Magdalen Chapel that the miracles were performed by electricity. I later found out that he was an early modernist in theology.

By now I was more interested in the type of churchmanship in a church than in its architecture. I had no Ronnie Wright to accompany me on my expeditions; instead, one of my closest friends was Lord Clonmore (now Wicklow) who was an ordinand at St Stephen's House, Norham Road. We were both Anglo-Catholics. Through the offices of the Reverend Frederic Hood (who was then on the staff of Pusey House under the celebrated Dr Darwell Stone) I was instructed by the Reverend Miles Sargent in the Catholic faith,

---

* Extract from Chapter 9, 'The Opening World', of *Summoned by Bells*.

which was nothing like the abbreviated Matins I had enjoyed daily in the school chapel at Marlborough.

When I left the gentle charge of the Reverend J. M. Thompson, my tutor was C. S. Lewis who was then in what he would have called his 'unregenerate days'. Breezy, tweedy, beer-drinking and jolly, he was very popular with extrovert undergraduates. He found the liturgy very funny and delighted in pointing out *non sequiturs* in it; moreover, he ruined Coleridge's 'Kubla Khan' for me by wondering whether the pants in the line 'As if this earth in fast thick pants were breathing' were woollen or fur. Now I knew dons were cleverer than any school-master, even than a headmaster, I realised that when Lewis asked me to read three books of *Paradise Lost*, he had not only read them all himself but had enjoyed them and even knew what they meant.

Oxford was divided for me into two groups: hearties and aesthetes. Hearties were good college men who rowed in the college boat, ate in the college hall and drank beer and shouted. Their regulation uniform was college tie, college pullover, tweed coat and grey flannel trousers. Aesthetes, on the other hand, wore whole suits, silk ties of a single colour and sometimes – but only for about a week or two while they were fashionable – trousers of cream or strawberry-pink flannel. They let their hair grow long and never found out, as I never found out, where the college playing fields were or which was the college barge. Aesthetes never dined in hall but went instead to the George restaurant on the corner of Cornmarket and George Street, where there was a band consisting of three ladies and where punkahs, suspended from the ceiling, swayed to and fro, dispelling the smoke of Egyptian and Balkan cigarettes. Mr Ehrsam, the perfect Swiss hotelier, and his wife kept order and knew how much credit to allow us. I was an aesthete.

The chief Oxford aesthete when I went up in 1925 was Harold Acton who, with his brother William, was at Christ Church but was never seen inside the college in my day. He was a frequenter of restaurants and his own lodgings were somewhere in the High. Michael Dugdale, another aesthete and a friend of mine at Balliol, always used to walk into Brasenose – an entirely athletic college – with the aid of a stick and limping, because he knew that the athletes would be too sporting to attack a lame aesthete.

AESTHETES*

1960

No wonder, looking back, I never worked.
Too pleased with life, swept in the social round,
I soon left Old Marlburians behind.
(As one more solemn of our number said:
'Spiritually I was at Eton, John.')
I cut tutorials with wild excuse,
For life was luncheons, luncheons all the way –
And evenings dining with the Georgeoisie.
Open, swing doors, upon the lighted 'George'
And whiff of *vol-au-vent*! Behold the band
Sawing away at gems from *Chu Chin Chow*,
As Harold Acton and the punkahs wave:
'My dears, I want to rush into the fields
And slap raw meat with lilies.'
But as the laughs grew long and loud I heard
The more insistent inner voice of guilt:
'Stop!' cried my mother from her bed of pain.
I heard my father in his factory say:
'Fourth generation, John, they look to you.'
    'Harry Strathspey is coming if he can
After he's dined at Blenheim. Hamish says
That Ben has got twelve dozen Bollinger.'
'And Sandy's going as a matelot.'
'I will not have that Mr Mackworth Price;
Graham will be so furious if he's asked
We do *not* want another ghastly brawl' . . .
'Well, don't ask Graham, then.' 'I simply must.'
'The hearties say they're going to break it up.'
'Oh no, they're not. I've settled *them* all right,
I've bribed the Boat Club with a cask of beer.'

---

* Extract from Chapter 9, 'The Opening World', of *Summoned by Bells*.

Moon after parties: moon on Magdalen Tower,
And shadow on the place for climbing in . . .
Noise, then the great, deep silences again.

Aesthetes used to gather at the very fashionable sherry parties largely attended by Anglo–Catholic and a certain number of Roman Catholic undergraduates – given on Sundays at noon by George Alfred Kolkhorst, lecturer in Spanish at Exeter College and later Reader in the university. He had been born in Chile, which would explain why he knew Spanish, as I cannot imagine him ever taking the trouble to learn it. We nicknamed him 'Colonel' Kolkhorst, as he was so little like a colonel. He was very tall, with a slight stoop, and had rooms on the first floor at No. 38 Beaumont Street. When he first came up as an undergraduate, the Colonel had been known as G'ug: the apostrophe, he thought, implied deference and gave the impression of a slight yawn when pronounced. He wore a lump of sugar hung from his neck on a piece of cotton 'to sweeten his conversation' and at some of his parties would be dressed in a suit made entirely of white flannel, waistcoat and all. Though people never got drunk at the Colonel's parties, it was a habit to form a circle round him and slowly gyrate, calling out 'The Colonel's tight, the room's going round!' And we used to stick stamps on his ceiling by licking them and throwing them up on up-turned pennies. After one of his merrier sherry parties, the Colonel accompanied Robert Byron and Lord Clonmore and some other undergraduates to the top of St Mary Magdalen's Tower in the Cornmarket, where they sang hymns and began spitting on the people on the pavement. The Proctors★ were called and waited at the bottom of the Tower for the delinquents to descend, which they eventually did, headed by the Colonel in his white suit. As a graduate of the university and lecturer in Spanish, he was immune from punishment but the others were fined.

★ University officials responsible for discipline.

COLONEL KOLKHORST*

1960

What mist of buds about the guardian elms
Before St John's! What sense of joys to come
As opposite the Randolph's Gothic pile
We bought the Sunday newspapers and rush'd
Down Beaumont Street to Number 38
And Colonel Kolkhorst's Sunday-morning rout!

> D'ye ken Kolkhorst in his artful parlour,
> Handing out the drink at his Sunday morning gala?
> Some get sherry and some Marsala –
>   With his arts and his crafts in the morning!

The over-crowded room was lit by gas
And smelt of mice and chicken soup and dogs.
Among the knick-knacks stood a photograph
Of that most precious Oxford essayist,
Upon whose margin Osbert Lancaster
Wrote 'Alma Pater' in his sloping hand.
George Alfred Kolkhorst, you whom nothing shocked,
Who never once betrayed a confidence,.
No one believed you really were a don
Till Gerard Irvine (now a parish priest)
Went to your lecture on *Le Cid* and clapped.
You swept towards him, gowned, and turned him out.

The Colonel disliked dons, believing that they took themselves
too seriously. He regarded Spanish as hardly a subject at all and not
worth learning. He thought Cervantes the only outstanding
Spanish author though he liked the Nicaraguan poet Rubén Darío,
whose name we would pronounce at sherry parties with a tremendous rolling of 'r's. The one thing the Colonel detested above all

---

* Extract from Chapter 9, 'The Opening World', of *Summoned by Bells*.

else was research. It might be justified in reputable subjects like 'Literae Humaniores' and biology and the physical sciences, he said, but in Modern Spanish, a subject with very little literary history, research meant nothing but scratching around inventing subjects to increase the self-esteem of examining professors and did no one any good.

If anyone talked about their subject or held forth with a lot of facts at his parties, the Colonel would open his mouth to simulate a yawn, tapping his upper lip as he did so. He carried a little ear trumpet for 'catching clever remarks' but would swiftly put it away and yawn if they were not clever. I never heard of anyone seeing him in Exeter College and it was a frequent practice of his friends to ask at the Lodge whether the Colonel had been in lately.

Magdalen College, to which I was admitted through the kindness of the President, Sir Herbert Warren, had been the best college – in the social sense – because Edward VIII had been an undergraduate there when Prince of Wales. It had a very famous steward of the Junior Common Room, named Gynes, who saw to it that the under-graduates had the best food and wine when they entertained in their rooms. I remember giving a luncheon party at which constant glasses of Tokay were the only drink from the hors d'oeuvre to the coffee. I must have seemed an impossible person to poor C. S. Lewis but he had his revenge, for he wrote me a reference when I was trying to become a private schoolteacher which was so double-edged that I withdrew it after my first unsuccessful application for a post.

However, the best college in my time – it probably still is – was Christ Church, known as 'The House'. There, blue blood prevailed; it was the Mecca of all the socially ambitious. Indeed, one under-graduate who had rooms in the college backing on to a public highway would let down a rope ladder from his windows after the bell in Tom Tower had finished striking its 101 notes – which meant that all college gates were closed. This undergraduate allowed people from other colleges to use his rope ladder if they were acceptable to him. Thus it was said that he had climbed into society by a rope ladder.

There was always an atmosphere of leisure surrounding Christ Church undergraduates. They gave the impression that they were just dropping in at Oxford on their way to a seat in the House of Lords, shortly to be vacated on the decease of their fathers, or that they were coming in for a term or two but mostly staying away from college in country houses. They hunted, fished and shot. They may even have rode. But I never heard of them playing football or hockey, or even cricket, though cricket was sometimes played in the grounds of country houses within motoring distance of Oxford, and men from The House might have been called upon to swell a village team. Then it was not unusual for a rich undergraduate, and there were many such at The House, to chuck out the Bursar's furniture and all the humdrum college fittings in his rooms and have the whole place redecorated at his mother's advice and expense. Edward James,* for instance, had rooms in Canterbury Quad whose ceilings were black and whose walls were gold and around the frieze in Trajan lettering ran the words 'Ars longa, vita brevis'. They outstayed Edward's tenure of the rooms.

SEZINCOTE†

1960

Oxford May mornings! When the prunus bloomed
We'd drive to Sunday lunch at Sezincote:‡
First steps in learning how to be a guest,
First wood-smoke-scented luxury of life
In the large ambience of a country house.
Heavy with hawthorn scent were Cotswold lanes,
Golden the church towers standing in the sun,

---

* A wealthy student friend of Betjeman's at Oxford who supported the Surrealist movement and paid for the publication of Betjeman's first book of poems, *Mount Zion*. He was hurt that Betjeman later dropped him in favour of John Murray.
† Extract from Chapter 9, 'The Opening World', of *Summoned by Bells*.
‡ An early-nineteenth-century country house in Gloucestershire, designed in an exotic Indian style with onion-shaped domes and owned by the parents of Betjeman's friend John Dugdale.

And Gordon Russell with his arts and crafts,
Somewhere beyond in Broadway. Down the drive,
Under the early yellow leaves of oaks;
One lodge is Tudor, one in Indian style.
The bridge, the waterfall, the Temple Pool –
And there they burst on us, the onion domes,
Chajjahs and *chattris* made of amber stone:
'Home of the Oaks', exotic Sezincote!
Stately and strange it stood, the Nabob's house,
Indian without and coolest Greek within,
Looking from Gloucestershire to Oxfordshire;
And, by supremest landscape-gardener's art,
The lake below the eastward slope of grass
Was made to seem a mighty river-reach
Curving along to Chipping Norton's hills.

    Crackle of gravel! in the entrance-hall
Boot-jacks and mattocks, hunting mackintosh,
And whips and sticks and barometric clock
Were Colonel Dugdale's; but a sheaf of bast
And gardening-basket told us of his wife.
'Camilla Russell – Bridget King-Tenison –
And Major Attlee – Patsy Rivington –
Shall we go in? I think it's rather late.'

    Dear Mrs Dugdale, mother of us all,
In trailing and Edwardian-looking dress,
A Sargent portrait in your elegance,
Sweet confidante in every tale of woe!
She and her son and we were on the Left,
But Colonel Dugdale was Conservative.
From one end of the butler-tended board
The Colonel's eyes looked out towards the hills,
While at the other end our hostess heard
Political and undergraduate chat.
'Oh, Ethel,' loudly Colonel Dugdale's voice
Boomed sudden down the table, 'that manure –
I've had it shifted to the strawberry-beds.'
'Yes, Arthur . . . Major Attlee, as you said,

Seventeen million of the poor Chinese
Eat less than half a calory a week?'

> How proud beneath the swelling dome
>   I sang Lord Ullin's daughter
> At Mrs Dugdale's grand At Home
>   To Lady Horsbrugh-Porter.

So Sezincote became a second home.

Of course, there were also ordinary lay undergraduates – that is, those who were neither peers nor very rich – at Christ Church. There was the clever, bespectacled historian from Cornwall, A. L. Rowse, whom I was not to know till later. My chief friend among the laymen was a tow-haired boy from Gresham's called Wystan Auden, who was reading English and was tutored by Nevill Coghill of Exeter College. Coghill was an inspiring tutor who rendered Chaucer into readable English and was a keen producer of Shakespeare at the OUDS.★

There must have been dons at Christ Church too, though apart from Professor Lindemann (later Lord Cherwell, the scientist, and friend of Winston Churchill) and Gilbert Ryle the philosopher and J. C. Masterman, the Senior Censor and historian, I do not remember them . . . except for Roy Harrod, a young don who looked about my own age. He, as Junior Censor, was in charge of undergraduates' behaviour.

Balliol was, as I have mentioned, the cleverest college but it was more ascetic than aesthetic. Balliol was associated with brains. Our hero Aldous Huxley had been there in rooms papered plain grey, looking out on frosty stars above the Waterhouse block's Scottish baronial turrets. The whole tone of the college was Scottish and frugal but like all things Scottish it had a side of unbridled exuberance reserved for parties. Lampoons would be sung outside the rooms of dons. Fortunately the dons at Balliol were far friendlier to undergraduates than at most other colleges. The don who dominated Balliol was 'Sligger' Urquhart who held court in summer on a

---

★ Oxford University Dramatic Society.

lawn of the garden quad near the dining-hall. He liked people to be well born and, if possible, Roman Catholic and he gave reading parties in Switzerland. I only knew him well enough to touch my hat to him or to give him an oily smile.

Balliol had good scouts,* the undergraduates gave good luncheons and teas in their rooms and it was the college where I had the most friends. Balliol people whom I knew were, like me, not college men and therefore were to be found in restaurants and other people's rooms. As well as John Edward Bowle there was Wyndham Ketton-Cremer, Norfolk squire, Old Harrovian and a gentle pastoral poet much admired by Bowle. An old distich (by Dennis Kincaid, a Balliol wit who was the life and soul of the Colonel's parties) hath it:

> John Edward Bowle
> Had a superflux of soul.
> He was more beautiful than Rima,
> But not as beautiful as Ketton-Cremer.

Exeter College was for me the headquarters of Anglo-Catholicism and I had many friends there too. The dons were mostly approachable and encouraging, like Professor R. M. Dawkins who had rooms on the ground floor and appeared delighted to welcome anyone who called on him, whatever his real feelings about the intruders. He preferred, however, tough sporting men to aesthetes. He was an unconventional man with a red walrus moustache, freckled bald head and gold wire spectacles. He was exactly one's idea of the absent-minded professor yet nothing escaped him. He was generally called 'Dorks' and was reputed to have known Baron Corvo though he never mentioned him to us undergraduates. The fact that he was Sotheby and Bywater Professor of Byzantine and Modern Greek was a matter of childlike wonder and delight to him. Although he was the son of a landowning family with military traditions, he was the least military of men. He had been put into the electrical engineering business in Chelmsford but had carried on with modern Greek regardless. How he moved from electricity to a fellowship at Emmanuel College, Cambridge, is a puzzle. He always thought of

---

* College servants.

himself as a Cambridge man even after Oxford had made him a professor. He once told me you could never depend on the aesthetic
opinions of classical scholars or philosophers – scientists were far
more reliable and humble-minded.

That was my second Oxford. It has lasted long. Still the colleges
retain their individuality. I could have gone on through every college
in Oxford and the halls and theological colleges but time and the
patience of readers press. I must conclude with a mention of what
has always been my favourite college – Pembroke, where Dr
Johnson's teapot was preserved in the library. In my day it was still a
college you could enter if the dons liked you. Examinations were not
all that important. Mr Drake, who was the senior tutor, was the greatest authority on port in England and Pembroke had the best cellar.
The last Lord Pembroke was at the college in my day and wrote
excellent racing news for the *Cherwell*★ when I was an editor. I don't
think he bothered much about exams. The master was the great Dr
Holmes Dudden, the most successful of all vice-chancellors. He had
been a popular London preacher at the fashionable and beautiful
Holy Trinity Church, Sloane Street. He and Mr Drake and Mr Salt,
a High Churchman and bursar, and dear old Dr Ramsden, a scientist who kept silkworms on the mulberries in the Fellows' Garden,
made the Pembroke Senior Common Room the most enviable of all.
Clipped ivy still grew on the walls and in summer the window boxes
were filled with pink geraniums, the college colour. Pembroke
retained, of course, its barge when all the 'withits' were building boat
houses of brick. With its creeper-hung walls, intimate quads and rich
chapel decorated by Kempe, Pembroke was the best-maintained and
most romantic Oxford survival. Even today its new buildings have
involved the restoration of little streets adjoining and no flashy add-
itions. Hurrah!

★ Oxford student newspaper.

PEMBROKE*

1960

And does an unimportant don
In Pembroke College linger on,
   With sported oak, alone?
Do nearby bells of low St Ebbe's
   Ring all unnoticed there?
Can only climbing ivy see
That he for weeks has ceased to be,
While hungry spiders spin their webs
   Between his desk and chair,
Where he is sitting very still
With all Eternity to kill?
How empty, creeper-grown and odd
Seems lonely Pembroke's second quad!
   Still, when I see it, do I wonder why
   That college so polite and shy
Should have more character than Queen's
   Or Univ. splendid in The High.

---

* Extract from Chapter 9, 'The Opening World', of *Summoned by Bells*.

4
GIRLS
Blue Eyes and Freckles

AUNT ELSIE

Extract from Chapter 8, 'Cornwall in Adolescence'
Summoned by Bells
1960

.   .   .

Aunt Elsie, aunt of normal Scottish boys,
Adopted aunt of lone abnormal me:
She understood us all, she treated us
With reason, waiting while we choked with rage.
'Aunt Elsie, surely I could drive the car?'
The eucalyptus shivered in the drive,
The stars were out above the garage roof,
Night-scented stock and white tobacco plant
Gave way to petrol scent and came again.
A rival, changing gear along the lane,
Alone disturbed the wide September night.
'Come in, John, and I'll tell you why you can't.'
Thick carpets, Whistler books and porcelain,
There, in that more-than-summer residence,
She would explain that I was still a boy.
　'Was still a boy?' Then what, by God, was this —
This tender, humble, unrequited love
For Biddy Walsham? What the worshipping
That put me off my supper, fixed my hair
Thick with Anzora for the dance tonight?
The Talbot-Darracq, with its leather seats
And Biddy in beside me! I could show
Double-declutching to perfection now.

What though the Stokeses were a field away?
Biddy would scream with laughter as I'd charge
Up the steep corner of Coolgrena drive,
And slip from top to second, down to first,
And almost seem to ram the bungalow,
And swirl around the terraced plateau, brake –
Then switch the headlights off and we would wait
While the recovering engine ticked to quiet
In comfortable darkness. If my hand
By accident should touch her hand, perhaps
The love in me would race along to her
On the electron principle, perhaps . . . ?
'So surely, John, it's sensible to walk?'

TEA DANCES AND NIGHTCLUBS

Extract from the series *Music and People*
'London Calling Asia' (BBC General Overseas Service)
24 July 1954
Producer: Sunday Wilshin

•　•　•

The song 'Tea for Two'★ recalls to me portable gramophones on the river and scratchy needles, thé-dansants in seaside hotels, the innocent flickerings of early love. One heard it everywhere. It was

---

★ From the London musical comedy *No, No, Nanette* (1925). Music by Vincent Youmans, lyrics by Irving Caesar and Otto Harbach. In 1950 it was made into a movie, *Tea for Two*, directed by David Butler and starring Doris Day and Gordon MacRae.

the beginning of the new cheerful note, now that the 1914 war really was over and we all read such books as *Tell England* and *If Winter Comes* and only a few people had heard of T. S. Eliot. The words are ingenious. I like that bit where it says:

> Far from the cry of the city
> Where flowers pretty
> Caress the streams.

I always think that that must have been somewhere down in Maidenhead on the River Thames in the days when the river was still faintly fashionable and the flowers, in order to do such an odd thing as caress the streams, must have been artificial ones from a musical comedy set in the garden of an actress's hideout.

INDOOR GAMES NEAR NEWBURY

New Statesman and Nation
18 January 1947

In among the silver birches winding ways of tarmac wander
   And the signs to Bussock Bottom, Tussock Wood and
                             Windy Brake,
Gabled lodges, tile-hung churches, catch the light of our
                              Lagonda
   As we drive to Wendy's party, lemon curd and Christmas
                              cake.

     Rich the makes of motor whirring,
     Past the pine-plantation purring
        Come up, Hupmobile, Delage!
     Short the way your chauffeurs travel,
     Crumbling over private gravel
        Each from out his warm garáge.

Oh but Wendy, when the carpet yielded to my indoor pumps
     There you stood, your gold hair streaming,
     Handsome in the hall-light gleaming

There you looked and there you led me off into the game of
                                                    clumps
    Then the new Victrola playing
    And your funny uncle saying
'Choose your partners for a fox-trot! Dance until it's *tea* o'clock!
    'Come on, young 'uns, foot it featly!'
    Was it chance that paired us neatly,
    I, who loved you so completely,
You, who pressed me closely to you, hard against your party
                                                    frock?

'Meet me when you've finished eating!' So we met and no
                                                    one found us.
  Oh that dark and furry cupboard while the rest played hide
                                                    and seek!
Holding hands our two hearts beating in the bedroom silence
                                                    round us,
  Holding hands and hardly hearing sudden footsteps, thud
                                                    and shriek.
    Love that lay too deep for kissing –
    'Where *is* Wendy? Wendy's missing!'
      Love so pure it *had* to end,
    Love so strong that I was frighten'd
    When you gripped my fingers tight and
Hugging, whispered 'I'm your friend.'

Goodbye Wendy! Send the fairies, pinewood elf and larch
                                                    tree gnome,
    Spingle-spangled stars are peeping
    At the lush Lagonda creeping
Down the winding ways of tarmac to the leaded lights of home.
    There, among the silver birches,
    All the bells of all the churches
Sounded in the bath-waste running out into the frosty air.
    Wendy speeded my undressing,
    Wendy is the sheet's caressing,
    Wendy bending gives a blessing,
Holds me as I drift to dreamland, safe inside my slumber-wear.

Ten years later, depravity had set in and I was beginning to over-smoke and to spend the allowance my father gave me for my education on meals and social climbing. The tune, 'My Heart Stood Still',* seemed terribly modern to me and rather difficult but the words said exactly what we all meant, and still mean, when we fall in love. To this tune I became engaged to be married and we still have the music at home. But of course it doesn't go with musical comedies like *Tea for Two*. It goes with jogging round in smoky, over-crowded nightclubs. 'Hullooooooo, Wanda. Divine to see you, my deah. Are you going on to the Blue Lantern? We'll join you there at about half-past one.' It was the sort of tune that was thumped out by pale men with cigarettes in their mouths and another dry martini waiting for them on the piano. The late 1920s are nearing the swan song of the Bright Young Things before their fathers went bust and their allowances were stopped for ever.

COUNTRY-HOUSE PARTIES

Extracts from letters to Patrick Balfour

• • •

4 September 1928

Thank you for the helpful letter you sent to me at the beginning of my visit to Clandeboye.† Oh how peaceful were those first few days . . . But the peace was rudely shattered by the arrival of two girls in that Classical library, one of them carrying a gramophone

---

* Music by Richard Rodgers, lyrics by Lorenz Hart (1927).
† The large eighteenth-century house in County Down owned by Betjeman's Oxford friend Basil, Marquess of Dufferin and Ava.

record – a new one to be tried. Then we all started to practise the Charleston. We moved the gramophone into the saloon where there was a parquet floor and tried them. I was miserable. Edward* tried to get his own back (not without success) on Bloody[†] and me because we had laughed at his poetry. But it was over in a little while when Edward departed. I found that by altering my plane of thought I could get on quite well with Veronica[‡] . . . I have got to go out with a lot of jolly girls now – oh God I wish I were dead.

5 August 1929

I have discovered a rather beautiful girl here[§] aged thirteen and like a Shepperson[¶] drawing and my sex becomes rampant. Blue darting eyes and beautiful voice and figure. I think I must be a bit heter.

16 August 1931

I ought to tell you that I proposed marriage to a jolly girl last weekend and got accepted.[**] It has left me rather dippy. It occurred at two in the morning – suddenly two arms were raised from the floor and put around me, for I was sitting in a chair in an old-world Tudor manor house and then I was accepted and I kissed first the tip of the nose and then the neck and then the forehead and we took off our shoes in order to go upstairs quietly and we turned off the lights and stood on the stone floor of the hall and suddenly two cool little hands were in mine and then a subtly unresisting body pressed against me and I kissed her full on the lips for the first time. Since then there have been other kisses. Patrick, don't say anything about it because the parents are certain to object and with my reputation it would be very trying if it got about.

---

* Edward James.
[†] 'Little Bloody' was Betjeman's nickname for Basil Dufferin.
[‡] Lady Veronica Blackwood, a sister of Basil Dufferin.
[§] Holidaying with his parents at Trebetherick, in Cornwall.
[¶] Claude Shepperson (1867–1921), book illustrator.
[**] Camilla Russell.

LOVE'S YOUNG DREAM
Letters to Camilla Russell

• • •

6 August 1931

Alas! I cannot stay at Sezincote this weekend because a lot of people and relations are staying there, John* says. What an awful bore it is. I fear that as my holidays start next week I shan't see you for ages. This is hell because the more I see you the deeper my devotion to you becomes. I forgot to thank your aunt for that nice dinner which I take this opportunity of doing by writing to her. I think I shall spend part of my holidays at Sezincote.

I am writing to the Longfords† today about you and I hope also to work a visit to little Bloody for you. This is going to require a certain amount of tact what with childbirth and one thing and another.

I enclose a postal order for 3/- which I owe you. Do not spend all this at once but save it for a rainy day. Didn't I tell you to get a decent bandeau for your summer dresses? It's no good telling you anything. I do think, dear, you might pay some attention to what your mother asks instead of just being so vague. PEOPLE WOULD LIKE YOU MUCH BETTER. Write to me in my exile in this filthy office‡ and tell me how long and when you are going to be at 𝔜𝔢 𝔬𝔩𝔡𝔢 𝔏𝔦𝔱𝔱𝔩𝔢 𝔒𝔬𝔪𝔭𝔱𝔬𝔫𝔢 𝔐𝔞𝔫𝔬𝔯𝔢 in order that my visit to Sezincote may coincide with your being at your aunt's. If you're very lucky you may be allowed to stay at CATBALL§ but you must be very nice to your mother to obtain such a privilege.

---

* John Dugdale.
† Frank Pakenham, later the seventh Earl of Longford, was an Oxford friend and introduced Betjeman to his various brothers and sisters, who also became friends.
‡ *The Architectural Review.*
§ Catball was the Gloucestershire home of Camilla Russell's aunt, to whom Camilla was sent by her mother Lady Russell to get her away from Betjeman, an expedient

12 August 1931

Müller, duckie, I have written to your aunt explaining at some length and at the risk of giving offence, that it is essential for you to remain in England and not to go to Cairo* there to be on Dromedaries and divans and be scolded. I now await with anxiety the news about whether they will have me at Sezincote.

London is as usual in the hot weather like an unorthodox woman after a party – bled white by an unmerciless sun. I long for Salzburg and Hanover and München and that gay old jade Dresden and that sweetly intimate caf in the Boulevarde St Germaine des Prés where the artists and gendarmerie express themselves as only the Latin races can with a 'bonhomie' that is almost 'de trop' it is so metaphysical (or mystical if you will have it so) and 'lebewohl'. Glorious certainty of continental self-expression! Au clair de la lune, Mon ami Pierrot. Au bien revoir, Gutentag, Austen Coghlan.

There is no need to write to me unless you wish because (1) I hope to see you on Saturday or Sunday (2) writing letters is such hell unless one is in the mood to do it. My hat! I am crazy about you with those see-saw-like eyes.

14 August 1931

In case I do not see you tomorrow – which seems to me extremely likely considering the violent avalanche of circumstances against us – I have got the faithful old Lionel† to act as emissary. He is elderly and dear to me and utterly reliable. Give what messages you like to him. I have an awful feeling that our correspondence may be tampered with. Thank God you leave that incommodious little Catball on Sunday. I must know what line to take with your aunt.

---

that forced the pair to devise ways of writing to each other – when not meeting at country-house parties, especially at Sezincote – without being discovered.

* Camilla Russell lived in Cairo, where her father Sir John was head of the police.

† Lionel Perry, with whom Betjeman had shared rooms at Oxford in 1926.

If Anthony* has his heart in the right place he will let me stay at ye old Ridgewaye next weekend when you are there; I have written to him an appealing letter. In that case we can concoct endless plans. This sudden blow is no more than an incentive as far as I am concerned. Why the Ethel M. Dell[†] are you not allowed to see who you like? I shall come down in a car with Lord Alfred Douglas,[‡] Tom Douglas, Norman Douglas, Horatio Bottomley and Mrs Hearn and set light to Catball when dear little Red Nose[§] and her blasted textiles are in it. I wonder if she is at the bottom of it all? I must confess that I have never loved you so deeply as I do now. It takes circumstances like this to get me on the annoyance, I think I shall have Red Nose exiled from Egypt and from England for receiving and dealing in stolen woven goods.

Would you be so kind as to imprint a piece of paper with a lipstick kiss for me, to go back with Lionel as a token of good faith and fellowship and the work of each for weal of all. I hear that they have balanced the budget. This will only increase class hatred (hatred of the lower classes for the middle, not the upper classes) because of the 10% off the dole and will also do no more than put off the collapse until next year's budget [which] will have to meet an ever greater deficit owing to the . . . oh enough of it. You will be back again then. I shall whisk you off to Ireland when the collapse comes and there two enormous eyes will roll around the emerald fields and purple hills and a cool hand will clasp my clammy one and together we will walk to the Lake Isle of Innisfree or Pakenham Hall[¶] or Furness or Shelton Abbey. Darling I love you I love you I love you Dorothea and Dorothea every day.** It's hell. But my God it's exciting, ain't it duckie?

---

* Anthony Arthur Russell was a friend of Betjeman's and probably the person who introduced him to Camilla. He was two years older than Betjeman and an undergraduate of Balliol when they met.
† 'Hell'. Ethel M. Dell (1881–1939) was a writer of popular romantic novels.
‡ Oscar Wilde's 'Bosie'.
§ 'Red Nose' was Betjeman's and Camilla Russell's name for Lady Russell, Camilla's mother.
¶ Home of the Longford family.
** 'More and more every day'. Dorothea Moore was a popular writer of fiction for girls.

Clean up your little face and go and be nice to everyone, because I love you and don't care what happens.

23 August 1931

There has been the TT or something over here. I know that but semi-conscious from a hideous journey with toughs in mackintoshes and old school scarves I was whistled off to a prominent position on a grandstand to see a lot of small and noisy cars go down a rather boring piece of road. One of the drivers – a Sir Henry Birkin – was staying here so the talk has been motorcars only so far. It is going to stop soon I think. I owe that frightful Mrs Graham ten shillings – I clean forgot about it and am sending it to your aunt by the next post. This is a very grand party I must confess and I can't think why I have been asked. It consists of all the richest and most titled of the Guinnesses and little Bloody and Veronica. I have painted a very nice picture in watercolours on the plate-glass window in the Library here of little Bloody.

It is a lovely evening now and except for the fearful distant noise of motors carrying people to Belfast it might be as lovely as Sezincote. I do wish you were here. My God I do. Those enormous blue eyes must be rolling along the page now but I wish they could roll over my pale green face and unshaven chin.

How many times have I told you not to leave your things about? Why the hell don't you take them up to your bedroom and put them away instead of cluttering up the space here? And haven't I told you not to write to that young man? Who are his people? Do you know him well? If so you have seen enough of him – at any rate, I have. Was it all all right when we parted in Sedding Street to leave here on Thursday morning for PAKENHAM HALL, CASTLEPOLLARD, COUNTY WESTMEATH, IRELAND (Is that big enough for you to read it, duckie?) where I shall be for a week. I shall write to you before I leave here. I find to my horror that John Sparrow★ knows I have fallen in love. But how? The Longfords and the Dugdales alone

---

★ An Oxford friend. Edited Betjeman's *Selected Poems* in 1948.

know the state of my affections and Maureen* guessed it today. They must be silenced. But if Sparrow knows the Dean† does and there's no silencing him – 'though next to old Li and Dotty and AP-J‡ he is about my most cherished friend. Darlin', I am sorry – but I don't think they know it is you – and anyhow all will be well. The Willans at least have left you and I love you I love you I love you I love you I love you I love you I love you.

Undated

It's been such an effort to restrain my emotions in the enclosed letters which is to carry out your brilliant plan suggested today, that I want to see you so much I am almost tempted to go to the Castlepollard post office and telephone to you. My angel, God has prospered us. I found – not a little to my horror – that since the Dean knows all he lost no time in telling Evelyn Waugh. I see the Dean today and will try to shut him up. Anyhow I coped with Evelyn and I know I can trust him to remain quiet. He asked me where you lived and who you were and I said that you lived in Glos. He said that Alastair G§ – a great friend of his – has taken a house near Banbury and he will get A to ask you to stay there at – I suggest – the end of September, and that I will be asked, too. If this can be arranged will you be allowed to go? Darling, your letter was heaven and as I have to catch the last post before 3.30 on Monday I cannot say all I want as it is already 3.15 and your bogus letter has taken some time.

I will certainly arrange about Sezincote on the 11th–14th. What about little Red (Riding) Nose? Will she permit you to see me? You had better not say I am coming. Do what you can about Anthony. Your photograph is a bit of all right, I must confess. My God, I do love you, you little brute. The elephant in my other letter is close beside me here and if I pat him on the head I can delude myself by shutting my eyes and not noticing the anxious rough texture of his

---

* Maureen Guinness, who married Basil Dufferin.
† Maurice Bowra, Dean of Wadham. See p. 94.
‡ Alan Pryce-Jones, another Oxford friend and a writer.
§ Alastair Graham, a diplomat.

skin into thinking you are by me. I shan't be able to go to Sezincote when you have left for Cairo – it will be bitter melancholy. You need not worry about Mrs D.* She knows all without a doubt and will play up like anything. She is absolutely trustworthy.

'Virginia Creeper' is a stroke of genius. Bloody little boiling bitch! Why should she sit in a boat with you and be oily and malevolent while little Red Riding Nose stands in our way and the Irish Sea adds to the difficulty. Thank you, darling, for your plans. I should like the addresses you will be at. On Thursday I leave here for Cornwall to visit my hypochondriac mamma. She has written a complaining letter to me but kindly enclosing a silk handkerchief. My address in Cornwall will be: Trebetherick, Wadebridge, Cornwall.

Do write to me there as I get very depressed with my mother. I shall be back in London by the following Monday – or Tuesday – they call me for the post.

Darling – Darling – I must see you soon. I love you. Circles and sticks and bird and a tree when will my 'milla come back to me. I love you. I have kissed the spot marked X. Think of me at 11 and write. Kisses.

MYFANWY

New Lights for Old Chancels
1940

• • •

Kind o'er the *kinderbank* leans my Myfanwy,
White o'er the play-pen the sheen of her dress,
Fresh from the bathroom and soft in the nursery

---

* Mrs Ethel Dugdale.

Soap-scented fingers I long to caress.

Were you a prefect and head of your dormit'ry?
  Were you a hockey girl, tennis or gym?
Who was your favourite? What had a crush on you?
  Which were the baths where they taught you to swim?

Smooth down the Avenue glitters the bicycle,
  Black-stockinged legs under navy-blue serge,
Home and Colonial, Star, International,
  Balancing bicycle leant on the verge.

Trace me your wheel-tracks, you fortunate bicycle,
  Out of the shopping and into the dark,
Back down the Avenue, back to the pottingshed,
  Back on the house on the fringe of the park.

Golden the light on the locks of Myfanwy,
  Golden the light on the book on her knee,
Finger-marked pages of Rackham's Hans Andersen,
  Time for the children to come down to tea.

Oh! Fuller's angel-cake, Robertson's marmalade,
  Liberty lampshade, come, shine on us all,
My! What a spread for the friends of Myfanwy,
  Some in the alcove and some in the hall.

Then what sardines in the half-lighted passages!
  Locking of fingers in long hide-and-seek.
You will protect me, my silken Myfanwy,
  Ringleader, tom-boy, and chum to the weak.

LETTER TO MYFANWY PIPER
Extract

5 May 1943

• • •

Oh darling Goldilegz I often wish
That you were Margaret Short. I seem to see
Your strong blonde body curving through the reeds
At Shiplake while I await you in the punt
And Mr Piper sketches in the fields
Oh darling Goldilegz I write this down
Dunsany-wise, straight off, so full of sex
That as I write even my fountain pen
Becomes symbolic to me. Goldilegz
Still do you sweep your short hair off your brow?
Still do you run barelegg'd across the yard?
Still would you pillow with athletic curves
My bald, grey head upon your breasts?
Your stalwart body still excites me much
The thought of you, now spring is coming on,
Requires that I should exercise control . . .

SENEX*

Old Lights for New Chancels
1940

. . .

Oh would I could subdue the flesh
   Which sadly troubles me!
And then perhaps could view the flesh
As though I never knew the flesh
   And merry misery.

To see the golden hiking girl
   With wind about her hair,
The tennis-playing, biking girl,
The wholly-to-my-liking girl,
   To see and not to care.

At sundown on my tricycle
   I tour the Borough's edge,
And icy as an icicle
See bicycle by bicycle
   Stacked waiting in the hedge.

Get down from me! I thunder there,
   You spaniels! Shut your jaws!
Your teeth are stuffed with underwear,
Suspenders torn asunder there
   And buttocks in your paws!

Oh whip the dogs away my Lord,
   They make me ill with lust.

---

* Latin: 'old man'.

Bend bare knees down to pray, my Lord,
Teach sulky lips to say, my Lord,
　That flaxen hair is dust.

YOUTH AND AGE ON BEAULIEU RIVER, HANTS

New Statesman and Nation
6 October 1945

•　•　•

There comes a certain amount of poetry that reflects one's feeling as one gets older that there's no chance of anyone loving one again – and love played a large part in my writings of poetry. Now you know how when you've been ill, everything is more beautiful and more wonderful than when you're ordinarily quite well. Well this was my state when I went to stay on the Beaulieu River and I rowed out in a dinghy. It was a hot day and I was lying back in the boat recovering from having rowed when suddenly a sharpie passed – a sharpie is a small sailing boat – with the most beautiful girl you can imagine in it, and she asked me the time. There was a young man with her in the boat, too. She asked me the time and in order not to disappoint her, although I hadn't got a watch on me, I just made up the time so as to get a nice smile from her. And then she sailed out of my life. And I thought, well, there'd be no chance of her ever loving me and so I shall put myself into – her name was Clemency by the way and she was the daughter of a General Buckland – I shall put myself into the position of some old lady sitting by the lakeside, by the riverside, and seeing her go by. It's called 'Youth and Age on Beaulieu River'. And I may tell you one further point: when you're in the sailing world and messing about with small boats,

everybody else who messes about with small boats is very critical of you;
and along the Beaulieu River there are various houses where people
look out from their houses and see sharpies passing and criticise them.*

Early sun on Beaulieu water
　　Lights the undersides of oaks,
Clumps of leaves it floods and blanches,
All transparent glow the branches
　　Which the double sunlight soaks;
　To her craft on Beaulieu water
　Clemency the General's daughter
　　Pulls across with even strokes.

Schoolboy-sure she is this morning;
　　Soon her sharpie's rigg'd and free.
Cool beneath a garden awning
　　Mrs Fairclough, sipping tea
And raising large long-distance glasses
As the little sharpie passes,
　Sighs our sailor girl to see:

Tulip figure, so appealing,
　　Oval face, so serious-eyed.
Tree-roots pass'd and muddy beaches.
On to huge and lake-like reaches,
　　Soft and sun-warm, see her glide –
　Slacks the slim young limbs revealing,
　Sun-brown arm the tiller feeling –
　　With the wind and with the tide.

Evening light will bring the water,
　　Day-long sun will burst the bud,
Clemency, the General's daughter
　　Will return upon the flood.
But the older woman only
Knows the ebb-tide leaves her lonely
　　With the shining fields of mud.

---

* Introduction taken from *Trains and Buttered Toast* (2006).

5

FRIENDS

Bears and Boys

The 'Varsity Students' Rag (1927)
Archibald Ormsby Gore (1931–3)
Maurice Bowra: A Formative Friend (1974)
For Patrick, Aetat: LXX (1974)
W. H. Auden at Oxford (1975)
Interior Decorator (1964)

THE 'VARSITY STUDENTS' RAG

Cherwell
29 October 1927

•   •   •

I'm afraid the fellows in Putney rather wish they had
  The social ease and manners of a 'varsity undergrad,
For tho' they're awf'lly decent and up to a lark as a rule
You want to have the 'varsity touch after a public school.

CHORUS:
> *We* had a rag at Monico's. *We* had a rag at the Troc.,★
> And the one we had at the Berkeley gave the customers
> quite a shock.
> *Then* we went to the Popular, and after that – oh my!
> I *wish* you'd seen the rag we had in the Grill Room at
> the Cri.†

I started a rag in Putney at our Frothblower's Branch‡ down
there;
We got in a damn'd old lorry and drove to Trafalgar Square;
And we each had a couple of toy balloons and made the hell
of a din,
And I saw a bobby at Parson's Green who looked like
running us in.

★ The Trocadero.
† The Criterion.
‡ A network of drinking and charitable clubs set up in the early 1920s, defunct by
the early 1930s.

CHORUS:

We had a rag at Monico's. *We* had a rag at the Troc.,
And the one we had at the Berkeley gave the customers
quite a shock.
Then we went to the Popular, and after that – oh my!
I *wish* you'd seen the rag we had in the Grill Room at
the Cri.

But that's nothing to the rag we had at the college the other
night;
We'd gallons and gallons of cider – and I got frightfully tight.
And then we smash'd up ev'rything, and what was the
funniest part
We smashed some rotten old pictures which were priceless
works of art.

CHORUS:

We had a rag at Monico's. *We* had a rag at the Troc.,
And the one we had at the Berkeley gave the customers
quite a shock.
Then we went to the Popular, and after that – oh my!
I *wish* you'd seen the rag we had in the Grill Room at
the Cri.

There's something about a 'varsity man that distinguishes him
from a cad:
You can tell by his tie and blazer he's a 'varsity undergrad,
And you know that he's always ready and up to a bit of a lark,
With a toy balloon and a whistle and some cider after dark.

CHORUS:

We had a rag at Monico's. *We* had a rag at the Troc.,
And the one we had at the Berkeley gave the customers
quite a shock.
Then we went to the Popular, and after that – oh my!
I *wish* you'd seen the rag we had in the Grill Room at
the Cri.

ARCHIBALD ORMSBY GORE*
Letters to Camilla Russell and Alan Pryce-Jones (1931–3)

• • •

Letter to Camilla Russell
26 August 1931

Archibald, my bear, has accepted a call to the Congregational Church on Wanstead Flats where he has been doing the duty of lay reader for some years. He is also very keen on solo dancing.

Letter to Camilla Russell
21 December 1931

> There once was an elderly bear
> Whose head was the shape of a pear
> He sat in deep gloom
> And longed for the tomb
> As he'd lost nearly all of his hair.

Archibald has accepted the Incumbency of Raum's Episcopal Chapel, Homerton, E17. It is a proprietary chapel and in communion with a part of the Church of England. It has always been associated with the Evangelical party and he will have to wear a black gown in the pulpit as the Surplice is considered ritualistic. He will distribute Holy Supper at the Lord's Table after the 7 o'clock evening service every fourth Sunday in the month. I hope, as do we all in

---

* Betjeman and his teddy bear Archibald Ormsby Gore ('born' 1908) are said to have been the inspiration for Evelyn Waugh's depiction of Sebastian Flyte and his teddy bear Aloysius in *Brideshead Revisited* (1945). Why Betjeman gave Archibald the surname Ormsby Gore is not known. The Ormsby Gores are a real family, originating from Wales, and possessors since 1876 of the hereditary title Baron Harlech.

Homerton, Clapton, Walthamstow and Hackney Marshes, that his ministry will be successful and fruitful.

Letter to Alan Pryce-Jones
18 February 1933

Archie has been very drunk lately. He was asked to talk at the Young Men's Welfare Centre in Colchester last Tuesday and arrived reeling with sherry. I don't know why he should do this sort of thing. His Homer is still unfinished. He has ringworm.

MAURICE BOWRA:
A FORMATIVE FRIEND

From *Maurice Bowra: A Celebration*.
Edited by Hugh Lloyd-Jones
Duckworth, 1974

• • •

Stand with me on a moonlit night in the late twenties in the front quad of Wadham College seen from the porter's lodge. At the top right-hand corner of this pleasant, three-storeyed manor-house of a quadrangle, the work of Somerset masons, are the rooms of the Dean. Raised and cheerful voices may be heard. Above them all, and louder, is the voice of Maurice, the Dean of Wadham, audible even from here. One did not have to look for Maurice, one only had to listen.

So lovable, loyal and formative a friend must be written about without a waste of words. Maurice despised journalism and pitied journalists. He was a stickler for grammar. There must be no hanging clauses, no verbless sentence in what I write about him here. He also despised television and refused to appear on it.

If one wants to hear an echo of Maurice's voice it may be heard sometimes in the conversation of Isaiah Berlin, Patrick Kinross and Osbert Lancaster – 'Couldn't agree with you more,' 'Yers, yers – splendid!' But his resonant voice is needed and that 1914 army slang punctuated with 'old boy' and 'old man' to bring back the feeling of safe elation as the glass was thrust into one's hand and the introductions made to people one knew and liked already but given different titles in the fantastic hierarchy Maurice invented for them.

And then there were his clothes. 'Why do you dress like an undergraduate, Betjeman?' he said to me some years after I had gone down. This was because I still wore a tweed coat and grey flannel trousers. Maurice himself was always in a suit, generally dark blue.

The Oxford of the late twenties, which was when I first came up, seemed to me to be divided, in so far as undergraduates were concerned, between aesthetes and hearties. I was an aesthete. There would have been no hearties at the parties that I attended. Maurice's were always dinner parties. On the other hand we all knew he was a great 'college man' and was held in high favour by the rowing men of Wadham; and he may have known Blues – provided they came from Wadham. But he kept us all as sets and very much apart.

The guests I met at Maurice's dinner parties were generally intellectuals, with a few young peers who may have been sons of his friends of the 1914 war generation to which unexpectedly Maurice belonged. We could not believe that anyone so free and easy and unmilitary and scandalously entertaining could ever have fought the Huns in trench warfare. He never mentioned it in the twenties. We thought he was our own age.

I think his way of speaking with a strong emphasis on certain syllables partly came from Winchester. Maurice, though a Cheltonian, was at New College, which was then an Oxford branch of Winchester. I think it also came from Cambridge and such friends there as Dadie Rylands and Adrian Bishop. It was a King's Cambridge way of talking. Adrian Bishop was his closest and most reckless friend in the twenties. Under the pleasure-lover, as with Maurice, so with Adrian, there was the ascetic. Adrian, whose real name was Frank, became an Anglican–Benedictine monk and took the name of Brother Thomas More in religion. Maurice reconciled himself to this change by referring to Adrian as 'Brother Tom'. I still possess *A Sixteenth-Century Anthology* edited by Arthur Symons that Adrian gave me with this inscription: 'To John Betjeman, hoping that his thirty-first year may bring an increase in tact, wisdom and courage. With love, from Frank Bishop.' The censoriousness was characteristic of the stern self-discipline that Maurice, Adrian and many of that generation imposed on themselves.

Because Wadham had an Evangelical tradition going back to the time of Warden Symons who had arranged times of Chapel so that undergraduates could not attend Newman's sermons in St Mary's, Maurice also proclaimed himself an Evangelical. But his Evangelicalism was only skin deep. One of his closest friends among the Fellows of Wadham was Father Brabant, the Wadham chaplain for many years, who was most distinctly Anglo-Catholic. So were many of Maurice's friends. It was through one of these, Lord Clonmore, that I first met Maurice. Pierce Synnott, an Irish Roman Catholic, was about the only Papist friend of Maurice in these days. Maurice and I went to stay with both of these people and I remember on one occasion Maurice coming into my bedroom when we were changing for dinner and saying, 'I say, old boy, shall we roger the skivvies?' The gift of exceeding the bounds of good taste was to me one of his endearing characteristics. There was a streak of Gowing in *The Diary of a Nobody* about Maurice that either attracted or repelled.

So outspoken a man contracted enemies. Sometimes it may have been simply a matter of genes. The rival host to undergraduates in the late twenties was the University Lecturer in Spanish, G. A. Kolkhorst, then known as 'G'ug' and later as 'Colonel' Kolkhorst because he was so little like a colonel. 'Charming fellow, Kolkhorst,' said Maurice. 'A pity he's got a touch of the tarbrush.' To which Colonel Kolkhorst, who was wholly white, replied by always referring to Maurice as 'Mr Borer'. It was a good early lesson in diplomacy to be acceptable to both Maurice and the Colonel, as neither of them stood any nonsense and exposed mockingly any pretension. Maurice, who was so alarming on first acquaintance with his machine-gun fire of quips and sudden slaying of popular idols, was kindness itself when one was in trouble.

When I was rusticated he commiserated and had me to dinner and even drove out with congenial friends to Thorpe House, Oval Way, Gerrards Cross, where I was working my passage as a private schoolmaster. He came to see my parents and induced them to continue an allowance to me and he secured for me, through his friendship with the owners of the Architectural Press, a position on the *Architectural Review* that enabled me to keep myself independent of my parents. What he did for me, who was not of his College, he did for all the Wadham under-graduates. He was their adviser and friend who gave practical help. During the last war he gave practical help to the victims of the Nazi Government and found them positions in England. Politically I should have said he was left but not doctrinaire. Hugh Gaitskell was a close friend and many a wrangle over economics to which I did not listen did I hear at Maurice's table in my undergraduate days.

His most endearing quality was his power to build one up in one's own estimation. He did this by listening and either agreeing or sug-gesting a similar train of thought. In the same way he took one's own troubles on his shoulders. Firmly and kindly he separated me from those he regarded as unsuitable. Cautiously and slowly he made friends of the opposite sex who then became as close as his own gen-eration had been. I think particularly of Enid Starkie, Audrey Beecham, Dame Janet Vaughan and my wife, to whom he was devoted, and Pam Hartwell, Celli Clark and Ann Fleming. He forgave because he understood. What he could not forgive was dis-loyalty and ruthlessness. He was surprisingly kind and unshockable. Maurice continued his kindness to the children of his friends.

But his greatest loves were Oxford as a place and Wadham College as a society. He liked their buildings. My life is emptier without those afternoons when he would ring up and say, 'What about a look at Hertford and some Anglo-Jackson?' We would set off in search of the many works in Oxford of the architect Sir Thomas Jackson. Maurice would hear no word against him, for Jackson had been a Fellow of Wadham. His favourite colleges to visit when in architectural mood were Hertford because of the Jackson work, Keble because of Butterfield and his friend Crab Owen, and Pembroke because he admired the members of its Common Room and Dr Holmes Dudden, its Master.

In the twenties and thirties Maurice would venture further afield in hired cars driven very fast and dangerously by undergraduates. He did not drive himself. He took us to Garsington and Lady Ottoline* and Sezincote and of course we went out very fast to dine at the Spread Eagle at Thame when it was run by John Fothergill.

Once, when the car I was driving waltzed around in the road near Moreton-in-Marsh and buckled its wheels, he was quite unmoved. But I remember once taking him to see the inside of the Cowley Fathers' Mission House in Marston Street. That was the only time I knew him alarmed.

In later life he liked walking in North Oxford, especially in places like Belbroughton Road where he would look at houses in which he might retire. Another favourite walk was Holywell Cemetery, where he looked at the headstones to great brains and Heads of Houses now dust in erstwhile meadowland. He is buried there himself.

Shall any of us who knew him enjoy life as much as we did in his company? I can hear him say 'Definitely *no*.'

FOR PATRICK, AETAT: LXX†

Times Literary Supplement
15 November 1974

• • •

How glad I am that I was bound apprentice
To Patrick's London of the 1920s.

---

* Lady Ottoline Morrell, an artistic and political hostess, lived at Garsington Manor near Oxford.
† On the occasion of Patrick Balfour's seventieth birthday.

Estranged from parents (as we all were then),
Let into Oxford and let out again,
Kind fortune led me, how I do not know,
To that Venetian flat-cum-studio
Where Patrick wrought his craft in Yeoman's Row.*

For Patrick wrote and wrote. He wrote to live:
What cash he had left over he would give
To many friends, and friends of friends he knew,
So that the 'Yeo' to one great almshouse grew.
Not a teetotal almshouse, for I hear
The clink of glasses in my memory's ear,
The spurt of soda as the whisky rose
Bringing its heady scent to memory's nose
Along with smells one otherwise forgets:
Hairwash from Delhez, Turkish cigarettes,
The reek of Ronuk on a parquet floor
As parties came cascading through the door:
Elizabeth Ponsonby in leopard-skins
And Robert Byron and the Ruthven twins,
Ti Cholmondeley, Joan Eyres Monsell, Bridget Parsons,
And earls and baronets and squires and squarsons —
'Avis, it's *ages*! . . . Hamish, but it's *aeons* . . .'
(Once more that record, the Savoy Orpheans).
Leader in London's preservations lists
And least Wykehamical of Wykehamists:
Clan chief of Paddington's distinguished set,
Pray go on living to a hundred yet!

* A street in South Kensington between Harrods department store and the Victoria and Albert Museum.

W. H. AUDEN AT OXFORD

From *W. H. Auden: A Tribute*
Edited by Stephen Spender
Weidenfeld & Nicolson, 1975

• • •

When we first met we were Oxford undergraduates. I was ado-
lescent enough to think that learning was the accumulation of
facts and getting dates right. I greatly reverenced dons and thought
that schoolmasters were men who were not full enough of facts to be
made fellows of an Oxford or Cambridge college. When at
Marlborough I had had the run of a little-used part of the library that
contained, bound in leather, the whole run of Alfred H. Miles's *Poets
and Poetry of the Nineteenth Century*. The short biographies and clear
criticisms of these excellent volumes, together with the selected
examples of the poets, are still fresh in my mind. At school and at
Oxford I generally had with me the *Oxford Book of English Verse* and
Quiller-Couch's still unsurpassed *Oxford Book of Victorian Verse*. I felt I
knew as much about poetry as a schoolmaster, nearly as much as a don
and certainly much more than my fellow undergraduates.

Witness then my horror on being introduced to a tall, milky-
skinned and coltish member of 'The House' who contradicted all my
statements about poetry, who did not think Lord Alfred Douglas was
a better sonneteer than Shakespeare, who had read Ebenezer Elliott
and Philip Bourke Marston and other poets whom I regarded as my
special province and who was not in the least interested in the grand
friends I had made in The House – such as John Dumfries, Christopher
Sykes, Edward James, Harold and William Acton and Bryan Guinness;
who dismissed the Sitwells in a sentence and really admired the boring
Anglo-Saxon poets like Beowulf whom we had read in the English

school; and who was a close friend of John Bryson and Nevill Coghill, real dons who read Anglo-Saxon, Gutnish,* Finnish and probably Swedish and Faroese as easily as I read the gossip column of the *Cherwell* of which I was then an editor.

And yet there was an oracular quality about this tough youth in corduroys that compelled my attention. He was very attractive and quite unselfconscious and already a born schoolmaster and lecturer. He would not come to the fashionable luncheons with peers and baronets and a sprinkling of dons that I liked to attend and sometimes gave myself. He was not a member of the 'Georgeoisie' like Alan Pryce-Jones and Mark Ogilvie-Grant, who dined every night at the George restaurant to the strains of a string band. (Mark Ogilvie-Grant once came into the restaurant in a bathing dress with seaweed in his hair and carrying a looking-glass.) He didn't belong to the OUDS like Osbert Lancaster or Peter Fleming. He belonged to no clique. When he asked me to tea in his rooms high up in the north-west corner of Peck I felt I was district-visiting so snobbish was I, so other-worldly he. There it was that I found out where his heart was. He had quite enjoyed his life at Gresham's School but did not seem to have retained Greshamian friends in Oxford. At this time it was fashionable, in my set, for undergraduates to regard their parents as brutal philistines. Auden, on the other hand, much reverenced his father. They lived in Edgbaston and his mother was High Church as I was. He often spoke with affection of his parents and brother, of Birmingham and the country around it and was very proud of a relation who had written the decidedly antiquarian Methuen *Little Guide to Shropshire*. He was interested in sanitation as his father had been and was, even after I had gone down from Oxford, always asking me for the return of a book with coloured illustrations of soil-pipes and domestic privies for the working classes that he had lent me and that I had lost.

Wystan (the name is that of a Saxon saint whose church Wistanstow is fully noted in Auden's *Little Guide to Shropshire*) was unaware that he represented the new type of Oxford undergraduate. I was the old type: trivial, baroque, incense loving, a diner

---

* An almost defunct dialect of Swedish, related to Old Norse and possibly Gothic, spoken on the island of Gotland.

with a great admiration for the landowning classes and the houses and parks in which they were lucky enough to live. Wystan was already aware of slum conditions in Birmingham and mining towns and docks. But he combined with this an intense interest in geology and natural history and topography of the British Isles. He liked railways and canals and had a knowledge of Bradshaw's timetables. He liked visiting churches old and new. He loved the Isle of Man, its railways, trams and trains, and first encouraged me to go there. Above all he liked poetry, chanting it aloud after tea. In this he enjoyed the complicated internal rhymes in Irish hedge poetry and the alliteration of Anglo-Saxon poetry. The alliteration of Swinburne seemed false by comparison. The two friends of his I recall meeting in his rooms at this time were Gabriel Carritt (later Bill Carritt the politician) and William McElwee who became a schoolmaster at Stowe. They must have been interested in the music, a side of Wystan's life I was never able to share except in the appreciation of verbal rhythm.

Wystan and I much enjoyed discovering unknown poets, preferably of the last century and the Edwardian age, and reading out our discoveries to each other. This was how we stumbled on the works of the Reverend Dr E. E. Bradford, DD, whose lyrics, innocent and touching about the love of 'lads', as boys were so often called by scoutmasters in those days, used to bring us uncontrollable mirth.

> Once a schoolboy newly come,
>   Timid, frail and friendless,
> Feared to face a footer scrum
>   Oh! the taunts were endless.
>
> Suddenly he drew apart
>   Soon they heard him crying.
> With a penknife in his heart
>   Home they brought him dying.

This was the Auden I knew at Oxford and whom I was to meet later in the documentary film world and at home, when I was first married, in Uffington, Berkshire, where he rapidly wrote in some parts for a village play that my wife was producing. We never lost touch with him. The last two times we met were in the Refreshment Room of the Great Central Railway on Marylebone Station, before it was ruined by re-decoration and, more conventionally, at a poetry recital given by the BBC.

INTERIOR DECORATOR*

London Magazine
June 1964

• • •

Eternal youth is in his eyes;
  Now he has freshened up his lips;
He slicks his hair and feigns surprise,
    Then glances at his fingertips.

'My dears, but yes, *of course* I know,
    Though why you think of asking *me*
I can't imagine, even though
    It rather *is* my cup of tea.

You see, my dears, I'm old – so old
    I'll *have* to give myself away –
So don't be flattering when you're told –
    But I was *sixty* yesterday.

And so, of course, I knew them *all*,
    And I was with them when they went

---

* Originally entitled 'Period Piece'.

To Basil's marvellous *mâtelot* ball
    At Bedstead, somewhere down in Kent.

I was in decorating then,
    And Basil said the job was mine,
And, though I shouldn't say it, when
    I'd finished, it was just *divine*.

A *hideous* house, inside and out –
    And Basil's mother – well, not *quite* –
But still, I'll say for the old trout
    She paid my little bill all right.

I *stripped* the hideous painted wood,
    Stippled the corridors and halls,
And *pickled* everything I could,
    And *scumbled* nearly all the walls.

I put Red Ensigns on the seats
    And hung Blue Peters down their backs,
And on the beds, instead of sheets,
    Enormous pairs of Union Jacks.

My dears, just *everyone* was there –
    But oh, how *old* it makes me feel
When I recall that charming pair
    In *mâtelot* suits of *eau de nil*!

One was Kilcock, Clonbrassil's son,
    Who died in nineteen thirty-three
(God rest his soul!), the other one –
    Can you believe it – tiny *me*.

Bug Maxwell, Ropey, Rodney Park,
    Peter Beckhampton, Georges de Hem,
Maria Madeleine de Sark –
    I wonder what became of them?

Working in some department store –
    That was the last I heard of Bug.

Ropey was always such a bore,
    And didn't Rodney go to jug?

And Georges de Hem collaborated
    So that's the last we'll hear of him!
And Pete and I, though we're related,
    Are out of touch, now he's so dim.

And what's become of poor Maria?
    Patrick, I'd like another drink.'
He gazes sadly at the fire,
    And solemnly pretends to think.

Eternal age is in his eyes;
    They watch the countless parties pass,
And, as the conversation dies,
    His consolation is the glass.

6

ARISTOCRATS

Peers and Parties

The Anglo-Irish Aristocracy (1930–1)
Peers without Tears (1933)
The Earl of Rosse (1939)

THE ANGLO-IRISH ARISTOCRACY

Letters to Patrick Balfour and Camilla Russell (1930–1)

. . .

Letter to Patrick Balfour
1 September 1930

Lord Trimlestown's seat is called Bloomsbury near Kells and near this very remote place, as you know. We devised a very clever scheme for calling on him. We made out a petition to prevent the demolition of Dublin Places of Worship – which, by the way, are of course not going to be destroyed – and took it for him to sign. Bloomsbury is very difficult to find and when you do reach it, is very small. We asked about Lord Trimlestown in the district and no one had heard of him. There we found Bloomsbury, an unpretentious William IV structure in the Roman manner and painted light mauve and brown. We learned at a lodge near the grass-grown drive and ruined gates that Lord Trimlestown had left it fourteen years ago – 'Those were grand days,' the old man said. His eldest daughter is a Mrs Ratcliffe who lives in an even smaller Georgian house near Kells. That is all. Four of his nine sisters are nuns and the rest have not married very well. I am so sorry.

On the way back, heart-broken and stricken, we found an interesting sight in the roadside: an old man who lived in a wheelbarrow with a mackintosh and umbrella over the top, all year round. He was deaf and drunk but not dotty. I think he was a brother of Lord Trimlestown.

Letter to Patrick Balfour
13 September 1930

I have gathered quite a lot about Lord Trimlestown, his ancestors

and his sisters and daughters now living. I have made up a little
poem:

> -curry, -brock and -mell are gone,
> Soon 'twill be farewell to Clon;
> Little known they were before,
> They are even less with -more.

The other day we went to the Cavan Tennis Tournament. It was all
organised by Lord Farnham who did the umpiring, carried a bucket of
sand to the place where competitors serve and arranged that a subscription dance should take place in his house.

His house is called Farnham and, as he has had to sell most of his
furniture, it is a little bare but the acetylene gas makes a brave show;
so do Lady Farnham (who has the unfortunate habit of winking) and
his two daughters Verbena and Verbosa. They all told us it was very
sporting of us to come several times. Lord Farnham is just like a pear.
Very tall and slim. Do write to him as he is so badly off and Verbena
and Verbosa are so pretty. I fell in love with Verbena and danced with
her. She is very London.

Letter to Camilla Russell
29 August 1931

I feel obliged to write so soon on top of the other letter simply to
complain of the hellish people staying at Clandeboye, to praise the
heavenly people here. There was Seymour Berry about whom I have
complained to you in the past. He is the typical social success – dear
old Seymour, so witty you know and so influential – the sort of chap
it's well to keep in with, you know – the son of Lord Camrose. Oh!
He's so epigrammatic that the whole table hangs on his words. Then
there's dear old Buzzy – both he and Seymour have got six-litre
Bentleys, topping little buses, they can rev up and change down in
less than twenty minutes – splendid shock absorbers too. Dear old
Seymour – dear old Buzzy. I can't understand why little A★ surrounds
himself with them.

★ Ava – that is, Basil Dufferin.

Here there is Maurice Bowra coming with his Homburg hat on horizontally and his fists clenched and his untiring energy, kindness and humour. David C,* who is off his rocker, and Mary Pakenham,† to whom I am devoted, is here also. It was she who heard, when she was a girl at school, another girl say 'Lady Mary – *and* knows it.' Pansy her sister and Henry Lamb – good painter and funny chap who smokes Irish cigars – Pansy's husband, Evelyn Waugh with his eyes blazing with religious fanaticism and Frank whom you know and Eliza Harman his fiancée, with whom he is walking out, and her sister who seems dim and not unnaturally frightened. The Longfords are delightfully mad this year. Edward (L.) struck a man in the face at the Dublin Horse Show because he was a hearty and sang 'God Save the King' when people were not supposed to. There was a free fight all over the stand and Edward had to leave. There is an old family toy here of whom I am very fond . . . but not so nice as my old bear Archibald . . . who is very interested in Temperance Work at Clacton-on-Sea.

PEERS WITHOUT TEARS‡

Evening Standard
19 December 1933

• • •

I think the English, Scottish and Irish peerage lives up to its reputation of eccentricity. It was a peer, not known to the world at large, who rushed round an Oxford quadrangle shouting 'I'm as drunk as

---

* Lord David Cecil.
† A sister of Frank Pakenham.
‡ Published on the occasion of a Parliamentary debate about House of Lords reform.

the lord that I am.' There is another of equal eccentricity who takes off his hat when passing any Protestant churches or Nonconformist chapels. And I often think, as a serious student of the peerage, that there are probably many more just as peculiar whose oddities are concealed behind some simple statement in *Who's Who* like '*recreation:* all outdoor sports'. I have seen the son and heir of an Irish peer hooked by his braces to the spikes of a high iron railing. This is outdoor sport.

Victorian novels were always full of 'mad lords' and 'dissolute earls', while baronets were almost exclusively 'wicked'. And only the other day someone spoke to me of a friend as being 'mad as a peer' which, considering several peers are locked up in asylums, shows how such popular catchphrases have a foundation of fact.

Not for the world would any of us in our senses have such peers degraded. They are nearly always cleverer than commoners. A Lords debate, for those who bother to read *Hansard*, is much better than a debate on the same subject in the Commons. And peers, where they have not been taxed out of them, have their estates to attend to as well as their debates.

Of course not all peers sit in the House of Lords. Many Irish and Scotch ones are not even allowed to. The last Lord Cloncurry (who in his will left some of his money to a Protestant archbishop and some to a Romanist archbishop) travelled all the way over to London from Dublin to hear a Lords debate. When he reached the House he was refused admission because no one knew who he was and had to go to a relation to have papers signed proving his identity.

His brother, the previous Lord Cloncurry, was the unwitting cause of a setback in the history of Ireland. Gladstone was anxious to put through some sort of Land Bill for Ireland of the utmost importance. He was told that the man he ought to consult was Lord Cloncurry. There were at that time several Irish peers with the prefix 'Clon' to their titles. Gladstone's secretary got the name wrong and sent for Lord Clon—— instead of Lord Cloncurry. Lord Clon——, though not in the least interested in any Irish Land Bill, was overcome with excitement at getting a summons to see Mr Gladstone. He showed the letter to his friends at the club. His friends advised him to go and gave him several glasses of port before he set off. On seeing him, Mr Gladstone immediately held forth on the Irish Land question for half an hour. At the end he said, 'Well, what do you think of that?' Lord Clon——, still under the influence of port, said 'I think it's all tommy rot.' Thus was an Irish Land Bill never passed.

There are hundreds of foreign and papal counts, frequently bogus, who are of little interest. There are the well-known peers – the Dukes, Lord Lonsdale, Lord Derby and most political peers. They are also not of interest to a thorough student. My interest lies in the comparative rarity of British peers and the extraordinary obscurity of some of them. There are those peers whose ancestors were well known and who must have an awful time trying to live up to their forebears. Among them are Lord Nelson, the Reverend the Lord Byron and the Duke of Wellington. Then there is at least one peer who should be known for his name alone. He is the Marquess of Downshire and his Christian names are Arthur Wills Percy Wellington Blundell Trumbull Sandys Hill. And who knew about Lord Sherard until he died? I think that I was the only person. He lived in Western Australia as 'Mr Castle' and when he died the papers said that a Bournemouth clergyman had succeeded to the title. But the whole thing was so muddy that it was not until some time afterwards that it was discovered that the Bournemouth clergyman had been dead for months.

Lord Harberton is the author of two brilliant books that Sir John Squire reads every night at his bedside. They are called *Worse than Scripture, or the Truth about Science* and *How to Lengthen our Ears*. Lord Harberton lives in Brittany and is said to have taken a taxicab right across France to see his brother who was staying on the shores of the Mediterranean. Another author peer was the late Lord Westmeath whose recent publication *Stephen Montressor* (Talbot Press, Dublin), though not at all similar to the work of Lord Harberton, should be on every bookshelf alongside the work of John Oxenham and Wilhelmina Stitch. Lord Westmeath added a wing to his house in Ireland, which was already rather large, and then, with a fine sense of symmetry, added another wing at the other end, to balance. This is in the eighteenth-century tradition.

Several peers have no addresses and but the briefest notice in *Who's Who*. They always interest me. Among them are Lords Cork, Haldon, Langford and Massy. I met Lord Massy in a little cottage on the Wicklow hills. Lord Belmore, on the other hand, occupies more than half a column of *Who's Who*. He is a trustee of Enniskillen Savings Bank and a Conservator of Fisheries for Enniskillen district, among other things.

Some lords do not mention their particular interests. For instance, Lord Clonbrook (the peerage is now, alas, extinct) did not like to see the stumps of trees about his park. He used to get his men to dig a hole round the tree to be removed and then saw it off deep down near the root. Though this way of cutting down trees was possibly expensive, it was certainly tidy. Then there is Lord Ashbourne who wears a saffron kilt and generally speaks Gaelic or, failing that, French but never English. Lord Roden is extremely interested in high explosives and blows up bits of his estate. Lord Trimlestown (whose peerage was created in 1461), though over seventy, is still – thanks to a hard early life before the mast – keen on dancing and racing.

Of course, all this reads rather like a gossip column. But it is not a gossip column of an ordinary kind because few of the peers I have mentioned appear in the newspapers. Their work and their hobbies are carried on behind the scenes. Do not let it be supposed that they do nothing. Lord Talbot de Malahide is the owner of some priceless Boswell manuscripts relating not only to Dr Johnson but to Boswell's private life. A deputation of literary professors from the universities sent a letter asking Lord Talbot de Malahide to let them see the manuscripts. The reply was described to me as 'short and unambiguous'. It must have taken a good deal of hard thought to make such a reply as that.

Three very interesting peers are Lord Taafe, Lord Newburgh and Lord Gardner. Lord Taafe is an Austrian, just as Lord Newburgh is an Italian. Because Lord Taafe fought in the Austrian army against England he had his peerage taken away from him; Lord Newburgh, being on the Allies' side, is still a member of the House of Lords. Poor Lord Taafe is only Count Taafe now. Surely it would be polite to give him back his peerage? Lastly there is Lord Gardner. If you look in *Who's Who* or *Debrett* you will find no mention of his name. Some publications say the peerage has lapsed. Actually Lord Gardner is a Eurasian engine-driver in India. Possibly the engine-driver is a picturesque addition. Anyhow, Lord Gardner, like some of the peers I have mentioned, cannot often be seen helping to govern the country in the House of Lords.

THE EARL OF ROSSE

Letter to Michael Rosse
10 September 1939

• • •

Those castellations
 Like Constellations
And wide plantations
 Mid crags and moss
Do guard Birr Castle
A fine example
To all and sundry
 Like the Earl of Rosse.

'Tis he abides there
Likewise he hides there
And entertains there
 At his own expense
He's built an arbour
With his own labour
Of beech and maple
 For a defence.

The green arbutus
And greener yew there
In plann'd confusion
 Do sweetly grow
And there the dahlia
Like royal regalia
With never a failure
 For ever blows.

'Tis there the telescope
Just like a periscope
Or Grecian Penelope
   So loyal and grand
Waits twixt its arches
For all researches
Of astral bodies
   The Earl's command.

Were I the Keeper
Or e'er the creeper
About each window
   And antique boss
I would embrace them
And interlace them
Those ancient buildings
   For the Earl of Rosse.

7

FOREIGNERS

Sitzbaths and Hookahs

Correspondence (1930—9)
The Costa Blanca (1971)
Turks (1955)

CORRESPONDENCE

Letters to Patrick Balfour, Diana Guinness and Alan Pryce-Jones (1930–9)

• • •

Königshof Grand Hotel Royal, Bonn, Germany
To Patrick Balfour
15 April 1930

It is useless to pretend that I enjoy myself abroad. The continual difficulty of overcoming a foreign language which the meanest children in the public gardens opposite can speak with fluency, the constant frustration of natural impulse through inability to communicate with the object of one's desires, overcomes the spirit as much as it mortifies the flesh. For instance I have drunk tea in my life but never have I wanted to drink it so much as in this town. It is obtainable but I do not know how to ask for it; it is waiting steaming hot, but I have not the courage to depend upon my *Hugo's Simplified Course* . . .

To Diana Guinness
12 August 1932

I am sorry to hear that you are ill in the South of France with pleurisy. It is probably not true but if it is I am very, very sorry for you, not so much because of your disease, as because you are in the South of France which has always been in my mind as something worse than Maidenhead although I admit I have never been there.

To Alan Pryce-Jones
17 September 1939

My dearest Bog, What a joke about your being a Captain, if it is really true. But how distasteful for you, having to go over to France. Abroad is so nasty. I would rather die in Wolverhampton than Aix-la Chapelle. But then you prefer abroad, don't you? I hope your job is as nice as it sounds and I hope you will end up as a Colonel and come through quite safely . . .

THE COSTA BLANCA
Two Sonnets

Saturday Book: Volume 31
1971

• • •

SHE
The Costa Blanca! Skies without a stain!
Eric and I at almond-blossom time
Came here and fell in love with it. The climb
Under the pine trees, up the dusty lane
To Casa Kenilworth, brought back again
Our honeymoon, when I was in my prime.
Goodbye democracy and smoke and grime:
Eric retires next year. We're off to Spain!

We've got the perfect site beside the shore,
Owned by a charming Spaniard, Miguel,
Who says that he is quite prepared to sell
And build our Casa for us *and*, what's more,

Preposterously cheaply. We have found
Delightful English people living round.

HE (*five years later*)
Mind if I see your *Mail*? We used to share
Our *Telegraph* with people who've returned –
The lucky sods! I'll tell you what I've learned:
If you come out here put aside the fare
To England. *I'd* run like a bloody hare
If I'd the chance, and how we both have yearned
To see our Esher lawn. I think we've earned
A bit of what we once had over there.

That Dago caught the wife and me all right!
Here on this tideless, tourist-littered sea
We're stuck. You'd hate it too if you were me:
There's no piped water on the bloody site.
Our savings gone, we climb the stony path
Back to the house with scorpions in the bath.

TURKS
First programme in the experimental series 'Foreigners'

BBC Home Service
20 February 1955
Producer: Joseph Weltman

• • •

The questions that I'm going to ask Dr Iz are not intended to be insulting. They're being asked from the point of view of an insular fool, which I am. When you were naughty and self-willed as a child, I wonder if your parents ever called you a 'regular Turk' and when you hear the word 'Turk' do you think of that or do you think of Turkish cigarettes? Do you think of 'the terrible Turk' or of Turkish delight? Do you think of 'the Sick Man of Europe' or do you think of baths and carpets? We all of us have a number of these mental associations with a mere word and they seem to form a confused general picture of the terrible Turk and now that I've got one with me in the studio – Dr Iz, a real live Turk – I'm going to ask him for his comments on some of our popular notions about his people. Now I don't think I've ever met a Turk before and therefore there's one question that strikes me: they're very rare. Are there many in England? How many?

IZ: There are about 200 Turks in England. Most of them are students scattered all over England, mostly in Northern or Midland industrial towns.

BETJEMAN: Only 200?

IZ: Yes.

BETJEMAN: That's extraordinary. Well now, there's another thing I'm going to do and that is describe you because you don't look at all Turkish. You've got a fair skin and dark hair and I expected you to be wearing a fez.

IZ: Well you see, when people think of Oriental countries, they lump all the Oriental countries together. Of course Turks don't look what you would call Oriental; they look more European and you might easily come across fair or fair-haired, blue-eyed and tall Turks whom you'd think sort of not European even. So they are a mixture. And as to wearing a fez, until thirty years ago Turks used to wear a fez. Apart from the fez, the whole dress was European; but in 1925 the fez was also abolished.

BETJEMAN: If you were to wear a fez in Turkey now, you'd be considered as an extreme conservative, is that it?

IZ: No, that would be an offence, because it's not allowed.

BETJEMAN: You'd go to jail, would you?

IZ: Well, perhaps you'd be warned not to wear it. It isn't wise.

BETJEMAN: Now another question, quite irrelevant, but, er, do you eat sweets all the time? There's a packet there, I notice.

IZ: Yes, well, I just brought them back from Turkey just to show you.

BETJEMAN: What is it? Turkish Delight? May I have a bit?

IZ: Please do.

BETJEMAN: Oh thanks very much.

IZ: Well, as to eating a lot of sweets, we do eat lots of sweets but rather sweet pastries and very little chocolates. In Turkey chocolates are eaten by children rather than the grown-up people.

BETJEMAN: Go on talking for a minute because I can't speak.

IZ: Yes, well, you see we eat lots of pastries, sweet pastries and all sorts of boiled sweets and this Turkish Delight.

BETJEMAN: This Turkish Delight doesn't taste anything like – if you can hear me speaking properly – doesn't taste anything like the kind of stuff I buy in sweet shops. It's much more chewy and it seems to have nuts in it.

IZ: You can have plain Turkish Delight with nuts and sometimes it has cream in it.

BETJEMAN: Lovely stuff. Can I take some more back with me afterwards because I must resist it for the moment. Now is Turkish coffee, what we call Turkish coffee, half sugar and half coffee as it is here?

IZ: You can have it as you like. You can order a plain Turkish coffee which is without sugar, or medium Turkish coffee which is half sugared, or a sweet Turkish coffee which is half sugar, half coffee.

BETJEMAN: Is the coffee a different kind of coffee from French?

IZ: It has got like a powder. You can buy it fresh in London in some shops. You can buy it at Harrods, for instance.

BETJEMAN: Oh yes. By the way we'll get into trouble for advertising!

IZ: I see. Well then, you can buy it in some other shops!

BETJEMAN: Now another question on this subject of eating and drinking. Do you eat your food lying down on a long sofa and not in the presence of women?

IZ: Well, I thought Romans did that.

BETJEMAN: So did I.

IZ: Yes, but the Turks don't. But in the old days, up to the last century, Turks ate their food sitting on cushions on the floor round a low table, but that was of course a long time ago. You can find this almost ceremonial eating in villages nowadays, but in towns they eat at tables.

BETJEMAN: Like we're sitting at a table here and me eating Turkish Delight, yes. Now is the food – I've got an idea, I've never had Turkish food to my knowledge – but is it all oil and spices, which is what I imagine it to be?

IZ: Turkish food is not spicy, that's of course a confusion with Indian and Arab food. We can put sometimes spice as you put here in England, but we do use oil.

BETJEMAN: What oil?

IZ: Olive oil.

BETJEMAN: Olive oil?

IZ: Olive oil is used to make some special dishes which are eaten cold.

BETJEMAN: Oh yes. And why are turkeys called turkeys?

IZ: I think they thought they were brought from Turkey. We all call them 'Hindi', which means simply 'India', because this was originally an Indian hen, because we thought that turkeys were brought from India, as you think that they were brought from Turkey.

BETJEMAN: So Turks eat a lot of turkeys, do they? Yes? They don't have Christmas but do they eat them all the year round?

IZ: Yes, they eat them any time.

BETJEMAN: Like we eat chickens.

IZ: Yes, and they call them 'India'.

BETJEMAN: I see, yes. Now, er, when you're in Turkey, I should imagine you couldn't do it in the Underground, but when you're in Turkey do you smoke a hookah?

IZ: Personally, I don't. I don't even smoke cigarettes. But people do smoke a lot in Turkey, smoke Turkish cigarettes, and some people smoke hookah, which we call 'nargile', by the way. This smoking hookah is going out of fashion.

BETJEMAN: What sort of tobacco is it that's smoked in a hookah?

IZ: It's a special tobacco imported from Persia.

BETJEMAN: Do you know what is the difference between Turkish tobacco and Virginian tobacco — I mean apart from the ones grown in America?

IZ: I can only tell you what people say, because I'm a non-smoker. They say they find, some people find, Turkish tobacco stronger than American tobacco for instance.

BETJEMAN: Anyhow it's different. And are your baths entirely of steam?

IZ: We have two kinds of baths: in the house, as you have a bath, and in the market in the street, a public bath, as you have Turkish baths here. The Turkish bath, of course, is entirely of steam but in our houses we have just an ordinary bath.

BETJEMAN: Oh you've got a bath with hot and cold?

IZ: Yes.

BETJEMAN: But does everybody go to the public baths very often?

IZ: No, not everybody.

BETJEMAN: And are there as few Turkish baths in Turkey as there are in the big towns in England, let's say one or two?

IZ: No, there are many. Every district has its public bath.

BETJEMAN: And do people go to sleep all night in them?

IZ: No, they're not allowed to sleep the night. They have to leave the bath at twelve.

BETJEMAN: Oh well, now do let me give you some advice. In England if you're absolutely stumped for hotel money, I've done it myself, a Turkish bath is cheaper and you can spend the night there, at least you can in some.

IZ: I must go and try.

BETJEMAN: Now are your carpets? what we call Turkey carpets – there's a special kind of Turkey carpet in England: very thick, rather hideous, generally red and blue and very much favoured in old-fashioned hotel lounges and boarding houses.

IZ: Yes, I know. I'm very surprised to hear that they're called Turkey carpets because I've never seen one in Turkey. Turkish carpets or Turkey carpets – genuine ones – are exactly like what you call Persian carpets or Bokhara carpets with this difference: that the design and the colour may be slightly different, peculiar to Turkish.

BETJEMAN: Are red and blue prevailing colours?

IZ: Yes.

BETJEMAN: That's possibly why we call them Turkish here, but we mean a great thick thing for deadening the sound of one's hob-nailed boots. Now there is a lot of magic in Turkey. We always hear about flying carpets in connection with Turkey.

IZ: I'll tell you why you connect Turkey with flying carpets: because they appear in *A Thousand-and-One Night* tales which originated from Baghdad, which used to be a Turkish province until thirty years ago. So all this magic and flying carpet in Turkey could easily be associated.

BETJEMAN: Oh I see.

IZ: But in present-day Turkey, magic not only doesn't exist but, er, is prohibited by law.

BETJEMAN: Oh, oh, isn't that sad. Well, I've got a lot more questions I'm going to ask. I see you've got a pen in your hand. Now when you write, does your writing come out like fretwork?

IZ: It used to until 1928. We used to write from right to left and in Arabic script. This is now abolished and in Turkey now what we use is an alphabet which is based on the Latin alphabet and we use exactly the same letters except for instance C is J, C with a cedilla is CH, and S with a cedilla is SH, and we have one I without a dot on it.

BETJEMAN: Oh, what is that? How do you sound that?

[Noises indicating sound of letter I without the dot.]

BETJEMAN: Oh, and your name is spelt 'Iz' but I notice it's got a dot on it.

IZ: Yes, 'Iz' without a dot would be 'Uz'.

BETJEMAN: Yes, I've got it. Now there's a character that we all know about: the Sick Man of Europe. Was he Abdul the Damned? There was a film about him.

IZ: The expression 'Sick Man of Europe' was, as far as I know, used for the first time by the Czar of Russia in the middle of the nineteenth century at a party. The Czar addressing the British Ambassador said, 'We have a sick man who may die and you must see him off at his funeral'; and he meant Turkey.

BETJEMAN: Oh I see.

IZ: This is how this expression 'Sick Man of Europe' started, because the Ottoman Empire was sort of disintegrating.

BETJEMAN: Well!

IZ: Well, Abdul Hamed is of course nothing to do . . .

BETJEMAN: . . . He's Abdul the Damned. Why was he damned?

IZ: Because his rule was despotic and many people disliked him so that sometimes they called him 'Abdul the Damned'.

BETJEMAN: Oh I see: it was a term of abuse.

IZ: Of course, not by Turks: this expression is not a translation of a Turkish expression.

BETJEMAN: Oh I've got it, yes, it's some Englishman or somebody. Now is your Parliament, the thing that was also very popular in England as a romantic thing, 'The Sublime Port'?

IZ: 'Sublime Port' was the name of the Ottoman Government – or rather, the sea, the place, or the building of the Ottoman Government, was called 'Sublime Port'.

BETJEMAN: Rather like the Houses of Parliament?

IZ: Not exactly: it wasn't a Parliament but rather the central Government, sort of the Prime Minister, sort of Downing Street.

BETJEMAN: Is it still there?

IZ: It's still there but the Turkish Parliament is in Ankara.

BETJEMAN: And what is in the 'Sublime Port' now?

IZ: The seat of the Governor of Istanbul.

BETJEMAN: Oh I see, yes. And it's called that to this day.

IZ: Yes, it is.

BETJEMAN: Yes, I see. Now there's one or two questions I'd like to ask you about yourself. Where were you brought up?

IZ: I was born and brought up in Istanbul which was called Constantinople.

BETJEMAN: It's the same thing.

IZ: Yes, until 1928 when the Latin alphabet was accepted in Turkey. But Turks called Constantinople always Istanbul.

BETJEMAN: Oh, they always have done?

IZ: They've always called it Istanbul. This change sort of happened in Europe.

BETJEMAN: When you went for a holiday when you were a child, did you go into the country in Turkey, do they do that, do they go to the sea?

IZ: They do, but in Istanbul they don't need that because Istanbul is so scattered and so vast that it's very easy to go to the country in the town itself.

BETJEMAN: Oh yes I see; and did you when you were a child, did you ever go into the country to a lake beginning with X or Z?

IZ: Oh you mean Van. Well it's too far but I went to, for instance, Uludag which is a mountain resort near Istanbul which is a wonderful country like Switzerland with pine trees and lakes and waterfalls. It's just a few hours from Istanbul.

BETJEMAN: One further question about Turkey: is there lots of grass there or is it very barren and tree-less like we imagine the Holy Land to be?

IZ: It depends. The centre of Anatolia is rather desert and barren but the north Anatolian coast, west Anatolian southern coast and Istanbul are not barren, they're green.

BETJEMAN: And you have grass in the squares?

IZ: Oh yes.

BETJEMAN: Now is there such a thing as a Turkish garden? – that does interest me, the gardening in Turkey. Have you got a garden yourself?

IZ: Yes, Turks are very fond of flowers and gardening and you'd be surprised to find how Turkish gardens are similar to English gardens. They are very informal, just the opposite of geometric French gardens, and we have vegetable gardens and walled gardens.

BETJEMAN: Is there any particular Turkish flower that we know over here?

IZ: Well of course the tulip is almost a national flower because in Turkish history there is a period which is called the 'tulip age' when the tulip was very popular. As a matter of fact, the name 'tulip' in English is from Turkish.

BETJEMAN: It's a Turkish word, is it?

IZ: From a Turkish word and it was brought from Turkey.

BETJEMAN: By the Dutch?

IZ: By the Dutch.

BETJEMAN: And then to England. Oh yes, I see. Right. I've got a certain picture. And is there such a thing as the Turkish theatre?

IZ: Until the middle of nineteenth century, we used to have Shadow Plays as in China or Commedia dell'Arte as in Italy – sort of improvised theatre on fixed patterns. But towards the end of the nineteenth century we took from Europe, from France, the modern theatre and now we have theatre as in England, translated from Western languages sometimes.

BETJEMAN: You've got your own Turkish dramatists?

IZ: Yes we have.

BETJEMAN: And have you got Turkish opera?

IZ: Turkish opera is very young. Some twenty to twenty-five years ago, Paul Hindemith* was invited to come and found a School of Opera and now we have a young Turkish Opera in Ankara.

BETJEMAN: But before that there was no equivalent of opera in Turkey?

IZ: No.

BETJEMAN: And is there ballet in Turkey?

---

* Prolific composer and violist, he visited Ankara in 1935–7.

IZ: Ballet is also a new thing. Miss de Valois★ came from England and started a Ballet School in Turkey which hasn't started yet to perfect anything but they're hoping in a few years' time they're going to start.

BETJEMAN: Now do they make films in Turkey?

IZ: They do.

BETJEMAN: I mean the Turks.

IZ: Yes they do. Twenty years ago we used to have one or two films a year, now they make nearly fifty films a year.

BETJEMAN: And do the people go to the cinema a lot? Are there cinemas in every town?

IZ: Cinema is very popular.

BETJEMAN: Yes, and more popular than the theatre, I suppose. Now another question – about Turkish art. I have an idea that it's all patterns and that it's probably considered wrong to represent the human form. Is Turkish art all patterns or does it show people?

IZ: No, it shows people.

BETJEMAN: Has it always done so?

IZ: Yes, it has always done so but in miniature form, without perspective. Until a century ago, Turkish painting had hardly any perspective and it was old-fashioned style, just miniatures. Yes – but now we have a modern school of painting, under the influence of French Impressionists first and then more recent French schools and it's a very flourishing school of painting and it has several first-class painters.

BETJEMAN: Now there's a phrase in our *Book of Common Prayer* that talks about 'Jews, Turks and Infidels'. Why are Turks stuck in?

★ Dame Ninette de Valois, founder of the Royal Ballet.

IZ: I think the reason why 'Jews, Turks and Infidels' are put together is that, for many countries, Turks represented the invading Muslim armies. Muslims also meant infidels in the eyes of Christian Europe and for Christians in Europe of course all infidels, which meant here Turks and Jews who were disliked, were lumped together.

BETJEMAN: Oh yes I see, and therefore something to do with the Crusades, you think – yes, of course – it goes back to that age.

IZ: And later, of course, the Ottoman invasions in Central Europe. Remember, Turks put siege to Vienna twice, as late as the end of the seventeenth century, so the memories of these Turkish invasions had a reaction in Europe.

BETJEMAN: Why do we talk about a tough child as being 'a regular Turk'?

IZ: I think for similar reasons, I mean in French they have a proverb: 'strong as a Turk'. I think the reason must be the words Turkish and Turk and Turkey were associated for several centuries with strength and fighting capabilities.

BETJEMAN: Oh yes I see. And now there's a sort of corollary to that because Turks are always thought to be great gentlemen. 'The Turk is a gentleman': you always hear that said by officers of the 1914 war.

IZ: Even before that. Several English and Central European travellers went to Turkey from the sixteenth century onwards and their reports have been mostly in favour of Turks. Lady Montague, the wife of some English Ambassador, I think, sent letters from Turkey, with several pages in praise of Turks and Turkey. Of course in the 1914 war, the behaviour of Turkish soliders was so liked by the British in Gallipoli and the Dardanelles that they called them 'Johnny Turk' and 'gentleman Turk'.

BETJEMAN: There's one rather more intimate question; you may think it's insulting. But have you got a harem?

IZ: Well, unfortunately not! (*Laughter*)

BETJEMAN: Is it usual for Turks to have harems?

IZ: Well, I must tell you about this. Of course the Sultan had a harem. He had several wives and pashas who imitated him had also several wives but for the Turkish to have more than one wife in Turkish society is something very unusual. But to Europe, of course, the main person in Turkey was the Sultan, the Grand Turk, and the pashas, that's how the concept of harem was passed to Europe: from the palaces of viziers and grand viziers. But the ordinary Turk in the street had rarely more than one wife, although polygamy was allowed by Islam.

BETJEMAN: Oh yes, I was going to say – yes – bigamy is a crime in this country; it's not a crime even now in Turkey.

IZ: It is now. It wasn't a crime until 1925 but by special law bigamy or polygamy was abolished and prohibited. But this prohibition was not a hard thing on Turks because the institution did not exist, so to speak, in 1925.

BETJEMAN: Yes. So you won't know any very, very old man with about thirty very, very old wives?

IZ: Well, you can come across old men who have more than one wife in Turkey but very rarely.

BETJEMAN: Yes, I see. Now do the women wear yashmaks?

IZ: No. Yashmaks disappeared about sixty years ago completely and they were replaced by the petchah which means a kind of veil – yes! – and Turkish women in towns used to wear this petchah veil. But from 1920 onwards the petchah disappeared in Turkey; and in towns Turkish women are wearing dresses exactly like European women except, of course, in the country where some old women still keep on the traditional veil.

BETJEMAN: Now there's one other thing that always interests me very much. St Sophia was turned into a museum. Does that mean that religion doesn't now play a part in Turkish life?

IZ: Turkey is a secular state; religion and state have been separated in 1925 and the state doesn't interfere in any way in religious affairs. Atatürk wanted St Sophia to be turned into a museum to avoid all sort of religious friction between Muslims and Christians.

BETJEMAN: Well, thank you very much indeed, Dr Iz. I think you've been most patient with me asking these inane questions and answering them so interestingly and so politely. Can I have another piece of Turkish Delight and would you like another piece? You certainly earned it.

8

DECADENTS

Divines and Divans

THE EIGHTEEN NINETIES
Extract

Introduction to *The Eighteen Nineties: A Period Anthology of Prose and Verse*
Edited by Martin Secker
The Richards Press, 1948

•   •   •

Draw the curtains, kindle a joss-stick in a dark corner, settle down on a sofa by the fire, light an Egyptian cigarette and sip a brandy and soda as you think yourself back to the world that ended in prison and disgrace for Wilde, suicide for Crackanthorpe and John Davidson, premature death for Beardsley, Dowson, Lionel Johnson, religion for some, drink and drugs for others, temporary or permanent oblivion for many more. Of all that brilliant company only Sir Max Beerbohm survives today, his complete eighteen-ninety self. What, for instance, happened to Theo Marzials, so famous once for his drawing-room songs, for his poems and his company? He it was who, Sir Max told me, was a clerk in the British Museum Reading Room with Edmund Gosse in the time of the great Librarian Panizzi. One still day, when learned heads were bent over books in that great circular room, Marzials was in the gallery when Panizzi came in. Marzials leaned on the rail and addressed the room thus: 'Am I, or am I not, the darling of the Reading Room?' We see him at a private view in the Grosvenor Gallery on page 17 of Max's essay in this book. We have a glimpse of him looking into a cage of stuffed birds in the South Kensington Museum and with chocolate creams loose in his pocket 'he had eaten five large chocolates in the space of two minutes; in his young days the handsomest, the wittiest, the most brilliant and the

most charming of poets, he had a tragic career in the extreme.' Thus
Ford Madox Hueffer in *Ancient Lights*. And only lately I read in a book
of reminiscences by H. de Vere Stacpoole that Marzials led an exotic
life in Paris. What really happened to him? Mr Secker learned from a
friend of Marzials that he died, cheerful to the last, but poor and forgotten, as a paying-guest in a farmhouse in Colyton, Devon. Are his
remains in Colyton churchyard? What, if any, was his tragedy?

What furnished rooms, what rest-homes for the aged, what bungalows, what little inns and smelly public houses, what *pensions* in the
south of France, have roofed over the last hours of other nineties
writers whose fame died with the twentieth century? Some I have
known myself who, with the stimulus of hospitality and a sympathetic ear, have flashed their old fire. In little flats I have seen them,
surrounded by the relics of former fame and riches, leather luggage
and silver-framed photographs. Some, connected with art, not
letters, I have found in real poverty. To very few was justice ever done
except in those happy last ten years of the old Queen's reign.

Another sip of brandy and another Egyptian cigarette; a whiff of
opium and we can see the mood of the time. Carriages from Mayfair
to Belgravia, sun-blinds on verandahs in Park Lane, stable-smells in
the mews behind and stretching in front of us the plane-trees, the
grass, the pedestrians and the riders in the Park. The scene will serve,
for I quote from *The Londoners*:

> 'Really! There is no art except Paris, no possibility of dining out of
> Paris, no good dressmakers beyond the limits of Paris, no perfect
> language except the perfect language of Paris, no gaiety, no verve,
> no dancing, no love-making worthy of the name, but in Paris.'
> 'Then, Mr Ingerstall, why on earth do you always live in London?'
> said the Duchess heavily.

And although Mr Ingerstall replied with a *bon mot*, his answer
would have been 'Because I like to shock and to rebel. Because I read
Baudelaire, because I hate the conventionalism of English life and like
the supposed looseness of the French.'

Ah, the wheels of the well-sprung carriages of those British conventions knew their place, bowling along on the ground under the
weight of the élite who sat in the cushioned seats.

> The rich man in his castle,
> The poor man at his gate,
> He made them high and lowly
> And ordered their estate.

That verse of the hymn was not omitted (as it often is now) in fashionable London churches. The tenantry bobbed in the villages, only money could buy a position equal to that of good birth. An economist – and they were as rare in those days as were their invitations to smart parties – an economist might say the world was cracking. But most of those who sat back in the carriages saw nothing wrong with the horses. For was not the pair that pulled them along sound? Was it not Money and Birth? And did not the road stretch on in the everlasting sunshine of those days when most people thought everything was getting better and better, with the Queen on the throne and the millennium in the offing?

What the Duchess believed in Park Lane, the knight's wife believed in South Kensington and Mr and Mrs Pooter believed near the Holloway Road. In the villages it was easier still to trust in a settled order of things – squire, parson, tenant, labourer. 'Oi knows moi place,' said the last as he took off his rustic hat, and 'I know mine,' said the squire's lady as she came round with the jellies to his sick wife.

Of course there were shades of opinion. There were Liberals and Radicals as well as Conservatives but the majority even of the first two did not think that anything was so seriously wrong that it could not be cured by model cottages, the advance of science, baths, sanitation, votes for women and raising the school-leaving age.

In this materialist world that had forgotten Original Sin, in this unwieldy industrialism grafted on to the dying roots of agricultural feudal life, where was the place for the artist? The true artist is always a rebel and in advance of his time. So he delighted to shock. And because the conventions of the time now seem so remote, the shock of his revolution seems so feeble.

> "Tell me not of Philosophies
> Of morals, ethics, laws of life'

sang Lord Alfred Douglas in a poem he afterwards regretted. In 1892 such thoughts must have seemed startling indeed, from one in his position. You might think and do outrageous things but you should never write them.

So the nineties' writers delighted to outrage the Duchess, the knight's wife and Mr and Mrs Pooter. And the measure of these people's delight at being outraged is the fame at the time of the nineties' authors. The Wilde scandal was a blow from which the writers who delighted to tell of Sin, to create an atmosphere of Evil and to deny their Maker never fully recovered. For these writers were in advance of their time, in that most of them were beginning to believe again that there really were such things as Sin and Evil and that there might be a Maker to deny.

Our ears, deafened by 'socially conscious' writers, by realism, reportage and propaganda, will hardly be able to hear their rebellion at all. It was largely formulated by the Paterian dictum that Art should not be 'socially conscious' and should have nothing to do with philosophies, morals, ethics, laws of life. It was, as it were, the equivalent in prose and verse of the abstract painting of more recent years. But if we do not recognise the note of rebellion, we will hear – those of us who can hear rhythm and rhyme – the accompaniment of sound craftsmanship. Never was English more carefully written than in the nineties. Infinite pains were taken to use balanced sentences in prose, to create atmosphere, to write mellifluously, to delight in language. Henry Harland's story 'Castles near Spain' is a forgotten piece of light romance, so delicately and beautifully written and constructed that it hangs like intricate lace over solid truth and by its very lightness and intricacy enhances the quality of that which it overlies. The writers seem not to have minded so much what they wrote about as that they wrote well. Such fastidiousness proclaims Housman a nineties poet. He published so little in his lifetime and what appeared posthumously was a long way short of it. John Davidson's poem 'The Ballad of a Nun', about a sort of nineties Lady of Shalott, seems melodramatic if read to oneself but if read aloud, the sound of the words gives the poem another life. By the same standards of sound, Yeats writing merely sonorously and decoratively in his early poems is but half the poet he became when he emerged from the sunflowers and Morris patterns of Bedford Park, untwisted his Celtic knots and became the great poet of his later years.

The time has come to open the windows, quench the joss-stick and Egyptian cigarette and substitute cocoa for brandy and soda. We are in the present. Once more, what happened to most of these writers? As Mr A. J. A. Symons has said: 'Some doubtless found salvation in the Fabian Society, others in the Catholic Church; but a minority remained that, despairing of truth outside itself, looked inward to the only verities that had not seemed to crumble while it watched: the cultivation of the self, the consolations of art.'

ON SEEING AN OLD POET IN THE CAFÉ ROYAL

Old Lights for New Chancels
1940

• • •

I saw him in the Café Royal.
 Very old and very grand.
Modernistic shone the lamplight
  There in London's fairyland.
'Devilled chicken. Devilled whitebait.
  Devil if I understand.

Where is Oscar? Where is Bosie?
  Have I seen that man before?
And the old one in the corner,
  Is it really Wratislaw?'

Scent of Tutti-Frutti-Sen-Sen
  And cheroots upon the floor.

OSCAR WILDE

Foreword to *Oscar Wilde: A Memoir* by Theodore Wratislaw
From the series *Makers of the Nineties*, edited by G. Krishnamurti
The Eighteen Nineties Society, 1979

• • •

These rhymes of mine, wrung forth by weariness
Of weary life among these fools, may bring
Me in my lifetime nothing; let it be.
But God! I pray Thee in after time to bless
Me with some poet-lover who may sing
My name, my lady's and our memory.
                    ＿THEODORE WRATISLAW

Every word of these lines must have been savoured and repeated
out loud. In the woods around Goring-on-Thames, in the
Warwickshire meadows and in a dream of the Mediterranean shores,
and by the wine-dark deep of the Aegean. They were written to echo
from the 1890s until today.

Do you think he repeated those lines to his hero Oscar Wilde
when he came down by train to visit him on the banks of the
Thames? And what, I wonder, would Dr Arnold of Rugby,
Theodore's headmaster, have thought of this decadent and revolu-
tionary pupil? A Bohemian nobleman by heredity and a Count of
the Holy Roman Empire. None of it goes with the shires and the
healthy hunting sets of those days. The only photograph of

Theodore Wratislaw I have seen shows a big egg-shaped face above a high collar and conventional suit, a clean-shaven man with pince-ncz. He looks like a foreign languages master at an Edwardian public school and he was in fact the descendant of the foreign languages master at Eton. Dr Krishnamurti, who likes the by-ways as well as the highways of the nineties, has done us a favour by publishing this poet whose words should be chanted out in a melancholy autumn garden.

I doubt whether Wratislaw, who was a qualified solicitor, committed any of the purple sins he liked to hint at in his lyrics. I think they were a tease to the establishment and I fear the books waited too long in the stock of Over's celebrated bookshop in Rugby. The melancholy and evil are skin deep. The buttoned-up figure with a high collar and conventional suit was obviously longing to burst out of his narrow neatness. He was a punk before his time, a hot-house flower left down in those soggy playing fields of Rugby where Tom Brown is said to have inaugurated Rugby Football.*

The delightful thing about this essay that has been recently unearthed is the happy light it throws on the last few weeks of Oscar's life before the onslaught of the implacable Carson.† Goring and Pangbourne are still heavy with the nineties right up to the Seven Deadly Sins as those detached houses are called along the reach of the river at Pangbourne. We see Oscar confident, benevolent and witty, still writing *An Ideal Husband*, the favourite guest of many a country house, idolised by Lady Desborough. There he is in a white flannel suit on Goring Station meeting his young Rugbeian guest. This is a last streak of sunlight. Let us bask in it.

---

* Actually said to have been inaugurated by William Webb Ellis in 1823.
† Sir Edward Carson, counsel for the Marquess of Queensberry at Wilde's trial.

THE ARREST OF OSCAR WILDE AT THE CADOGAN HOTEL

Oxford and Cambridge
June 1933

•   •   •

He sipped at a weak hock and seltzer
  As he gazed at the London skies
Through the Nottingham lace of the curtains
  Or was it his bees-winged eyes?

To the right and before him Pont Street
  Did tower in her new built red,
As hard as the morning gaslight
  That shone on his unmade bed,

'I want some more hock in my seltzer,
  And Robbie, please give me your hand –
Is this the end or beginning?
  How can I understand?

'So you've brought me the latest *Yellow Book*:
  And Buchan has got in it now:
Approval of what is approved of
  Is as false as a well-kept vow.

'More hock, Robbie – where is the seltzer?
  Dear boy, pull again at the bell!
They are all little better than *cretins*,
  Though this *is* the Cadogan Hotel.

'One astrakhan coat is at Willis's –
  Another one's at the Savoy:

Do fetch my morocco portmanteau,
    And bring them on later, dear boy.'

A thump, and a murmur of voices –
    ('Oh why must they make such a din?')
As the door of the bedroom swung open
    And TWO PLAIN CLOTHES POLICEMEN came in:

'Mr Woilde, we 'ave come for tew take yew
    Where felons and criminals dwell:
We must ask yew tew leave with us quoietly
    For this *is* the Cadogan Hotel.'

He rose, and he put down *The Yellow Book*.
    He staggered – and, terrible-eyed,
He brushed past the palms on the staircase
    And was helped to a hansom outside.

VENUS AND CHAMPAGNE

Harper's Bazaar
March 1939

•　•　•

London still smelled of straw and stables; black smoke choked one on the Underground; in a wakening glow of a single coil of dimly burning wire, electric light peeped from its curly glass shade on to a waiting world. Gas shone green and warm on to ferns and slabs of plaice in eating-houses; oriental cigar divans were yellow with the new lighting; the clubs changed boldly over from gasolier to electrolier; in the suburbs, behind fanlights of then still-standing Regency terraces, the fishtail jetted yellow and blue in its wire frame. Lemon-coloured horse-trams slid between the plane trees. Fogs were pea-soup and Victorians remembered their youth. Baths were enclosed in a mahogany surround; washing-basins and lavatory basins were decorated with floral patterns glazed into the porcelain. Hansoms jingled over the streets and dust blew into one's eyes.

Bachelors lived in Jermyn Street (pronounced Jarmin Street) and walked round to the clubs, caressing their fine moustaches. A glance at the sporting news, a chuckle over Binstead in the *Pink 'Un*, a good sleep in the leather chair, the *Globe* or the *Pall Mall Gazette* in case one woke up; a little dinner party in Berkeley Square; mustn't forget to order those new boots from my boot-maker; a dozen more shirts from my shirt-maker; some studs from my stud-maker; what the deuce is the matter with my tailor? This is the third suit he's made for me too tight under the arms.

Plenty of leisure, Good King Edward on the throne, big financial men near it. An age of racing men, rich men, horses and Venus.

> Venus, Venus, we entreat you,
>> Come and live on earth again!
> Ringing songs of joy shall greet you,
>> AND A FOUNTAIN OF CHAMPAGNE!

The 'Venus on Earth' waltz swimming out of first-floor drawing-rooms down to the cab shelter in the Square. A nice arrangement of green lattice arches round the band, banked with sweet peas. From the pub in the mews at the back, a loud chorus from Public, Private and Jug & Bottle but not from the butlers sipping port in the Saloon.

> We don't want no war-ar –
> There never was a King like King Edward –
> We don't want no war-ar –
> For he hates that kind of thing.

The country within easy reach. Steam railway, suburban branches, still paying. 'Frequent trains to London and all parts.' Spring lengthened into summer and thinned the crowds in Rotten Row. The north-east Londoner went boating on the Lea; the artisan could walk of an evening among market gardeners beyond Fulham and

Shepherd's Bush; the artist and the poet went to stay with friends among the deep sandy lanes and old cottages of Surrey; the antiquary pedalled off on his bicycle, camera plates stuffed into the pocket of his Norfolk jacket. Cliftonville, Bournemouth and Eastbourne were beginning to fill up; donkeys drew bathing-machines into the sea; Volks' Electric Railway carried delighted cargoes from Palace Pier to Blackrock, Brighton; Hove looked askance at Kemptown. London was empty of all but the poor.

Great Central, Midland or North Western for the shires but the South Western from Waterloo for the New Forest. At the third stop is the Junction where we have to change. Our host, that well-known and hospitable racing man Mr Algie Blank, would gladly have sent the De Dion Bouton to the Junction direct but it cannot manage that hill between Oakenhurst and the Junction. The local branch is rather slow. However, the officials of the line are most courteous to the first-class passengers, especially when they know they are for Oakenhurst. The porter brings us footwarmers. The inside of a first-class carriage is like a coach. Reminds me of my youth. What's that coloured photograph opposite? Torquay! Well, well, it might almost be Monte Carlo.

Warm luxuriance of an Edwardian country evening! In my mind's eye I see the timbered turrets of Oakenhurst, dark red against the sunset, rising above black conifers. The motorcar takes the gravel drive nicely and sweeps us past the rhododendrons. Probably they are still putting our luggage into the brake at the station – wonder of modern transport, the De Dion Bouton!

The butler has brought in the lamps, there is acetylene in the passages; they are having the electric light put in next year. The men are in the smoking-room. The women are already gone to dress. What a fine display of flowers! How well hydrangeas look against mahogany! I like those orchids – those, underneath the palm. Dear Lydia, she has always been fond of flowers. She smiles down at me from that clever Sargent, all gracious femininity. What was it that clever fellow Belloc wrote about her? Never mind, I'll be able to ask, if I'm sitting next to her at dinner. Can't make out why she married Algie. With all that money she could have married anyone – *anyone*. Beaten copper, thick carpets, mahogany Renaissance and bevelled glass; soft lights, tiger skins and those amusin' Spy caricatures in the men's lobby. I wonder whether I've been given the Pink Bedroom? Hope so. It's dull in the bachelor's wing.

There we were, all assembled for dinner – Chicken Hartopp, Erly Clonmell, Derry Rossmore, Hook and Eye Vivian, Sugar Candy and Algie, Lydia, Tiny, Doods, Mittie, Nettie and Mrs Cornwallis-West. Ireland well represented in the male sex. It takes an Irishman to tell a story and there's none better than an Irish peer, Lord Rossmore.

(The following anecdotes are taken from his *Things I Can Tell* – Everleigh Nash, London, 1912. The Lord Rossmore who wrote this marvellously entertaining book was the fifth baron. He died in 1921. I hope his widow will forgive a stranger quoting so familiarly about people who may well have been her friends.)

> Poor 'Erly'! He was his own worst enemy. One night at Dublin Castle, when he had indulged a little too freely, he went into the bathroom and sat down heavily on a stout dowager's brocaded satin lap that in his muddled confusion he had mistaken for an armchair.
>
> The dow was furious and no wonder. 'Get up, Lord Clonmell: you're drunk,' she cried.
>
> He looked round. 'I'll take my oath I'm not, I'm only tired, very tired,' and he settled himself down again.

And then there was Chicken Hartopp, a topper to hounds and as bald as a coot. In those days of peers and peasants they knew how to put the peasant in his place.

> I remember another of Chicken's exploits when he was MFH* in the south of Ireland. A certain beggar used to bore him to death with his demands for assistance so Chicken determined to stop it. The man, who was legless, used to push himself about in a go-cart with the aid of two sticks and Chicken told him that if he dared worry him under a month he'd dynamite him. The mendicant still persisted and Chicken promptly took away his sticks, tied an empty tin case underneath the go-cart and informed him that within ten minutes he would be blown up.

---

* Master of Fox Hounds.

The beggar expostulated, entreated, cursed and yelled blue murder but his tormentor kept the game up until eight minutes had elapsed when he untied the canister and returned the sticks to the man, who left the neighbourhood as though he were pursued by the seven devils.

Poor Hartopp died at the Sackville Street Club, the scene of so many of our 'jollies'.

I wonder what happened to the beggar.

Dear gay days when Claridge's and Mount Street rose red and new among the brown of Mayfair stock brick! Whorls of terracotta, bulging ironwork balconies, hanging baskets of fern and geranium, white shiny paint, silk-shaded electric lamp-stands, gilt Louis Seize furniture.

Excellent wine, excellent brandy, excellent cigars; the stars are out above the conifers and rhododendrons of Oakenhurst Park. It's two o'clock and time to stagger up to the Pink Bedroom, though the others may go on with their games and the balls may click till five in the billiard-room.

I sleep soundly in those linen sheets as smooth as water and I do not dream of the future. I do not see Trixie mourning for her son killed in the war, nor Oakenhurst turned into a hospital. I do not see the stained-glass windows and new chancels in their parish churches, memorials to my dead fellow-guests. I do not see those few drawing-rooms with their miniature and brown photographs, flock walls and empty chintz-covered chairs where the one or two survivors sit swamped among their treasures with nothing but the past to remember. I do not hear aeroplanes or help to dig an ARP* shelter. I see Venus, in pink tulle, swirling out of a fountain of champagne.

---

* Air Raid Precautions.

9

WRITERS

Savants and Stylists

Evelyn Waugh (1934 and 1946)
The Life of Le Queux (1939)
Sir Max Beerbohm: An Eightieth-Birthday Tribute (1952)

EVELYN WAUGH

Extracted from 'Evelyn Waugh', programme 11 in the BBC Radio series *Living Writers* (14 December 1946), produced by Gilbert Phelps and 'Architecture in Fiction', JB's review of *A Handful of Dust* in the *Architectural Review* (1934)

• • •

There is no living writer whose works I enjoy as thoroughly as those of Evelyn Waugh. I have read all he has written twice and much of it three times. Far be it from a cautious critic to say *this* man will last, *that* one will be forgotten, but here in the felted impersonality of a broadcasting studio, let me fling caution to the winds and say that Evelyn Waugh is the one English novelist of my own generation – that is to say, of us who are in their forties – who is certain to be remembered while English novels are read.

All the more irritating is it to find so few of his books in print. Of the nine works of fiction he has written, I find friends – if such they can be called – have borrowed five from my shelves and not returned them. Let me beg his publishers, Messrs Chapman and Hall, to put him back into print in a uniform edition worthy of a bookshelf – the nine fiction books, the four travel books, the two biographies and anything else they can collect. About twenty-two new novels are published each week. One in 300 matters and that, probably, not much. Let me beg them to put Evelyn Waugh into print, each of whose books is, to me at any rate, as a full glass of dry, still champagne-wine – delicate, invigorating, uplifting and healthily purging.

I do not think it is just because Evelyn Waugh is of my own world and age that he appeals to me. We have both known Oxford of the twenties, schoolmastering, country-house life in England and Ireland, chattering parties with the Bright Young Things in chromium flats and then piling into open cars to drive through midnight London and bathe by the moon in a Middlesex pond. No, that's not the reason. I think Evelyn Waugh will last and will always appeal to those who like the English language because he is a consummate user of it, an accurate and learned observer, a born storyteller possessed of a faultless ear for dialogue and because he is a whole person with a complete philosophy of life. He also cares about architecture.

Architecture has only recently come in for a mention in modern fiction. True, in the romantic novels of Scott, Monk Lewis and Mrs RadcliVe, Gothic formed not merely a chance background but a necessary background to the tales. This romantic convention persisted through the novels of Wilkie Collins and Le Fanu even to the days of Mrs Henry Wood, whose 'pretty drawing-rooms' were essential period settings for many an emotional scene.

But psychological novels of the late-Victorian era had no use for architecture. Even the historical stories of Stevenson set little store by architectural setting. In fact it is by the popular literature of a period that one is usually able to judge its taste in buildings. The last fifty years have been blind to architecture. Drawing-rooms are merely drawing-rooms leading out of halls. If a novelist bothers to describe a room at all, he generally dismisses it as 'comfortable'. When we learn elsewhere in the book that such a house is at Maidenhead or Muswell Hill, there seems no further need to describe the style. Indeed the style defies description. Then we all know the appalling ugliness of Sherlock Holmes's rooms in Baker Street. The novels of the late Anthony Hope cover almost every variety of pre-war fiction: the adventurous, the smart and the psychological. I think I have read almost every book this able writer has written yet I can think of no passage where he pays attention to architecture.

The first rebirth of architectural consciousness in fiction writers occurs in the novels of E. F. Benson and the ghost stories of M. R. James. They both show a taste for the Queen Anne style. It remained for Aldous Huxley to like Georgian. In *Antic Hay* he went so far as to poke fun at the Gothic revival and in other novels he has shown appreciation of the work of Sir Charles Barry.

But with Mr Evelyn Waugh came a real understanding of architectural style. *Decline and Fall* put jazz-modern in its right place.

And now comes *A Handful of Dust*, which has fine satire on the bluff of interior decorators. The repulsive character of Mrs Beaver may be taken as the interior decorator *in excelsis*. This woman 'does up' airless little mews flats in Mayfair. When she arrives at a nice large country house in good old Deane and Woodward Early English, she decides to cover the drawing-room with chromium plate. She sees 'some hope' for the room when this is done. It says much for the perception of the author that he makes Tony Last, the owner of the house, decide to put back the Deane and Woodward decoration after Mrs Beaver has faded from the story.

Mr Waugh sets the lead to his countless imitators. Architecture is fashionable again and Mr Waugh is largely responsible for making it fashionable. I only hope that those imitators who have missed the point of their master's humour up till now will not also miss the point of his architectural settings. He writes with a real knowledge of architecture, as displayed in his travel books and as covered in his early researches into the Rossetti family. It would be a tragedy if his imitators started to praise the work of benighted architects or worse still to glory in the extravagances of jazz-modernistic decoration. We see enough of the latter tendency in the cinema to wish it banished from the background of modern fiction.

THE LIFE OF LE QUEUX*

Sunday Times
22 May 1939

• • •

Every year young people who were 'good at school' or who learned Anglo-Saxon and Northumbrian, which is mostly taught in the name of English literature at Oxford – every year such literary aspirants come to London under the impression that they will do well in journalism. Poor innocents, they have no idea what journalism is. I would advise them to read this life of a successful journalist and then take to farming.

William Le Queux (pronounced 'Le Kew') was not at Oxford; he was not even 'good at English'. 'I am, alas! only too well aware of my own failings, or my hopeless grammar . . .' Yet he was able to write a story of four thousand words in four hours. Mr Sladen, our author, confesses with a naivety that distinguishes his book and will enchant the sophisticated, 'I do not know what gave the late Harry de Windt the impression that he dictated his novels by telephone, as he wrote everything by hand . . .'

Perhaps he got the impression from the fact that Le Queux wrote over a hundred novels and many non-fiction books, as well as count-less newspaper articles. And perhaps it was because the exchange cut him off in the middle of a novel that he sometimes changed the name of a character halfway through a book. However he did it he was able to get an expenses sheet of £3,000 paid by Lord Northcliffe for a four months' tour of East Anglia. He was able to make a name for himself

---

* Review of *The Real Le Queux* by N. St Barbe Sladen, FRSL (Nicholson & Watson, 1939).

even among those who never read his books, among which I must include myself.

Making a name for himself was what mattered to Le Queux more than money. He started journalism after a pat on the back from Emile Zola, as a police-court reporter for an Eastbourne paper. When he died he had spoken to people as diverse as Dr Crippen and the King of Montenegro.

The royalty section is perhaps the funniest of this work. Prince Nicholas of Montenegro waived all ceremony and 'produced his well-worn case of lizard-skin, offered Le Queux a cigarette . . . "Of Tennyson, too, I am great admirer. I am very fond of his poems."' He even sent a poem from his royal pen, six stanzas long, to Le Queux. The King of Italy talked of Ouida to him: 'I think I like *Pascarel* best of all and *Signa* next.' Queen Elizabeth of Rumania told him 'how she modelled some of her own verses on Austin Dobson's poems, especially "The Sundial"'. Even Abdul the Damned was a writer. '"Though the world is ignorant of it, he has written some of the finest poetry in our language," replied Noury, "and two historical romances."'

After all this literary conversation with royalty, after a daring expedition to brigands in Albania, after propaganda on behalf of misrepresented monarchs and nations, is it surprising that Le Queux's broad bosom clanked with foreign orders? Mr Sladen describes him here a little unhappily. 'He was an ardent and experienced criminologist and his influential contacts were numberless. I think he thoroughly enjoyed consorting with kings.' 'As Consul of the Republic of San Marino,' we are told, 'Le Queux had a gorgeous green and gold embroidered uniform and a cocked hat with a white ostrich feather.' 'He was always armed and his hand in his pocket was always ready for a sudden emergency.' At a dinner of a club called 'Ye Olde Tripe Eaters', he appeared wearing tinted glasses; 'in that way he had been able to have a long conversation at the dinner with a notorious continental spy.' What a man! He was so much a journalist that his life became one long news story.

I can imagine his study at the Villa Le Queux, bristling with relics and signed photographs. I can see him at one of those dining clubs

Mr Sladen mentions, making the eyes of the boys of Fleet Street goggle with his tales of adventure and contacts with famous people. His finest achievement seems to have been his forecast, in 1906, of the Great War, with the help and encouragement of Lord Roberts. He was also a pioneer of flying and wireless. As an amateur spy he was famous.

After reading this book I felt that Le Queux had had no private life at all. His time was spent in adventure and cigar-smoke — 'the press smoked three thousand cigars'; jollity, good food, how to avoid a hang-over, plenty of 'old man' and 'what-ho!', a good deal of boasting, 'the line of demarcation between friend and acquaintance in Le Queux's eyes was at times very slender', great courage — and in the midst of this electric-lit, smoke-laden life a certain pathos.

This is not journalism as our undergraduate sees it. Indeed, some undergraduates staying at an hotel in Switzerland in 1924, when Le Queux was also a guest, formed an 'Anti-Le Queux Club', poured ink over the poor old man and trussed him up like a fowl. He was not their idea of an author.

Their reaction is marked. And even if these were not literary gentlemen, let those that are visit the bars of Fleet Street. There they will find the unsuccessful versions of Le Queux, the same proud boasts, the same anxiety to be on Christian-name terms with those who are high up in the newspaper world. And the newspaper world, as far as these poor journalists are concerned, is one that talks in terms of thousands of words, not thousands of pounds.

Mr Sladen has managed to convey in a peculiar book that is little more than a series of almost unconnected facts the horror and adventure of journalism.

SIR MAX BEERBOHM: AN EIGHTIETH-BIRTHDAY TRIBUTE

Daily Telegraph
23 August 1952

. . .

It is pleasant to be asked to send him a birthday present. It is pleasant to think that these words may meet his eyes tomorrow. There, on the front steps of the villa in Rapallo among the empty chianti bottles or whatever it is that one puts outside an Italian villa for the equivalent of the milkman to collect, may be lying this morning's *Daily Telegraph*. Its familiar pages will be bleaching in the Mediterranean sun. Someone will carry it up to a tidy room whose French windows open on a terrace. And on that terrace he will be sitting looking down over olives and cypress trees to the 'wrinkled sea' below. Between sea and him the motor horns will be hooting along the road from Genoa to Viareggio that passes below his villa. Noise of internal-combustion engines will not disturb him.

As in his mind he belongs to an unhurried and polite age, so does he in his body. There will be none of that giving in to the heat with open collar and vulgar summer colours you can see at any English seaside resort. He will be correctly and coolly dressed in the sober shades we often see in his caricatures: pale greys and blues. And his dress, his slow, courteous speech, his quiet way of life are all part of that age around 1910 when he first came to live at Rapallo: the English exquisite, the calm perfectionist, famous then, even more famous today.

I suppose what he has better than all the rest of us is a sense of proportion. He can see the ridiculous in everything so he never loses his temper. He never hates. The nearest he comes to hate is pity. It is this sense of proportion that gives him those polite manners. You can hear them even in the model letter he wrote on 'How to thank author for inscribed copy of book' from *And Even Now*:

> Dear Mr Emanuel Flower – It was kind of you to think of sending me a copy of your new book. It would have been kinder still to think again and abandon that project. I am a man of gentle instincts and do not like to tell you that *A Flight into Arcady* (of which I have skimmed a few pages, thus wasting two or three minutes of my not altogether worthless time) is trash.
>
> On the other hand, I am determined that you shall not be able to go around boasting to your friends, if you have any, that this work was not condemned, derided and dismissed by your sincere well-wisher, Wrexford Cripps.

You can hear those good manners, too, in the French café in his story about the millionaire J. L. Pethel, from *Seven Men*:

> . . . squaring his arms on the little table, he asked me what I would drink. I protested that I was the host – a position which he, with the quick courtesy of the very rich, yielded to me at once.

A sense of proportion is the basis of all true humour. If it over-balances into anger, humour becomes satire. There is very little satire in Max Beerbohm. His rare wrath is righteous. He takes no pleasure in the knockabout and the pun. His fantasies – *Zuleika Dobson* and those even better stories in *Seven Men* 'Enoch Soames' and 'Maltby and Braxton' – are those of the fairy tale and ghost story.

It was his sense of proportion, too, that made him so distinguished a dramatic critic in his early days, when he wrote weekly for the *Saturday Review* for twelve years. One can read those criticisms in the rare collected edition and laugh oneself silly over ham acting in plays one has never seen nor will ever hear of again.

And what other gifts, besides this great one of proportion, have been given him to use these eighty years? Next most prominent is that ear for prose. He can imitate anyone. He can imitate almost too well. I believe that the only author who was offended among those parodied in *A Christmas Garland* was A. C. Benson, whose *From a College Window* he pilloried in 'Out of Harm's Way'. Do you remember the closing lines of that parody?:

A singular repose, a sense of security, an earnest of calm and continuity, as though he were reading over again one of those wise copy-books that he had so loved in boyhood, or were listening to the sounds made on a piano by some modest, very conscientious young girl, with a pale red pig-tail, practising her scales, very gently, hour after hour, next door.

One can hardly blame A. C. Benson for being offended.

And the other prominent gift is his eye for colour and of detail. You can see it in that pale red pig-tail. You can see it better in any of the caricatures. He notices dress as much as faces — the carelessly tied tie, the crease in the right place, the bulge in the wrong one.

The man endowed with such a highly developed sense of the ridiculous as Max usually becomes a cynic. To that temptation, he has not yielded. He is 'tough', a word he would not like me to use about him and I hope he will forgive it. But heaven knows, there must have been temptations. He makes no bones about his opinion of this century of the common man. He says he is much looking forward to the year 2000. There are probably many men in clubs, in chambers off Piccadilly, in the two remaining private rooms of their country houses, who have lapsed into cynicism or despair. For they, too, have known the London Max knew: the gaslights, Queen Victoria on the throne, puffed sleeves, bicycling in Battersea Park, riding in the Row, silly beauties in picture hats, aesthetes in velvet, port, cigars and unamalgamated railways. There can be none who knew so many of the intellectual and famous of the time. If they did, they have not left so much written or pictorial record of it.

We come back to that sense of proportion: Charterhouse, Oxford, a sound knowledge of Latin and Greek, a little French and presumably some Italian, a gift for drawing and writing; no 'deep' stuff, no Russian novelists, nothing abstract, no economics, philosophy and politics — Max has always kept within his range. He does what interests him, he describes things he loves and he uses all his talents all the time.

Max knew a civilised people, for he lived in civilised circles in London. He has determined to keep it alive in himself and in his art, the little part of it he knew, which happens to be a very interesting part. He has achieved it in himself, sitting there on the terrace at Rapallo. He has put them down, those last thirty years before the collapse of civilisation in 1910. It is in his books and drawings, which I can re-read and look at again and again because they are skilful, truthful, inspired and affectionate. By identifying himself with the period to which he belongs Max Beerbohm is making himself immortal. This, which should have been a birthday present and sounds unpleasantly like an obituary, is, I see, really a letter of thanks.

10

COMEDY
Gags and Guns

JOKE-ENGLISH*

New Statesman and Nation
22 October 1938

. . .

I wonder how many readers of the *New Statesman and Nation* light their favourite briars with the aid of an England's Glory match. These British-made, West Country matches have a joke printed on the back of every box. Many a hearty laugh have my chums and I enjoyed at their expense. The jokes are written in that special joke-English that prepares you for a smile from the start. 'A well-known Bristol angler', begins the joke on the back of the box I have in my pocket at this moment. The local touch is important. 'Bristol' helps to make the story vivid. Then 'A well-known Bristol angler' is so obviously a more comical character than a little-known Bristol angler.

I had always feared that joke-English was confined to England. I am delighted to discover from *The Speaker's Desk Book*, which was printed and compiled in America, that it is also in use across the Atlantic. It forges one more link, if I may coin a phrase, in the chain of Anglo-American fellowship. Here are 5,000 sparkling epigrams and 1,187 killing anecdotes, many of them almost new. The anecdotes are indexed under subjects so that, having regard for my public, I looked up 'LITERARY TENDENCIES'. Under this title I was happy to find a story written in a style as assured as that of the writer for England's Glory:

---

* Review of *The Speaker's Desk Book*, edited by Martha Lupton (Putnam, 1938).

He was engaged to the daughter of a literary man. He was bold as a wooer, but the veriest coward when it came to approaching the fair one's father.

This is an excellent start. Future fathers-in-law are as comical as plumbers' mates.

So he waited outside the great man's study while the 'fayre lady' did the tackling.

Here, the joke-English helps to keep the humour alive. A really good raconteur can imply these quotation marks round 'fayre lady' by giving a faint Elizabethan inflexion to his voice:

In five minutes she was out again, and on her dress was pinned a paper bearing the words 'With the author's compliments'.

Sometimes the audience does not get the full effect of a side-splitter at once. There is no harm in spinning out the anecdote for as long as possible and emphasising the final point. In dialogue jokes, for example, you may hammer home the wit with a penultimate or ultimate thud, thus: 'Came the reluctant rejoinder', 'was the smart reply', 'remarked that functionary, sagely'.

Imagine yourself, reader, as Managing Director of Consolidated Spare Parts, Ltd. The annual dinner of the firm is due and you will have to make a speech. *The Speaker's Desk Book* will banish all your fears, for the 5,000 sparkling epigrams are from authorities as divergent as Plautus and Benjamin C. Leeming.

I should advise four epigrams and one mirth-provoking anecdote for a short, snappy, after-dinner speech. Draw the long bow, if necessary. If the author of one of the epigrams is alive, say that he made the remark to you in the course of conversation. Your speech should open with a vague generalisation on business as a whole; it should then turn to the particular and a sparkler on Prosperity will be apposite; branch off into the general again or you will find yourself promising a bonus and Progress is a happy note on which to end the serious part of your speech. Now comes the humorous part. Again you must consult the *Desk Book* and look up 'WOMAN'. The staff are certain to have brought their wives and fiancées to the dinner. You can round off with an anecdote. I give here a specimen speech with the references to the page numbers on which the quotations may be found:

> Ladies and Gentlemen – I remember Ferdinand S. Schenk once told me a very wise thing. 'If the Golden Rule is to be preached at all these days,' he said, 'when so much of our lives is devoted to business, it must be preached specially in its application to the conduct of business' (p. 15). I think we can safely say that the Golden Rule holds together Consolidated Spare Parts, Ltd, and this has been the secret of our Prosperity. As Publius Syrus has it, 'Prosperity makes friends; adversity tries them' (p. 213). Let us hope that we will never have to give our friends a trial, for 'Progress never stands still' (p. 208). I am glad to see a goodly gathering of the fair sex tonight. 'Why is it we never hear of a self-made woman?' (p. 283) and that reminds me of a little story I heard the other day. 'An elderly man, of ultra-convivial habits but withal learned and bookish, was hailed before the bar of justice in a country town . . .' (etc., continue anecdote 826, p. 505).

And here, readers, I will leave you reaching for the empire wine, your faces wreathed in cigar-smoke and expectant smiles.

FUNNY BOOKS

New Statesman and Nation
3 December 1938

• • •

Any review of funny books must bristle with the prejudices of the reviewer and this review certainly bristles with mine. Were I, for instance, an English master who once taught me at a preparatory school, I should doubtless find *History Repeats Itself*, by J. Adrian Ross and J. E. Broome, a funny book. It owes a good deal to *1066 and All That* – which was not published in my day – and even more to W. S. Gilbert and the Gilbert A. Becketts:

> Boadicea, Queen of Britain,
> With the craze for speed was bitten.
> Chariots of different sorts –
> Landaulette and super sports –

This is just the sort of thing to read out to the junior boys when exams are over and you are prepared to unbend and show that you despise history as much as the boys do – this is just the thing for when there are ten minutes to spare before the bell goes for milk and biscuits.

Were I a fluffy river girl with a weakness for night clubs and Maidenhead, speed and Bing Crosby, and all the wild, wilful delights of this wild, wilful, delightful, funny old world, I would probably take my philosophy from *How about a Man* – 'full of sound but not too serious advice for every girl, whether she be sixteen or sixty'. But were I that English master, I would, of course, read it to the boys: or give it to the headmaster's wife for Christmas.

Were I somebody with the sort of humour one sometimes finds in a house one rents for the summer at the seaside, someone who likes putting up notices everywhere, little rhymes about not splashing in the bathroom, not dropping ash on the carpet, not leaving wet sand shoes in the hall, a real good, doggy, sporty sort not too keen about art, I would doubtless buy *Awful Weekends – and Guests*, by 'Fish', tear out the pictures and pin them up all over the house. As it is, drawings by 'Fish', though strongly individual, have never made me laugh. They are competent in a superficial, rather 1920 manner: eyes are like commas, curves of a decorative nature swirl about, everything is two-dimensional. Despite his pseudonym, 'Fish's' work smells to me of lavender soap.

The book that makes *me* laugh is *Take Forty Eggs*. It is a parody of a cookery and household management book and it seems to me to be spontaneous, unselfconscious and the result of perfect sympathy in humour between author and artist. It may not be everybody's idea of what is funny. Some may take this literally: 'Bloodstains, how to remove from newspaper. Newspapers in which meat or fish have been wrapped are often unpleasantly discoloured. To clean, soak for several hours in water and scrub vigorously.' Others may get more of a laugh from:

COOKERY FOR SADISTS

Devilled Sago

Tear a lettuce into pieces, fling them into boiling water and leave them till they blanch. Tear up a carrot by the roots and boil it in oil. Pound some sago to a jelly. Slash some turnips with a sharp knife, rub salt, curry powder and cayenne into the cuts and truss them tightly. Stuff with the other ingredients. Grill them. Baste them.

Eat them.

All these books appeal to individual types. But what shall we say of that organ that, as is well known, is appreciated the world over where clean fun and class distinction are decently honoured, that organ that is as essential to a household as the annual catalogue of the Army and Navy Stores? I refer to *Punch*.

I think *Punch* receives today severer knocks than it deserves. The glances at recent numbers that I have made during visits to the dentist show that a minor revolution is starting. On the one side is the old gang of artists and contributors: a certain type of drawing and 'joke' has so long been expected of it that it is unable to manufacture anything else. Mr Lewis Baumer draws fast, almond-eyed girls shocking elderly aristocrats or pokes fun at the rich or makes jokes about people keeping butlers and footmen; Mr G. D. Armour specialises in scratchy fences above which appears an 'angry MFH'; Mr Charles Grave remains resolutely nautical; etc, etc. On the other side there is the new gang of new artists and new kinds of humorists. It is not very strong and some of the artists' drawings are really hideous – as ugly as the worst work of the old gang. But there is an effort to break with the tradition of the late Sir Owen Seaman. The new gang labours under three disadvantages. The *New Yorker* exists and any jokes in the *New Yorker* tradition will be called plagiarism. Sex is taboo. The third disadvantage under which *Punch* labours is its public. The *Punch* public expects a joke that is 'good enough for *Punch*' and no better. Anything oddly humorous might lose a subscriber. Writing for *Punch* means writing for *Punch*'s public – almost as tricky and dangerous a task as writing for a periodical whose editor is under the advertisement manager.★

In *The Pick of Punch (1937–1938)* one finds the war fought out fiercely. There are 170 illustrations and I have made an analysis of those that were identifiable to me as jokes. Twenty-one were mostly cartoons that are not meant to be very funny or even satirical. The remaining 149 fell under the following subjects and I have given the number of jokes on each subject:

Class distinction (money, butlers, lack of education, ignorance, birth, incorrect accent, etc)	42
Unclassifiable and not funny	19
Professional (lawyers, 'modern artists', sailors, etc)	16
Funny (jokes whose drawings and words, if any, made me laugh and were not in the old gang tradition)	14
Precocious children (i.e. 'Where shall I wash, Mummy?' 'Why, in the bathroom of course.' 'No. Where on me?')	14
Sport (ignorance of rules of, inferiority in, etc)	13
Fairly funny	9
Colonels	5
Good idea, feeble drawing	4
History	4
Husbands (carrying parcels, etc)	4
Mildly satirical	3
Scottish	1
Funny drawing, feeble joke	1

Total 149

★ This can be taken as a reference to Betjeman's own situation as the new editor of *Decoration*.

The prose betrays the same symptoms as the illustrated jokes. I notice that the sort of story that starts ' "Well," I said to Angela, as I cracked my breakfast egg, "the Income Tax collector has called," ' is still popular.

The British Character, by 'Pont', consists of drawings that have appeared in *Punch*. 'Pont' is in the newer *Punch* tradition and he is good at drawing semi-imbecile clubmen, middle-aged ladies and vacuous 'modern' girls. Here and there the restrictions demanded by the *Punch* public appear but on the whole he has his own gentle sense of satire and sticks to it. I liked some of his drawings immensely, especially where one of the British characteristics is 'Love of writing letters to *The Times*'.

TORTURE AND DEATH

New Statesman and Nation
10 December 1938

• • •

How many vicious swings have gone socketing into midriffs, how many uppercuts have landed neatly on weak chins, how many lashes descended on trembling flesh, how many steel-blue eyes scanned open boyish faces, how many shifty dagoes have flinched before a steady gaze since first I started to read the twenty-two boys' books that it is now my pleasure to pass in review? We are told that the teaching of blood and violence is confined to the children of totalitarian states. Sir Humphrey Milford, Mr Thomas Nelson, Mr Blackie and his son and many another British publisher can bear witness that this is not true. I select at random from the nearest books to my desk:

Doran's automatic spat viciously though silently. Before he could press the trigger again, Colin's left had delivered a devastating blow on the bandit's solar plexus (*Standish Gets His Man*, by Percy F. Westerman).

This is, incidentally, a good specimen of the author's prose style. I am told that if all the words Mr Westerman has written in his many books for boys were stretched end to end, they would reach from Wareham (Dorset) to St Albans.

The point of Mazeus's lance never found a more fatal mark; it caught the Tuareg squarely in the throat and impaled him as cleanly as a butterfly is impaled upon a pin (*Biggles Flies South*, by Capt. W. E. Johns).

More of Biggles later.

A poor prospect for a fellow . . . no junior's head to punch for setting up sauce in the common room (*Jim the Dandy*, by S. M. Williams).

Here is a nice little torture to try on the milksop next door, next time you and your brother have got him alone. It comes from *Adventure Down Channel* 'and every boy with any sense knows what a splendid sailing yarn Percy Woodcock can spin' (publisher's blurb). I am afraid I cannot spin the yarn to chapter length as Mr Woodcock has done: it is briefly this. Lash your man by his ankles, wrists and thighs so that he cannot move. Now heat an iron bar on a stove well in view of your victim. When the bar is red hot, remove his shoes and socks and make as though to brand him on the soles of his feet. Now the skill comes in. When you have got the red-hot bar near his feet, substitute it for a block of ice without his seeing. Draw the ice across the soles of his feet. The nervous shock that results will cause yells of merriment.

I have not room to quote the many tortures and death blows at my disposal and I am afraid you may think I am a wretched coward who objects to such things in boys' books. I do not: as long as the story is improbable enough, the agonies and deaths are pleasantly remote. Only when a torture reaches the bounds of possibility does it not become so jolly. I advise those who give their sons *Adventure Down Channel* to hide the Primus and switch off the refrigerator for a week or two.

Two books demand separate notice, one on account of its superior merit, the other because it does not fall into any category. *Under Sealed Orders*, by 'Bartimeus', is nearly what its publishers claim it to be: 'The most important boy's book that has been published for a great many years.' I would qualify 'for a great many years' with 'this year' or 'the last two or three'. It is difficult to see why it is called a boys' book unless it be that the author is not concerned with explaining the reactions of his characters. Some chapters appended to the end of the book depict lurid adventures in the African jungle that may have led the publishers to think the book is only suitable for boys. For myself, I enjoyed it more than anything I have read for months. The best of the book is an account, written in unaffected and untechnical terms, of life on a man-of-war in the 1900s. It is full of amusing characters and good jokes, nor is it without a dark side. My only regret is that 'Bartimeus' found it necessary to launch off to Africa instead of keeping us anchored at Weymouth enjoying ourselves. *Explorers Awheel* is the story of four children who go bicycling with a pipe-smoking uncle who refers to them all, girls or boys, as 'you chaps'. They explore the West of England and do not seem to have noticed a single secular building or even a church, although at one place they had tea with the Vicar. There is much good-humoured banter in the Doone Valley and plenty of adventure. The visit of four inquisitive children to the Cerne Giant must have presented an awkward problem to their uncle but he does not mention any predicament and the artist, in his illustration of the giant, leaves it out.

The most prolific writers of boys' books recognise that the ingredients of a successful story are: (1) that the whole thing can be re-enacted in the garden with the summer-house as HQ and the least popular boy as villain; (2) that a fine flourish of technical terms will make the most far-fetched plot seem true – and anyhow, technical terms delight boys of all ages; (3) that jokes must be very simple. Most of the authors observe these rules.

I wonder whether even readers of the *New Statesman and Nation* can unravel all these technicalities:

The fuselage is of composite construction, being of a monocoque design reinforced by four longerons (*The Royal Air Force*, by Monk and Winter).

Then as their topmast, deprived of the support of its stay to the bowsprit end, was flogging about, they housed it (*Mixed Cargoes*, by Lawrence R. Bourne).

Pot-a-Pie glad you come. Mike Dubois um hit the hooch, so that um go plum crazy. Take up to tie-up (*Warden of the North*, by L. C. Douthwaite).

The use of 'historical' language may be described as an extension of the technical-terms device and is often employed in stories dealing with ye olden time. 'Queen Elizabeth was right royally angered that it could not be found, naught being known as to its whereabouts save an old tale that it had been bestowed in the caverns that turn the hill named Great Gallery into a veritable honeycomb.' (*Green Emeralds for the King*, by Constance Savery.) I wot this authoress will be right royally angered with me but, marry, her olden tongue and auncient speeches made me right hasty to skippe the leaves, albeit I tried to read them with a good wille.

Now and then an author will allow himself to draw a character. Martin Kent slips in an unusually observant passage: 'He was an intensely satisfied man, with his board meetings, committee meetings, golf on Saturday afternoons, and elaborate wireless sets.' (*A King from the Clouds*.) Lawrence Bourne draws likely merchant seamen and 'Bartimeus' excellent Royal Navy types. As for Biggles, the air detective, he can be haughty:

> The man bowed, and his right hand touched his heart with an obsequious gesture. 'Have I the honour of addressing the celebrated Major Bigglesworth?' he enquired, suavely. 'My name is Bigglesworth, if that's what you mean,' answered Biggles coldly.*

He can be witty:

---

* Betjeman's reading list included two Biggles novels and a Biggles omnibus. He quotes here from one of the two novels, *Biggles Flies South*.

'Yes; I fancy I saw a cairn of stones farther back —.' 'Listen, laddie,' interrupted Biggles. 'From what I can see of it, you are going to have plenty of time to trot about looking for heaps of stones. What we need is a nice heap of *scones*.'

(How does he know that the other man does not pronounce them *skonz*?) He can be righteously angry:

'. . . you murdering swine,' snarled Biggles, and before the others realised what he was going to do, he seized the abject half-caste by the back of the collar and began laying on the cane with all the power of his arm.

He has no time for archaeology:

Algy and Ginger looked with interest at the ancient ruins of such romantic association, but Biggles was more concerned with the present.

Readers will notice that school stories are on the wane, that the air is the thing now and that on the whole, the roughest, toughest sketch is all that is used.

THE DELIGHT OF LIGHT VERSE*

New Statesman and Nation
16 December 1939

•   •   •

Mr Auden defines light verse as the work of poets who 'have felt in sufficient intimacy with their audience to be able to forget themselves and their singing robes'. It has often happened that

---

* Originally published as 'Onwards from Dr Watts'.

people have written light verse who have not been poets. Consequently, we have come to think of light verse as that grisly, facetious stuff that introduces long words and an ingenious, jumpy rhyming scheme and appears in *Punch* and at end-of-term school concerts: a little tumty-tum on the piano, till ready, and then a waterfall of Latinised English. There is a splendid example in *Songs of Sherborne School*:

> When King Alfred was at Sherborne, he revelled in 'Unseens',
> He never said that 'Comps' were hard or dry,
> Repetition was his pleasure, and he spent his royal leisure
> In studying the verbs in -*mi*.

Chorus:

> So face Life cheerily, as Alfred did of old, etc.

I suppose that kind of thing is primarily the result of W. S. Gilbert.

Mr Belloc broke away from the facetious tradition years ago when he published his *Bad Child's Book of Beasts* in 1896. He was already a delicate, not over-complicated poet and he chose to base his light poems on the *Divine and Moral Songs* of Dr Watts (1715) and the *Original Poems for Infant Minds*, by Jane and Anne Taylor (1804). The only difference between the early Mr Belloc and Dr Watts and the Misses Taylor was that the first left out the moral from the poem or put in a ridiculous one. The result is humorous verse that makes one laugh on account of its deliberate naïvety:

> And even now, at twenty-five,
> He has to work to keep alive!
> Yes! All day long from 10 till 4!
> For half the year, or even more;
> With but an hour or two to spend
> At luncheon with a City friend.

This may be compared with Jane Taylor's

> Soft his existence rolls away,
> Tomorrow plenteous as today:
> He lives, enjoys, and lives anew,
> And when he dies – what shall we do!

The early semi-satire, semi-parody, depended a great deal on Lord Basil Blackwood's illustrations. When that talented artist was killed in the last war, Mr Belloc was driven to writing humorous verse that depended even more on the verse than on the illustrations. His early training in simplicity enabled him to avoid the facetious. The simple *Who's Who* entry of Herbert Keane's, a minor literary man, shows this sort of poetry, not requiring illustration, at its best:

> Clubs: Handy Dandy, Beagle's, Tree's,
> Pitt, Palmerston, Riviere,
> The Walnut Box, Empedocles,
> Throgmorton, Pot o' Beer.
>
> (The last for its bohemian lists
> Wherein he often meets
> Old Wasters, Poets, Communists,
> And Ladies from the Streets.)
>
> A strong Protectionist, believes
> In everything but Heaven.
> For entertainment, dines, receives,
> Unmarried, 57.

I doubt if there are better humorous verse writers in England than Mr Belloc. He has all the qualities needed – brevity, well-sounding lines, quotability and simplicity. He is never facetious, never obscure and he makes nice use of the unexpected:

> During a late election Lord
> Roehampton strained a vocal cord.

I used to be told, during the process of education, that 'to laugh is light, not to laugh is deep': that depth got you on in examinations and the Civil Service; lightness was definitely gamma and got you nowhere. The only sort of lightness permitted was post-examination gymnastics verse of the A. D. Godley type. Mr Belloc was a Brackenbury Scholar and got a first in History and he has yet produced a simple form of light verse of his own that all can understand.

This volume, which claims to be the collected humorous poems of H. Belloc, does not include all his humorous poems, some of the best of which are to be found in *Sonnets and Verse* (Duckworth, 7s 6d.). This book is, in fact, a reprint of those familiar large octavos for children, without the illustrations. Many of the lines refer to drawings that are not to be found in this book. Despite these disadvantages, here are nearly 200 pages of excellent light verse.

11

ENGLISHNESS

Hobbies and Hobby-horses

TEA TIME

Evening Standard
21 June 1935

• • •

Now is the time when imperious chauffeurs, like disappointed eagles, come flying by in splendid limousines; now the lesser cars go buzzing past, a golliwog hanging in the back window, father, mother and youngsters huddled together inside. A loudly dressed man with a long, low forehead comes hooting past everything in a long, low, loudly painted open car. Like the persistent whirr of a dentist's drill, the motorcycles thread in and out. The bicyclist, his hindpart highest, his eyes on the tarmac road, pedals silently on through the fumes of petrol. Did any snobbery over coats of arms, county families and peerages equal the snobbery of the road?

We are always talking about the open road, though few places are more exclusive, from the motorist who puts a large GB by his number plate (although he has never been abroad) to the bicyclist who covers himself and his machine with flags and badges.

And there is one form of roadside exclusiveness — for perhaps 'snobbery' is an unkind word to use — to which I have devoted the most careful study. It is the psychology of the roadside teashop.

I divide teashops into six kinds: Good Pull-in for Carmen; Teas and Minerals; Teas; Dainty Teas; Afternoon Teas; and Devonshire Teas, Farmhouse Teas, and Home-made Scones, etc.

'Good Pull-in for Carmen' is found on main roads only. Here the tea is strong, the china is as thick as the bread and butter and the visitor gets his money's worth. The surroundings are rarely pleasant.

More often than not the words 'Good Pull-in' are written up where most people would want to hurry by. 'Good Pull-ins' are open until sensible hours in the night, when they are patronised by people in tail-coats, and in the early morning, when they are patronised by the people for whom they are intended. I prefer a 'Good Pull-in' to most other varieties.

'Teas and Minerals' are not quite 'the thing'. There is apparently something wrong with the word 'minerals'. I asked a most refined lady who kept a teashop called the Jack O' Lantern in a cathedral city whether I could have some ginger beer. 'We keep no minerals,' she replied and I was conscious that I was not well shaved and not really a very nice person.

'Teas' is the sort of place for the adventurous motorist. You will not see such a notice up on a main road because there some well-informed man will have stopped to tell the proprietor that the 's' is the wrong way round. 'Teas', rather badly painted on a little board nailed to an oak tree, maybe seen in some deep green Devon lane. Or it may be stuck to the side of some warm brick farmhouse in an elm-surrounded Wiltshire village. The tea will be strong and there will be rock cakes, boiled eggs, a little meat and farm milk with the cream on it, all at a big farm table where, probably, some other strangers are munching self-consciously opposite.

'Dainty Teas' is almost entirely an urban word. The word 'dainty' has not reached the villages. 'Dainty Teas' are usually found on the first floor of a pastrycook's shop. There will be a hint of Tudor, a few jazz-modern cushions and the remains of a big pierglass bought cheap when the assembly rooms were sold. The tea will be Indian or China with bread and butter or cakes (these last somewhat elaborate in design and heavy on the stomach) called 'pastries'. There is something flyblown about 'dainty'.

'Afternoon Teas' means hotel tea. The afternoon is sleepy. The porter is having his nap. No one is about. 'Ring bell for waitress.' You ring. A long pause.

'May I have tea, please?'

'Will you have it in the lounge or in the coffee room?'

If you choose the coffee room, you will sit among tables laid for dinner, looking at someone's special bottle of sauce and someone else's bottle of spa water, not quite finished, waiting for the next meal. If you choose the lounge, be it wicker chair or palm variety or mahogany and stained glass, there will be out-of-date numbers of weekly periodicals to look at. Tea will be brought eventually and you will be glad to step out into the open air.

The last type of tea place, 'Devonshire Teas' etc, generally has some special name: 'Dame Nature's Pantry', 'Primula's Kitchen', 'At Ye Signe of Ye Olde Spynninge Wheele'. Hand-painted plates and cups rest on hand-painted tables. On the rush seats are all the higher-class inhabitants of a provincial town: a young man in bright green home-spuns with a batik-work tie, an old man in a Norfolk suit who exhibits the same view from different angles year after year at the Academy, one or two clergymen and their families, an elderly woman with a raffia-work basket full of shopping. Gentlefolk, tastefully got up as milkmaids, will bring tea. Tea will consist of all sorts of home-made goodies – rectangular things made out of porridge and treacle; flat circles called biscuits and tasting very sweet. Then the proprietress herself will come up, a fine big woman wearing a coat and skirt like a carriage rug or a dress of hand-dyed cotton. Perhaps she will take the visitor to the studio upstairs, for teashops of this sort often have a handicraft section. There she will show a view of the cathedral in poker-work, a design in poppies in leatherwork, a dumpy little piece of home-made pottery looking very like one of the home-made cakes downstairs, some tweed such as she is wearing herself.

Have I been occupying the attention of serious people with what may seem to be trivial matters? One of the Romantic poets – I wish I could remember which – has told us to pay attention to the gentlest roadside flower.

THE PAGAN MONTH OF MAY

Evening Standard
8 May 1936

• • •

With something of a shock I read the following notice on an elegant piece of cardboard in a tailor's window in the Strand today: 'There is a definite psychological stimulus in well-tailored clothes – but never more so than during spring.' I can hear yokels throughout the country croaking agreement. If we are still spring worshippers in London – and the May Queen ceremonies on Hayes Common should bear this out – how much more are country people spring worshippers?

It is unlucky that the merry month of May should be generally written 'ye merrie month of Maie' and that it should be associated with the arty-crafty folksiness that turns even a middlebrow sick. For despite its half-timbered associations, May is the month in the year when England's original nature worship comes uppermost to the surface. Little girls dress themselves up in ribbons and flowers; hobby-horses, Jack-in-the-Greens, morris dancers, teazers and furry dancers caper about. All sorts of people get a kiss who are not expecting one; the very churches are decorated – and if Easter falls late enough for May flowers, moss, cowslips and primroses hide the font, pulpit and window-sills of the most ill-attended country place of worship.

May ceremonies are almost all survivals of earth worship. Baal was the sun god worshipped on the tops of hills, Baalath was the earth god worshipped in the form of trees and flowers.

Naturally May, when the earth seems to come awake again, is particularly sacred to the earth god. The ceremonies connected with the earth god are also connected with fertility; indeed, the fertility ceremonies round May-poles and the odd heathen ceremonies not taken over by early Christianity became so licentious that the Puritans of Cromwell's time made strong efforts to put them down.

There are not the signs of licence in these old pagan ceremonies that there used to be. The vigour of the Puritans and the respectability of the nineteenth century put an end to them. For instance, there used to be a scouring of the White Horse in Berkshire (not, incidentally, a May Day celebration) when all the district used to attend revels on the White Horse Hill. This was stopped in the 1860s because it became so unrestrained.

In most places when May celebrations still continue there is a sort of official approval of them. At Helston, in Cornwall, today's Furry Dance is run by a committee. The Furry Dance, despite its committee, has still plenty of life in it and the dancers, in steeple hats, go in and out of the open doors of houses singing. This is said to be a survival of the festivities of the goddess Flora who was ever young and whose human frailty is well explained in dictionaries of mythology.

Hobby-horses, which have some connection with magic, still survive. The best I saw was the one at the little fishing port of Padstow, also in Cornwall. Here the First of May is heralded in a beautiful morning song sung at midnight in the streets of the town. One of the many verses haunts me still:

> The young men of Padstow they might if they would,
>> For summer is come unto day,
> They might have built a ship and gilded her with gold
>> In the merry morning of May.

The tune, with its extraordinary rhythm, can never be reproduced except by Padstow people. It seems as though the pagan gods are looking down on the town, so that even the old stone houses that tumble down the hill and pull up with a jerk at the quay seem new in comparison with this ancient ceremony. Then, next morning, the hobby-horses come out – more like Tibetan devil dancers' masks than horses. The song goes on and on, sung by the children, the women and the fishermen. The whole town sways to the tune. At every four verses there is a religious hush, the hobby-horse bows down, the teazer with his club bows down, the dancers bow down and the tune changes to a wailing tune half pagan and half plainsong. Then up springs the horse, up springs the teazer, up spring the dancers and the morning song is resumed. Green boughs are hung round the houses, the licensing hours seem to be mysteriously extended and during May Day Padstow goes mad so that a visitor realises that Cornwall is still a foreign country as remote from England as Ireland.

But England herself has her May ceremonies. The ghosts that haunt wells, made holy long before Christianity came to England, have to be propitiated. There are the ceremonies of well-dressing – notably at Tissington in Derbyshire – where the holy well is decorated so that it looks like some gilded shrine in a Continental church. Christianity has set its approval on this ceremony and you may see religious texts in flaring colours worked into the decoration of dressed wells.

The most sinister May ceremony occurs at Knutsford where there is a Jack-in-the-Green. This is a man in a wicker arrangement of green boughs. It has been suggested that he is a survival of the Druid worship. The Druids used to stuff a wicker cage with humans and set light to it.

Pagan ceremonies are not confined to May. But it takes Ireland to produce the best of the lot. This is the Puck fair at Killorglin, away in the west of Kerry. A he-goat is tethered for three days well above the heads of the people. The Puck fair is a fair in the true sense of the word with a goat-foot god presiding.

I WISH I WERE A STATIONMASTER

Evening Standard
20 August 1936

• • •

Though married men cannot unfortunately embrace the monastic life, there is nothing but competition to prevent their becoming stationmasters. Soon my imminent collapse will be upon me. As it is, the toot of a car sends a spear through my gizzard, the roar of a motor-bicycle spins the blood round in my head, while the incessant blare of the wireless gnaws my brain as a dog gnaws a bone. When the end comes and it is a question of a complete change of scene or the long white corridors of the lunatic asylum, I hope some kind railway company will offer me a life stationmastership.

If I may give the hint now, I should like a cut of the Somerset and Dorset Joint. And should there be no vacancy on any branch line of this company's secluded track, then may the Great Southern Railway of Ireland shelter me with its kindly patronage. I should like the stationmastership at Inny Junction, where the Sligo to Dublin train calls to take up passengers on Thursdays and Saturdays only. I think that at Inny Junction there would be no fear of my being troubled. No roads lead to the junction, though here and there the white walls of thatched Irish cabins decorate the bog and possibly a couple of goat tracks, not navigable in wet weather, lead to the lonely platforms.

The stationmastership of some important place has no attractions for me. The respect of a few donkeys and cattle round Inny Junction will mean more to me than a box of cigars from Sir Josiah Stamp or a smile from Mr Frank Pick. The noise of the four trains whiffling past from Street and Rathowen to Multyfarnham, and the other four rounding the bend from Float, varied by the occasional crunch of a distant turf cart, will be friendly enough intrusions into the sinking silence of the bog.

But these are happy dreams of the future. Now for the present. In this month of August everyone has a chance of enjoying the pleasures of railway travel and, as an inducement, I have summed up the advantages and disadvantages. First, the express train. Let us suppose you are travelling from Paddington. Already there is the atmosphere of the country when you reach the station, the prospect of pleasurable indigestion following radishes and Devonshire cider on top of the dining-car luncheon. People are standing about, shedding an aura of country-house comfort before stepping into their first-class carriages. Their gardeners, travelling third, carry specimen roses in little cardboard boxes. I have even seen a farm worker chewing a straw and leading a couple of Clydesdales about in the area before the departure platforms.

These are the advantages. You can see what remains of England from the carriage windows: fields and willows and elms; farms and cattle. Ugly villas are not so frequent along railways as they are along roads. The Victorians were the last people to take pride in 'Railway Terraces'. You can read in the train, eat in it, laugh in it, be spared the sight of cads with platinum cuties beside them passing you in racing cars and edging you into the ditch. You are not confronted with the mangled remains of birds and rabbits stretched out across the tarmac.

The disadvantages are as follows:

1. People who smoke manure in their pipes.
2. People who take off their shoes and rest their feet on the seat beside you.
3. People who talk to you.
4. People who talk to one another about their relations.
5. Uncontrolled children who try to hang themselves by the window strap.
6. Nervous women who get up and lean across you out of the window at every station and ask if the train they are in is really the train they are in or some other train and then continue looking out of the window under the impression that the engine driver when he sees their faces will immediately start the train moving again.

But disadvantages such as these are generally confined to main-line expresses. The true railway connoisseur prefers branch lines in the country – those little light railways that are fast disappearing. Here he can be sure of a carriage to himself and individual attention at the stations of his departure and arrival.

The London Passenger Transport Board has shut down the romantic Brill Tramway and now it has shut that useless yet beautiful bit of its line between Quainton Road and Verney Junction. But the time will come when branch lines come into their own again and that will be when silence is appreciated for its own sake. People who are children today will find a train journey at 15 miles an hour more exciting than a motor journey at 50 miles an hour, for they have not the memories that we have of the quiet little journeys in the heart of the country on a summer evening. They do not remember the farms and hedges high with flowers gliding by; the jolt alongside the quiet platform with its rambler roses and municipal-looking calceolarias; the country voice of the porter calling out the name of the station; the chatter of farm people getting into the compartments, loaded with bunches of flowers that they always seem to be taking to one another in the country; the rattle of a milk can and the noise of feet over gravel; then the silence before the train starts to puff its way on through the meadows.

If you look into that most informative of monthly publications, *Bradshaw's Guide*, you will find somewhere near the tide-table applicable to high water at London Bridge a list of 'Train Services Recently Withdrawn'. It is long and sad, for all the services are branch lines or else those little independent companies that have fought in vain against big combines. Before the grass grows up too high along the branch line where you are going for your holidays, take a farewell trip along it, say goodbye to the stationmaster and think of me.

SIGHTSEEING LONDON

Evening Standard
19 September 1936

• • •

The London sightseer of 250 years ago went round to see the sights in his own coach or on his own feet. He found it tiring. I went round in a charabanc with a guide. I was just as tired and saw less. I sat in the charabanc full of people from Leeds, Huddersfield, Bristol and Germany; and we threaded our way through the traffic blocks ferreting out the sights. I felt ashamed for the muddle London has made of itself and for the indignities it has suffered. The conductor of the tour tried to stimulate our imaginations by recalling medieval London in occasional sentimental reveries. But who cares whether Sebert, King of the East Saxons, built the first Westminster Abbey in 605 or whether the diameter of Big Ben's face is 22½ feet or whether Jack Cade struck his sword on London stone in 1450 when the noise of the traffic is deafening and the present so very present that the past is unimaginable?

In 1836 London must have been the most beautiful city in Europe. St Paul's dome rising out of a forest of Wren's white and black steeples; the bend of the river with the water lapping under the arches of Somerset House; gardens and trees and mellow brick houses along the water's edge to where the Abbey's twin towers dominated the landscape; the street full of handsome equipages, yellow, black and scarlet; the neat dresses of the gentry; Carlton House Terrace gleaming tall and stately over the newly planted St James's Park. Then there were that never-to-be-forgotten walk from the Duke's column up Regent Street, with the colonnade and the square-paned shop-fronts, culminating in that most splendid climax Portland Place, with Park Crescent beyond it, opening its arms to terrace upon terrace of fine houses along the edges of Regent's Park; the squares and straight streets dissolving into market gardens; the villages succumbing to the planned march of the new, magnificent Metropolis; the canals – but this was 1836.

London is gone; even pre-war* London is gone. A city has taken its place which is indistinguishable from any other big city except in its ancient monuments. Regent Street, Oxford Street, Holborn (even with its over-restored and rather poky medieval houses) might just as well be the main streets of Manchester, Sheffield or one of the foreign capitals – though foreign capitals add a certain spaciousness to the monotony of their commercial thoroughfares that London lacks. In place of the London of stucco stateliness has risen a town of overlarge stone buildings in an international Renaissance style: cumbersome columns clamped on to steel structures; interiors gleaming with

---

* Pre-First World War.

mahogany, plate-glass and the bogus efficiency, memo-writing, type-writing, red-tape and hygiene connected with big business. The present Regent Street, South Africa House, multiple stores and the new Bank of England are representative of the new international London. The open spaces are filled with flats and, as I write, the last stronghold of old London – Bayswater – is crashing into dust. And the approach is no less depressing from whatever direction you come. The new red houses just the same as those outside any other town, the windy white cemeteries, the wires, dumps, factories, arid recreation grounds and yet more sham Tudor villas extend out and out until there seems to be no England left to look at.

After Buckingham Palace we were shown Westminster Abbey (and the best parts of it are the lace-like Henry VII's chapel and the eighteenth-century monuments, especially Roubiliac's Nightingale Monument – which was not pointed out since it was round a corner among ladders and buckets). We saw the Houses of Parliament and the guide remarked disparagingly that it was 'modern' and took us off to St Stephen's Hall. Actually Barry's 'modern' (1834) buildings, such as the Victoria Tower, are far finer than the medieval. We then whisked down the Embankment (no time to see Somerset House, once the most famous building of London) and for some unknown reason were shown the Monument, now completely dwarfed and not half as interesting as Wren's City churches of St Mildred, Bread Street* or St Mary Abchurch. We shuddered a bit in the Tower, which of all London's recognised medieval sights is the one most worth seeing. At St Paul's Cathedral we paused for luncheon.

We were then taken for a long dreary drive down Holborn with a long, long look at ye olde houses. When we came out into Oxford Street we turned left down Regent Street. This part of the journey took a very long time so that by the time we reached Trafalgar Square our senses were deadened. We were taken down Whitehall, which came as a welcome relief though the guide was so fulsome about the Horseguards that we did not have time to look at the Banqueting House opposite, nor at the graceful little Treasury further on. We returned past the Cenotaph and then we were back where we had

---

* Destroyed by German aerial bombing in April and May 1941.

started. We had not seen London. Rather we had seen a hotchpotch of disordered and undigested history between traffic blocks.

I have come to the conclusion that it is useless to find London by seeing recognised sights. Those who like architecture will be disappointed and so will those who want to see the life of the city. A few archaeologists may be pleased.

Londoners may still be seen carrying on between their great Portland stone walls the life of shouting and bargaining. The visitor should walk in Soho; see Albany and the Edwardian solemnity of the Burlington Arcade;* find a fine spacious Victorian London behind the Albert Hall among the Museums; see the East End towards evening when the little shops and the stalls are bright; and end up the day in an old music-hall like the South London Palace so as to see what is left of Cockney life. Otherwise he will find the usual BBC accents and conversation and the usual industrial suburbanism of any other large English town. Those who like architecture should see the City churches, the Temple, the squares of Clerkenwell, Greenwich Hospital, the Regent's Park terraces – the most magnificent collection of buildings in England – and that wonder of engineering, the Crystal Palace. But I do not see how any stranger can hope to understand London without the company of a Londoner who knows the subtle difference between South Kensington and Mayfair and can pick out the real London from the commercial internationalism and the fake antique.

---

* Burlington Arcade dates from 1818–19 but its Piccadilly end was remodelled by Beresford Pite in 1911 (and remodelled again in 1930 and 1937).

12

OUTDOORS

Hiking and Hunters

A HIKE ON THE DOWNS*

Cherwell
30 April 1932

• • •

'Yes, rub some soap upon your feet!
   We'll hike round Winchester for weeks –
Like ancient Britons – just we two –
   Or more perhaps like ancient Greeks.

'You take your pipe – that will impress
   Your strength on anyone who passes;
I'll take my *Plautus* (*non purgatus*)
   And both my pairs of horn-rimmed glasses.

'I've got my first, and now I know
   What life is and what life contains –
For, being just a first year man
   You don't meet all the first-class brains.

'Objectively, our Common Room
   Is like a small Athenian state –
Except for Lewis: he's all right
   But do you think he's *quite* first rate?

'Hampshire mentality is low,
   And that is why they stare at us.

---

* Originally 'A Hike with a First'.

Yes, here's the earthwork – but it's dark;
  We may as well return by bus.'

THE CRICKET MASTER

From *Summoned by Bells*
1960

• • •

My undergraduate eyes beholding,
  As I climbed your slope, Cat Hill:
Emerald chestnut fans unfolding,
    Symbols of my hope, Cat Hill,
What cared I for past disaster,
Applicant for cricket master,
Nothing much of cricket knowing,
Conscious but of money owing?
    Somehow I would cope, Cat Hill.

'The sort of man we want must be prepared
To take our first eleven. Many boys
From last year's team are with us. You will find
Their bowling's pretty good and they are keen.'
'And so am I, Sir, very keen indeed.'
Oh where's mid-on? And what is silly point?
Do six balls make an over? Help me, God!
'Of course you'll get some first-class cricket too;
The MCC send down an A team here.'
My bluff had worked. I sought the common-room,
Of last term's pipe-smoke faintly redolent.

It waited empty with its worn arm-chairs
For senior bums to mine, when in there came
A fierce old eagle in whose piercing eye
I saw that instant-registered dislike
Of all unhealthy aesthetes such as me.
'I'm Winters – you're our other new recruit
And here's another new man – Barnstaple.'
He introduced a thick Devonian.
'Let's go and have some practice in the nets.
You'd better go in first.' With but one pad,
No gloves, and knees that knocked in utter fright,
Vainly I tried to fend the hail of balls
Hurled at my head by brutal Barnstaple
And at my shins by Winters. Nasty quiet
Followed my poor performance. When the sun
Had sunk behind the fringe of Hadley Wood
And Barnstaple and I were left alone
Among the ash-trays of the common-room,
He murmured in his soft West-country tones:
'D'you know what Winters told me, Betjeman?
He didn't think you'd ever held a bat.'

    The trusting boys returned. 'We're jolly glad
You're on our side, Sir, in the trial match.'
'But I'm no good at all.' 'Oh yes, you are.'
When I was out first ball, they said 'Bad luck!
You hadn't got your eye in.' Still I see
Barnstaple's smile of undisguised contempt,
Still feel the sting of Winters' silent sneer.
Disgraced, demoted to the seventh game,
Even the boys had lost their faith in me.
God guards his aesthetes. If by chance these lines
Are read by one who in some common-room
Has had his bluff called, let him now take heart:
In every school there is a sacred place
More holy than the chapel. Ours was yours:
I mean, of course, the first-eleven pitch.
Here in the welcome break from morning work,

The heavier boys, of milk and biscuits full,
Sat on the roller while we others pushed
Its weighty cargo slowly up and down.
We searched the grass for weeds, caressed the turf,
Lay on our stomachs squinting down its length
To see that all was absolutely smooth.

    The prize-day neared. And, on the eve before,
We masters hung our college blazers out
In readiness for tomorrow. Matron made
A final survey of the boys' best clothes –
Clean shirts. Clean collars. 'Rice, your jacket's torn.
Bring it to me this instant!' Supper done,
Barnstaple drove his round-nosed Morris out
And he and I and Vera Spencer-Clarke,
Our strong gymnasium mistress, squashed ourselves
Into the front and rattled to The Cock.

    Sweet bean-fields then were scenting Middlesex;
Narrow lanes led between the dairy-farms
To ponds reflecting weather-boarded inns.
There on the wooden bench outside The Cock
Sat Barnstaple, Miss Spencer-Clarke and I,
At last forgetful of tomorrow's dread
And gazing into sky-blue Hertfordshire.
Three pints for Barnstaple, three halves for me,
Sherry of course for Vera Spencer-Clarke.

    Pre-prize-day nerves? Or too much bitter beer?
What had that evening done to Barnstaple?
I only know that singing we returned;
The more we sang, the faster Barnstaple
Drove his old Morris, swerving down the drive
And in and out the rhododendron clumps,
Over the very playing-field itself,
And then – oh horror! – right across the pitch
Not once, but twice or thrice. The mark of tyres
Next day was noticed at the Parents' Match.
That settled Barnstaple and he was sacked,
While I survived him, lasting three more terms.

Shops and villas have invaded
    Your chestnut quiet there, Cat Hill.
Cricket field and pitch degraded,
    Nothing did they spare, Cat Hill.
Vera Spencer-Clarke is married
And the rest are dead and buried;
I am thirty summers older,
Richer, wickeder and colder,
    Fuller too of care, Cat Hill.

CHELTENHAM

The Listener
22 December 1938

• • •

F*loruit, floret, floreat!*
    Cheltonia's children cry.
I composed those lines when a summer wind
    Was blowing the elm leaves dry,
And we were seventy-six for seven
    And they had C. B. Fry.

Shall I forget the warm marquee
    And the general's wife so soon,
When my son's colleger* acted as tray
    For an ice and a macaroon,
And distant carriages jingled through
    The stuccoed afternoon?

---

* Mortar board.

Floruit. Yes, the Empire Map
    Cheltonia's sons have starred.
Floret. Still the stream goes on
    Of soldier, brusher* and bard.
Floreat. While behind the limes
    Lengthens the Promenade.

NORTH COAST RECOLLECTIONS

West Country Magazine
Spring 1947

• • •

No people on the golf-links, not a crack
    Of well-swung driver from the fourteenth tee,
No sailing bounding ball across the turf
And lady's slipper of the fairway. Black
Rises Bray Hill and, Stepper-wards, the sun
Sends Bray Hill's phantom stretching to the church.
The lane, the links, the beach, the cliffs are bare
The neighbourhood is dressing for a dance
And lamps are being lit in bungalows.
    O! thymy time of evening: clover scent
And feathery tamarisk round the churchyard wall
And shrivelled sea-pinks and this foreshore pale
With silver sand and sharpened quartz and slate
And brittle twigs, bleached, salted and prepared

---

* Schoolmaster.

For kindling blue-flamed fires on winter nights.
    Here Petroc landed, here I stand today;
The same Atlantic surges roll for me
As rolled for Parson Hawker and for him,
And spent their gathering thunder on the rocks
Crashing with pebbly backwash, burst again
And strewed the nibbled fields along the cliffs.

    When low tides drain the estuary gold
Small intersecting breakers far away
Ripple about a bar of shifting sand
Where centuries ago were waving woods
Where centuries hence, there will be woods again.

    Within the bungalow of Mrs Hanks
Her daughter Phoebe now French-chalks the floor.
Norman and Gordon in their dancing pumps
Slide up and down, but can't make concrete smooth.
'My Sweet Hortense . . .'
Sings louder down the garden than the sea.
'A practice record, Phoebe. Mummykins,
Gordon and I will do the washing-up.'
'We picnic here; we scrounge and help ourselves,'
Says Mrs Hanks, and visitors will smile
To see them all turn to it. Boys and girls
Weed in the sterile garden, mostly sand
And dead tomato-plants and chicken-runs.
Today they cleaned the dulled Benares ware
(Dulled by the sea-mist), early made the beds,
And Phoebe twirled the icing round the cake
And Gordon tinkered with the gramophone
While into an immense enamel jug
Norman poured 'Eiffel Tower' for lemonade.
    O! healthy bodies, bursting into 'teens
And bursting out of last year's summer clothes,
Fluff barking and French windows banging to
Till the asbestos walling of the place
Shakes with the life it shelters, and with all

The preparations for this evening's dance.

Now drains the colour from the convolvulus,
The windows of Trenain are flashing fire,
Black sways the tamarisk against the West,
And bathing things are taken in from sills.
One child still zig-zags homewards up the lane,
Cold on bare feet he feels the dew-wet sand.
Behind him, from a walk along the cliff,
Come pater and the mater and the dogs.

Four macrocarpa hide the tennis club.
Two children of a chartered actuary
(Beaworthy, Trouncer, Heppelwhite and Co.),
Harold and Bonzo Trouncer are engaged
In semi-finals for the tournament.
'Love thirty!' Pang! across the evening air
Twangs Harold's racquet. Plung! the ball returns.
Experience at Budleigh Salterton
Keeps Bonzo steady at the net. 'Well done!'
'Love forty!' Captain Mycroft, midst applause,
Pronounces for the Trouncers, to be sure
He can't be certain Bonzo didn't reach
A shade across the net, but Demon Sex,
That tulip figure in white cotton dress,
Bare legs, wide eyes and so tip-tilted nose
Quite overset him. Harold serves again
And Mrs Pardon says it's getting cold,
Miss Myatt shivers, Lady Lambourn thinks
These English evenings are a little damp
And dreams herself again in fair Shanghai.
'Game . . . AND! and thank you!'; so the pair from Rock
(A neighbouring and less exclusive place)
Defeated, climb into their Morris Ten.
'The final is tomorrow! Well, good night!'
He lay in wait, he lay in wait, he did,
John Lambourn, curly-headed; dewy grass
Dampened his flannels, but he still remained.

The sunset drained the colours black and gold,
From his all-glorious First Eleven scarf.
But still he waited by the twilit hedge.
Only his eyes blazed blue with early love,
Blue blazing in the darkness of the lane,
Blue blazer, less incalculably blue,
Dark scarf, white flannels, supple body still,
First love, first light, first life. A heartbeat noise!
His heart or little feet? A snap of twigs
Dry, dead and brown the under branches part
And Bonzo scrambles by their secret way.
First love so deep, John Lambourn cannot speak,
So deep, he feels a tightening in his throat,
So tender, he could brush away the sand
Dried up in patches on her freckled legs,
Could hold her gently till the stars went down,
And if she cut herself would staunch the wound,
Yes, even with his First Eleven scarf,
And hold it there for hours.
So happy, and so deep he loves the world,
Could worship God and rocks and stones and trees,
Be nicer to his mother, kill himself
If that would make him pure enough for her.
And so at last he manages to say
'You going to the Hanks's hop tonight?'
'Well, I'm not sure. Are you?' 'I think I may –
'It's pretty dud though, – only lemonade.'

    Sir Gawaint was a right and goodly knight
Nor ever wist he to uncurtis be.
So old, so lovely, and so very true!
Then Mrs Wilder shut the Walter Crane
And tied the tapes and tucked her youngest in
What time without amidst the lavender
At late last 'He' played Primula and Prue
With new-found liveliness, for bed was soon.
And in the garage, serious seventeen

Harvey, the eldest, hammered on, content,
Fixing a mizzen to his model boat.
'Coo-ee! Coo-ee!' across the lavender,
Across the mist of pale gypsophila
And lolling purple poppies, Mumsie called,
A splendid sunset lit the rocking-horse
And Morris pattern of the nursery walls.
'Coo-ee!' the slate-hung, goodly-builded house
And sunset-sodden garden fell to quiet.
'Prue! Primsie! Mumsie wants you. Sleepi-byes!'
Prue jumped the marigolds and hid herself,
Her sister scampered to the Wendy Hut
And Harvey, glancing at his Ingersoll,
Thought 'Damn! I must get ready for the dance.'

    So on this after-storm-lit evening
To Jim the raindrops in the tamarisk,
The fuchsia bells, the sodden matchbox lid
That checked a tiny torrent in the lane
Were magnified and shining clear with life.
Then pealing out across the estuary
The Padstow bells rang up for practice-night
An undersong to birds and dripping shrubs.
The full Atlantic at September spring
Flooded a final tide-mark up the sand,
And ocean sank to silence under bells,
And the next breaker was a lesser one
Then lesser still. Atlantic, bells and birds
Were layer on interchanging layer of sound.

HUNTER TRIALS

Time and Tide
5 January 1952

• • •

It's awf'lly bad luck on Diana,
   Her ponies have swallowed their bits;
She fished down their throats with a spanner
   And frightened them all into fits.

So now she's attempting to borrow.
   Do lend her some bits, Mummy, *do*;
I'll lend her my own for tomorrow,
   But today *I*'ll be wanting them too.

Just look at Prunella on Guzzle,
   The wizardest pony on earth;
Why doesn't she slacken his muzzle
   And tighten the breech in his girth?

I say, Mummy, there's Mrs Geyser
   And doesn't she look pretty sick?
I bet it's because Mona Lisa
   Was hit on the hock with a brick.

Miss Blewitt says Monica threw it,
   But Monica says it was Joan,
And Joan's very thick with Miss Blewitt,
   So Monica's sulking alone.

And Margaret failed in her paces,
   Her withers got tied in a noose,

So her coronets caught in the traces
    And now all her fetlocks are loose.

Oh, it's me now. I'm terribly nervous.
    I wonder if Smudges will shy.
She's practically certain to swerve as
    Her Pelham is over one eye.

        ★   ★   ★

Oh wasn't it naughty of Smudges?
    Oh, Mummy, I'm sick with disgust.
She threw me in front of the Judges,
    And my silly old collarbone's bust.

THE OLYMPIC GIRL

A Few Late Chrysanthemums
1954

•   •   •

The sort of girl I like to see
    Smiles down from her great height at me.
She stands in strong, athletic pose
And wrinkles her *retroussé* nose.
Is it distaste that makes her frown,
So furious and freckled, down
On an unhealthy worm like me?
Or am I what she likes to see?
I do not know, though much I care.
Eithe genoimen★ . . . would I were

(Forgive me, shade of Rupert Brooke)
An object fit to claim her look.
Oh! would I were her racket press'd
With hard excitement to her breast
And swished into the sunlit air
Arm-high above her tousled hair,
And banged against the bounding ball
'Oh! Plung!' my tauten'd strings would call,
'Oh! Plung! my darling, break my strings
For you I will do brilliant things.'
And when the match is over, I
Would flop beside you, hear you sigh;
And then, with what supreme caress,
You'd tuck me up into my press.
Fair tigress of the tennis courts,
So short in sleeve and strong in shorts,
Little, alas, to you I mean,
For I am bald and old and green.

SEASIDE GOLF

Punch
6 July 1953

• • •

How straight it flew, how long it flew,
It clear'd the rutty track

---

* 'Would I were' in classical Greek. Printed versions of this poem often quote the words in an approximation of their original form – εἴθε γενοίμην – but wrongly

And soaring, disappeared from view
    Beyond the bunker's back –
A glorious, sailing, bounding drive
That made me glad I was alive.

And down the fairway, far along
    It glowed a lonely white;
I played an iron sure and strong
    And clipp'd it out of sight,
And spite of grassy banks between
I knew I'd find it on the green.

And so I did. It lay content
    Two paces from the pin;
A steady putt and then it went
    Oh, most securely in.
The very turf rejoiced to see
That quite unprecedented three.

Ah! seaweed smells from sandy caves
    And thyme and mist in whiffs,
In-coming tide, Atlantic waves
    Slapping the sunny cliffs,
Lark song and sea sounds in the air
And splendour, splendour everywhere.

---

spelled and wrongly stressed. They appear in Plato ('*Eithe genoimen ouranos*') but are better known from Rupert Brooke's own quotation of them in his 1912 poem 'The Old Vicarage, Grantchester', which is what Betjeman refers to here.

13

TRAVEL

Brunel and Bradshaw

MY FAVOURITE HOLIDAY*

Everybody's
June 1954

• • •

Exploring Great Britain has always been more fun to me than going abroad. No language barrier except in parts of Wales and Scotland, different money troubles and infinite variety of scenery – these are some of the advantages. Give me a *Kelly's Directory*† and a town I haven't visited before, a warm-coloured room in some commercial hotel with a Bible by the bed and a view in the morning over chimney pots and tiles, factory chimneys and Victorian spires and I am happy. No town is so dull that it has not something to attract. I shall never forget waking in early dawn at Oldham to hear a noise like cavalry clopping down the cobbled streets outside my window. It was the clatter of clogged feet hurrying off to the mills.

So the best holiday I ever had was in these islands. Best of all, I hadn't planned it beforehand so there were none of the disappointments that anticipation produces. I had just been sacked from something – I have been sacked twenty-two times, if you include educational experiences – and I had received a little bonus in the form of conscience money from my late employers. I wasn't married; I had no children and no sense of responsibility. It was a hot August day in London. I was in Long Acre and went into the map shop there and saw displayed a large-scale map of the Isle of Man. I bought it

---

* This essay recalls a radio programme Betjeman made about a more recent solo visit to the Isle of Man in 1949, paid for by the BBC.
† A house-by-house street guide, no longer in existence.

and went to a travel agency and took an aeroplane due to leave that afternoon. I bought myself a dozen oysters at a fish bar near Victoria and studied the map. I decided to stay at the most unimportant-looking part of the island, judging by the map, and the place with the fewest main roads and yet near the sea. This appeared to be Ballaugh on the west coast of the island.

As the Isle of Man circled below us with a fringe of white and moving lace around its coast, I was able to see Ballaugh, its small fields and scattered farms below me. Of course I had brought *Bradshaw's* railway guide, which showed me there was an afternoon train to Ballaugh from Douglas, changing at St John's.

The silence at Ronaldsway airport after the noise of the aero-plane, the wet air blowing from the west across the grass, the Manx flag of three legs flying over the hut, the delightful gimcrack unim-portance of it all (for these were the early days of air travel), the tall grey Gothic buildings of King William's College (about which *Eric, or Little by Little* was written) nearby, the drive through tamarisk and veronica-hedged lanes to Douglas – it all reminded me of Northern Ireland.

I wish I could convey to you my joys in seeing a strange place for the first time. I get it from three things: buildings, scenery and people. I don't mind whether buildings are old or new. I have looked at them so long and noticed shapes of window panes, pitches of roofs and different varieties of stone and brick that are so infinite in these islands that I can work out the history of a place and am never bored. For instance, it was quite obvious from the aeroplane that Castletown, near the airport, was an ancient town, with narrow streets clustered round the sad castle and a Georgian main square with a column in the middle of it. It was obvious too that Douglas was only old round the harbour for here were the narrow streets of a fishing port and all round them stretched the long, straight or winding roads of modern houses. But you only see the map of a place from an aeroplane. You get no idea of its outlines, its colour and texture. The mountains and glens of the middle of the island looked brown and flat. The most northern point, which was sandy and marshy-looking with a few white cottages gleaming here and there, looked worth exploring.

I should say that I also bought a guide to the island in London
– a second-hand one as they are always more thorough if they are
pre-1914 – and had read the history of the island in the aeroplane.
So when the bus reached Douglas, I had an idea of what it was
going to look like – but only an idea. It was the height of the
holiday season and full of North Country people, the men in flannels and blazers, the girls in bright cotton dresses, walking up and
down the late-Victorian sea front where the crowded trams rumble
by the sand. There in the water was the romantic ruin called 'The
Tower of Refuge', built on a rock in the middle of the bay. Along
the front were bow-windowed boarding houses and flash hotels and
bathing things hung from sills; and hydrangeas bloomed in public
gardens and ices were being eaten by children and champagne was
being drunk in public bars – for there are bars in Douglas where
champagne only is served – and silver bands played in bandstands
and there was no sign of the country, except that behind the boarding houses of the front were the misty hills and on the nearest of
them were perched the Georgian castles and villas of an earlier
age when the island was a refuge for Regency bucks who would
not pay their debts and built themselves houses here for secret
retirement.

If you are a railway maniac, the Isle of Man is a paradise. The
lines are narrow gauge, the rolling stock is ancient and far too few
people have yet discovered its joys. The ticket I took to Ballaugh
was a thick, old-fashioned bit of cardboard such as one never sees
in England. The train ground slowly out of Douglas and past the
ilex trees of The Nunnery,★ the chief country house of the island
situated deep in Douglas, a bowery oasis in the noise. We went past
brown streams and through woody glens and at St John's I saw the
grass mound where once a year sits the Tynwald, the tribal gathering of the island, and where the laws are proclaimed in Manx and
English. The train into which I changed for Ballaugh was far older
and more countrified than that from Douglas. And here I was in
another land, a lace of fuchsia hedges and fields and Ireland in the
distance. The rhythm and safety and isolation of a train always help

---

★ A thirteenth-century stately home, now used by the Isle of Man Business School.

me to write poetry and I suppose if I was born to do anything it is to write poetry. And I remember how verses came springing to my head on the Isle of Man railway so that I almost forgot to get out at Ballaugh Station.

If you don't know the Vicar, ask the stationmaster where lodgings may be had – and this I did. Down the lane to the sea, which reminded me of Cornwall, I went to the farm he showed me. English people lived there. They kept bees. Already a Methodist minister and his family had rooms there but I was put up on a sofa in the drawing room. We had honey and wholemeal bread and Manx kippers for high tea and these kippers, smoked in wood chips, tasted more delicious than a peat-cured ham.

A man alone on a holiday is always an object of pity and affection. People think his wife may have died or he may be unhappily married or looking for a wife or be a famous man in disguise. So I knew great kindness on the island from the people at the farm, from the Methodist fellow boarders and from everyone I met. In the evenings I would go into Douglas by train after high tea and come back after visiting the great dance hall and watching those hundreds of couples doing elaborate steps in perfect rhythm so that the dance seemed like a complicated ritual. And sometimes in the evening I would go to Peel and stand on the sheltering island where the ruins of St German's Cathedral are and watch the fishing smacks sail out into the sunset. By day I would walk along the wild rock-and-bracken-covered west coast or into those primeval swamps known as 'corraghs', where the air was hot and still and the flowers and insects seemed enormous. There were electrical tramcars to travel in – one winding up the mountain of Snaefell, from which one can see five kingdoms: Ireland, Scotland, Wales, England and the mountainy island of the Kingdom of Man itself at one's feet. And all these pleasures were heightened and intensified so that they are still vivid in my brain, because I was alone and without responsibility. It was the last time I can remember being wholly unembarrassed.

THE GREAT WESTERN

Introduction to *The Book of the Great Western*
Edited by George Perry, assisted by Graham Norton
and Christopher Bushell
Sunday Times Magazine, 1970

. . .

It is a privilege to have been born in 1906 and therefore to have been old enough to remember the distinct personalities of English railways before 1923. Who were the great ones? The London and North Western, aggressive and independent with its Greek portals and castellated bridges and its carriages of purple-brown and broken white; the Midland, noted more for comfort than speed, with its scarlet livery and pinnacled terminus of St Pancras; the Great Northern, of record runs to York and Scotland and engines by Sturrock and Stirling; the Great Eastern, smokiest of all lines, whose austere suburban traffic prevented London from eating too far into East Anglia; the Great Central, glittering, nouveau riche and generous; the London and South Western, whose porters wore red ties and which tried to capture Devon and Cornwall after swallowing up Southampton Docks; the two rivals: the London, Brighton and South Coast, with its Pullman express to Brighton in one hour, and the South Eastern and Chatham, whose Italianate hotel at Charing Cross was patronised by Sherlock Holmes – these were the other greats of Southern England; and there were great lines of the North and Scotland and Ireland. There were even rival lines on the Isle of Man and Jersey.

But the greatest of the greats was the Great Western. In that sad year of 1923 when the scarlet paint of the Midland was poured over the purple-brown and broken white of the London and North

Western, when the rival lines of South London and beyond were painted a universal green, the Great Western retained its title, its livery and its personality. It mopped up some railways of South Wales but did so in no hectoring manner. The Great Western was great and could afford to be magnanimous.

Most railway writers are scholarly specialists on locomotives or signalling or mechanical engineering or history and Acts of Parliament. A few like Jack Simmons and that excellent writer and painter C. Hamilton Ellis and the humorist Paul Jennings have appreciated the personalities of the different lines. It is only with the personality of the Great Western that I am concerned.

A railway grows in one's affection if one has known it in early childhood and for the rest of one's life, as I have known the Great Western. For this reason this introduction to a Great Western Album must be somewhat autobiographical. It was the first line on which I took long journeys. There were two routes to North Cornwall from London. One was from Waterloo on the London and South Western by the ambitiously named 'Atlantic Coast Express'. It dawdled after Exeter (Queen Street), with a long wait at Okehampton and a still longer one at Halwill and Beaworthy (junction for Bude) and nothing to see but mist on the moor and washing hanging out in the garth of the Cottage Hospital. But by Great Western from Paddington there was variety. There were also comforting constants that survive to this day, like radishes and watercress after luncheon in the dining-car. There was what is still to me the most glorious bit of line in England – that from Exeter to Newton Abbot. The twin Norman towers of the cathedral disappeared behind one and the Exe began to widen. Barges on the embanked canal glided above the saltings. The Italianate red sandstone tower of a pumping-station for Brunel's unsuccessful atmospheric railway★ stood, as it still stands, by the shore's edge at Starcross and then we were at Dawlish with the sea right under the carriage window. In the tunnels through the hills I would pretend to myself that this was the Hampstead and Highgate line and then

---

★ Its trains were intended to be propelled by air pressure in pneumatic tubes – a popular new technology in the 1840s.

have the delightful self-induced surprise of seeing the English Channel. On rough days the water was milky pink for many yards out: even on calm days we could hear the crash and withdrawal of the waves as the train waited at Dawlish Station. Then came Teignmouth with its long bridge to Shaldon on the opposite bank; it was goodbye to seagulls and we were back with saltings and herons and ilex-shaded gardens of stucco villas at Newton Abbot. Through flowering banks we climbed until we were high on viaducts spanning woody valleys, yellow in spring with primroses. There was the long wait at Plymouth (North Road), dullest of stations and no less dull now it has been rebuilt in copybook contemporary. The general grey slate, grey cement and back gardens of Plymouth, as seen from the Great Western, made the surprise of Saltash Bridge all the more exciting. Up and down stream, grey battleships were moored in the Tamar and its reaches. Hundreds of feet below, the pathetic steam ferry to Saltash from the Devon bank tried to compete with Brunel's mighty bridge. Then it was Cornwall and even more splendid valleys and viaducts in the fading light and the oil-lit welcome of Bodmin Road Station, among conifers and ponticum. A slow branch line went to the Great Western terminus of Bodmin, then backed out and stopped at a very unimportant place on an empty hillside called St Lawrence Platform. Thence it rushed through the woody Camel valley, not stopping at oil-lit halts owned by the London and South Western, until here we were at Wadebridge at 7.51 p.m. and the Atlantic air instead of that of the English Channel.

THE CORNISH EXPRESS*

1960

Come, friends of Hygiene, Electricity
And those young twins, Free Thought and clean Fresh Air:
Attend the long express from Waterloo

---

* Extract from Chapter 4, 'Cornwall in Childhood', of *Summoned by Bells*.

That takes us down to Cornwall. Tea-time shows
The small fields waiting, every blackthorn hedge
Straining inland before the south-west gale.
The emptying train, wind in the ventilators,
Puffs out of Egloskerry to Tresméer
Through minty meadows, under bearded trees
And hills upon whose sides the clinging farms
Hold Bible Christians. Can it really be
That this same carriage came from Waterloo?
On Wadebridge station what a breath of sea
Scented the Camel valley! Cornish air,
Soft Cornish rains, and silence after steam . . .
As out of Derry's stable came the brake
To drag us up those long, familiar hills,
Past haunted woods and oil-lit farms and on
To far Trebetherick by the sounding sea.

So strong was the personality of the Great Western that even though it took me homesick to my preparatory school in Oxford, and homesick again to school at Marlborough, it did not lose its place in my affections. It was the last link with the civilised world. How many a breaking heart there used to be at Paddington Station on those days when school trains departed to the West, Wales and the Midlands. There the pupils stood in school clothes, with a grip containing pyjamas, a sponge-bag and health certificate, trying to look cheerful. They eyed each other's parents and dreaded the coming journey with strangers and potential foes in the carriage. For Marlborough we waited at Savernake and were pulled along the branch line to a terminus high above the town; then the long walk to the cold dormitories and it was farewell to the Great Western until the special took us home for holidays in early dawn.

BACK TO SCHOOL*

1960

Doom! Shivering doom! Clutching a leather grip
Containing things for the first night of term –
House-slippers, sponge-bag, pyjams, Common Prayer,
My health certificate, photographs of home
(Where were my bike, my playbox and my trunk?) –
I walked with strangers down the hill to school.
The town's first gaslights twinkled in the cold.
Deserted by the coaches, poorly served
By railway, Marlborough was a lonely place;
The old Bath Road, in chalky whiteness, raised
Occasional clouds of dust as motors passed.

As though aware of the coming motor age, the Great Western from 1923 onwards went in for new colour schemes for the insides of its carriages. This was the time of the 2.30 p.m. from Paddington, the 'Cheltenham Flyer', the fastest train in the British Isles. In the new third-class carriages the upholstering was of black and red rapp, without buttons and with black and red blinds that were meant to roll up out of sight during the daytime but often did not do so. The new firsts were a symphony of brown and gold lace with walnut panels and brass fittings and still that delightful loop of cloth, a survival of stage-coaches, for the corner seats.

The smarter undergraduates at Oxford in the twenties preferred to come by road from London in Aston Martin, Sports Bugatti or even round-nosed Morris. They thought it was faster than by train. It certainly is not now. It was always necessary to use the Great Western for a day trip to London from Oxford because one could return by what was known as the 'Flying Fornicator', the 9.50 p.m. from Paddington, which just reached Oxford in time to get back to one's college before they shut the gates at midnight.

---

* Extract from Chapter 7, 'Marlborough', of *Summoned by Bells*.

It was while at Oxford that I discovered the joys of the Midland and North Welsh sections of the Great Western and that unexpected terminus at Birkenhead. More delightful than these outposts were the branch lines in the Cotswolds to Shipton-on-Stour and Moreton-in-Marsh, to Fairford from Yarnton and the main line to Worcester. A station on this line, Adlestrop, summarises the country quiet of the Great Western on a hot day, in two stanzas by Edward Thomas:

> Yes I remember Adlestrop
> The name, because one afternoon
> Of heat the express train drew up there
> Unwontedly. It was late June.
>
> The steam hissed. Someone cleared his throat.
> No one left and no one came
> On the bare platform. What I saw
> Was Adlestrop – only the name.

Although not many people got out on these branch lines, the trains were always punctual, passengers and station staff were friends, stationmasters were part of the village community like the schoolmaster, the postmaster and the parson. People were very proud of the Great Western: engines were kept trim and shiny, carriages were clean, station gardens blossomed with flowers. The company kept itself a strict but happy ship. I wonder if there is any truth in that story of a Great Western employee who retired and was asked by the company what he would like for a leaving present. He said he would like a railway carriage to live in and was given one. When some friends went to visit him in his carriage on a wet day they found him sitting outside the carriage, under an umbrella, smoking a pipe. When they asked him why, he said the company had given him a non-smoker.

Motor traffic was already making London nasty to live in even in the late twenties. I moved out on to the Wycombe line at Seer Green Halt which had a look of St Lawrence Platform, Bodmin. Though it was adventurous to travel on the dying Great Central to Marylebone, I preferred trains to Paddington and motor-rail journeys over that only unsuccessful GWR venture, its London suburban service.

In the thirties I married and wanted to live in real country, yet it would be necessary for me to travel up every day to work on a newspaper. The Great Western provided the real country. Uffington, junction for Faringdon, was the farthest country station on any line from London that had trains to fit in with the hours that suited my employers and me. There were still people in Uffington village in the early thirties, when we lived there, who remembered the change-over from broad gauge. Swindon, the nearest large town, was still primarily a railway town and its social distinctions were railway ones. If you were in the works, you were said to be 'inside'. If you were 'inside', you were pretty safe with the benefits the company had provided for its workers ever since the days of Daniel Gooch the mechanical engineer, Brunel the civil engineer and Charles Saunders the secretary. They had decided that this flat part of North Wiltshire should be the site of their works. There were (and still are) the company's cottages in limestone in the Tudor style, the Institute with its library and theatre, the medical services and the church of St Mark from which the railway town has spread out. There was a village atmosphere about new Swindon. Mr Hawksworth, the Chief Mechanical Engineer, who is still alive, was a churchwarden at St Mark's. Daughter churches were built; one, called St Saviour's, was constructed by the railwaymen at their own expense in their spare time. Beyond the original limestone company's cottages, the red-brick villas, all two storeys high, climbed up to the Marlborough Downs where the market town of old Swindon crowns the hill. The more important you became 'inside' in Swindon, the more anxious you were to leave new Swindon and to have a smart villa on the outskirts of the old town. Despite this stratification, Swindon was warm-hearted and radical. There was a strong chapel element. The WEA* prospered under Reuben George, whom many will remember. It was an unashamedly ugly and friendly town. The only time not to go there was 'trip' week in the summer when the works were almost shut and all families of 'inside' people travelled at reduced rates for their holidays.

---

* Workers' Educational Association.

ON HEARING THE FULL PEAL OF TEN BELLS FROM CHRIST CHURCH, SWINDON, WILTS.

New Bats in Old Belfries
1945

Your peal of ten ring over then this town,
Ring on my men nor ever ring them down.
This winter chill, let sunset spill cold fire
On villa'd hill and on Sir Gilbert's spire,
So new, so high, so pure, so broach'd, so tall.
Long run the thunder of the bells through all!

Oh still white headstone on these fields of sound
Hear you the wedding joybells wheeling round?
Oh brick-built breeding boxes of new souls,
Hear how the pealing through the louvres rolls!
Now birth and death-reminding bells ring clear,
Loud under 'planes and over changing gear.

Railwaymen are organised rather like naval men, to whom many of them bear a physical resemblance, with red weather-beaten features. The admiral of the Great Western fleet in these last glorious days of the company was the General Manager, Sir Felix Pole. He had started as a telegraph clerk on Swindon Station. He was a born journalist and publicist for the line as well as an organiser. His successor, Keith Grand, kept up his tradition, so far as it was possible. I always felt that the pseudo-modern décor the GWR invented in its last days – that sans-serif monogram, the 'streamlining' of the inside of the Paddington Hotel and obliteration of P. C. Hardwick's fine Baroque coffee room, the chromium and plyboard – was an augury of that dread, dead bit of bureaucracy, 'British Railways'.

Almost the last public gesture the Great Western made was to the Wantage Steam Tramway Co. When that delightfully dim tramline ceased in May 1946 the Great Western took its ancient engine,

Shannon, to be repaired and then set it up on Wantage Road Station. For a time it shone bright on the down platform with its copper and green paint. Then there seems to have been nobody who thought it was his job to polish it. Then it disappeared. And now Wantage Road Station has disappeared too.

The Great Western tried to keep up its spirit after 1 January 1948. It was subjected to various petty insults. Some minor official spent much money changing the words 'Great Western' to 'British Railways (Western Region)' on all notices and boards. Trains were no longer punctual; but as though to compensate for this, a new timetable was brought out with the wasteful withitry of many pages of self-advertisement and officialese in illegible close-set sans-serif type. The 'Lawn' at Paddington was renamed 'main circulating area', just as 'refreshment facilities are available on this train' is the new officialese for 'there's a dining car'. Great Western employees were not actively discouraged from wearing the pill-box hat worn in the company's days by certain ranks but if they wanted one they had to pay for it themselves.

There is no doubt that the only comfortable and fast method of travel on this island today is by train. This has been caused by too many lorries and private cars on the roads. Perhaps from British Railways something will emerge as efficient, humane and exciting as was the Great Western.

14
SEASIDE
Sand and Sandwiches

Beside the Seaside (1969)

BESIDE THE SEASIDE

Sixth in the thirteen-part television series
'Bird's-Eye View'

BBC 2 Television
25 December 1969
Producer and Director: Edward Mirzoeff

• • •

They feared it most who knew it best,
  The sea that hits the rocky west.
To merchantmen it might bring wealth
But it was dangerous to health.
Far better live inland, and warm,
Out of the perilous wind and storm.
Safe from fresh air and suchlike harm
In sheltered mansion, cot or farm.

Quality sent its sons and daughters
In search of health to inland waters.
To Roman Bath or Cheltenham Spa
Where the Chalbeate fountains are.

To Cheltenham also came George III to be cured of biliousness, until his physicians advised him to take the sea-bathing cure in Dorset. So in July 1789 he went to Weymouth. It was then an unimportant fishing port, full of smugglers. The King stayed in a house belonging to his brother, the Duke of Gloucester. A statue on the front commemorates his visit. 'God Save the King' on ribbons was hung on bathing machines, on the bonnets of the ladies, around the waists of the girls. Fanny Burney wrote:

The King bathes and with great success; a machine follows the Royal one into the sea, filled with fiddlers who play 'God Save the King' as His Majesty takes his plunge.*

The country rejoiced in the King's recovery. The sea was no longer unfashionable. Moreover it was healthy.

Where the monarch led, his subjects followed. To Lyme Regis for instance, also in Dorset, came the genteel characters of Jane Austen's *Persuasion*. It was when jumping down on the Lower Cobb at Lyme – the Cobb is that stone wall that juts into the sea – that Louise Musgrove, you will remember, sprained her ankle, closed her eyes, and was taken by her companions to be lifeless.

Grander folk went further west to Sidmouth in South Devon. The Grand Duchess Helene of Russia set her double eagle there on Fortfield Terrace, whose cheerful stucco front looks on to a cricket ground swept by breezes from the English Channel. The wars against Napoleon stopped people going abroad – hence resorts like this.

Sidmouth is a sort of Cheltenham-on-Sea, the sea quite often as calm and gentle as the Thames. Behind that comely row of sunny lodgings, ornamental cottages were built, by men of means, out of sight of the water but within sound of the shingle shore. It was to Sidmouth that a younger brother of George IV came with his wife and infant daughter. He was the Duke of Kent. He despised the vulgarities of his brother's Brighton. He liked the country and the rock-strewn shore. One day in 1820 he got his feet wet, here at Sidmouth, contracted pneumonia and died – there, in that ornamental cottage he had built for himself, his wife and daughter, Princess Victoria. Could it have been her cradle memories of this southern shore that made Victoria, later England's Queen, build with her husband Albert, Prince Consort, this Italian palace – Osborne – on the English Channel? 'The dear Prince is constantly occupied in directing the many necessary improvements which are to be made,' wrote the young Queen Victoria in 1845.

---

* From *The Diary of Fanny Burney*.

It is impossible to imagine a prettier spot. Valleys and woods which would be beautiful anywhere; but all this near the sea – the woods grow into the sea – is quite perfection. We have a charming beach quite to ourselves. The sea was so blue and calm that the Prince said it was like Naples. And then we can walk about anywhere by ourselves without being followed and mobbed. Drove down to the beach with my maids and went into the bathing machine where I undressed and bathed in the sea for the first time in my life. It was delightful until I put my head under the water. And last but not least, we have Portsmouth and Spithead so close at hand that we shall be able to watch what is going on which will please the Navy.

The Isle of Wight prospered.
Ryde, so near to Osborne, grew in size.
The whole island was fired by the royal example.
Facing the Channel on the seaward side
Rose Ventnor's lodging houses, tier on tier;
The island's health resort in sunny pride
By terraces descending to the pier.

The Royal National Hospital for diseases of the chest, built just west of Ventnor in 1868 – empty, now that they've found other cures for consumption. How many a pale face looked its last out of these windows? How many prayers were offered for sufferers? How many prayers were made by suffering patients? Echoes of weak coughs along deserted corridors. Empty.

The sea as a cure for illness – 1868. In the next year the pier at Clevedon in Somerset was being built. The sea as a source of pleasure, for little steamer trips to Chepstow, Newport, Cardiff, Lynton and Lynmouth, Flat Holm and Steep Holm and other places of popular resort. At the opening ceremony they said, 'We believe it is the commencement of better times for our fair Clevedon.' It was. As the *Great Western Railway Guide Book* in 1884 said:

An excellent esplanade faces the sea. Good beaches, gardens, shrubberies, and large modern villas built along the edges of the lofty seacliffs, with churches and chapels, public schools, lodging and boarding houses, hotels, dining rooms, public gardens and excellent shops.

The sea as a source of pleasure.
Steamer trips round the bay!

These verses from long-forgotten songs remind me of the Victorian trippers' traditional fear of the sea:

> Those horrible pistons, they make my heart thump
> As the paddling wheels go round.
> Are they churning the ocean up into a lump
> Or will we all be drowned? Hey ho!
> Or will we all be drowned?

★   ★   ★

> Oh the paddle paddle steamer
> What a clever little schemer
> That ever she inveigled me from shore.
> Now I know I can't escape
> Perhaps we're sailing for the Cape
> And I'll never see old England any more.
> No more.

But if the truth be told, the man of wealth
Added some pleasure to his search for health.

Tropic Torquay overlooking historic Torbay: the balmy climate, the Palm Court orchestra. This was the time of the holiday hotels with commanding names: Grand, Imperial, Majestic, Palace.

Exclusive Bournemouth where the tide came twice
And children played with children who were nice
Where parents dozed in after-luncheon ease
And lovers longed to touch each other's knees.
Hydraulic power delights the old and young.
Steam traction! Let its praises now be sung.
Steam down the valley, steam below the hill.
The factories empty, lodging houses fill.
The long expresses glided by the shore
And towns grew where were never towns before.
Compartments packed and holidays begun,
It's Go Great Western to the coast and sun.

In fact it was the railways that made the mid-Victorian seaside
resorts. On bank holidays they were crowded out.

I want to take us off to somewhere where
The sun shines brightly and the tourists tarry.
Some people call it Weston super Mare
And others call it Weston super Maré.
Maré of course is Latin for 'the sea'
And Maré is what here it's said to be.

On this particular Whitsun, Weston's hey-day,
Excursion trains arriving every minute,
The town was cramm'd like rallies on a May Day,
You wouldn't have thought more people could get in it.
The roundabouts went round, the swings went swinging,
The warm sea sparkled and the earth was singing.

Yes, everything seemed paradise at Weston
That Whitsun afternoon beside the sea.
No one looked backward, everybody press'd on
To minerals and to ices and to tea.
Even the people walking on the pier
Were unaware of trouble waiting near.

How innocent and kindly was the funning,
All dedicated to the god of sport.
The driving and the diving and the running,
Fresh air and freedom – will they all be caught?
What thins the crowd, what darkens and what chills?
A mighty rainstorm from the Mendip Hills.

All put your macs on! Run for shelter fast!
Crouch where you like until it's fine again.
Holiday cheerfulness is unsurpassed,
Why be put out by healthy English rain?
Are we downhearted? No, we're happy still.
We came here to enjoy ourselves – *and* we will.

What's true of Weston's true of more than most,
No – *every* resort along the coast,

When everybody's feeling safe and warm,
Unheralded arrives the summer storm.
Those are the things the posters do not show,
Those are the headaches of the P.R.O.*

The model village shut and still it's raining;
Queues for the cafés and the sea-front's bleak.
Go to the pictures, then? I'm not complaining,
But didn't I see that film the other week?
As for our lodgings, we're in quite a fix
They never want us back till after six.

Yet this is quite the friendliest place I've hit on,
The air's a tonic and the sea's a treat.
Of all the merry coast resorts of Britain
Its sunshine record would be hard to beat.
Look on the bright side and we'll all feel better,
And if we're wet, well those out there are wetter.†

Escape – escape from the holiday crowds – over the Saltash Bridge.
Saltash Bridge by Isambard Kingdom Brunel, 1859: the first railway
link between Cornwall and England. Not another county: another
country. For years, an all-day journey by train and a wild reward at
the end of it. No piers; no pierrots. With what delight did late-
Victorian artists bring their oils and watercolours to paint the flaming
gorse and amethystine sea.

By train from suburbs of the big towns, by trap and wagonette,
past fern-stuffed hedges, from the oil-lit country station, schoolmasters came with promising pupils, undergraduates on reading parties,
doctors with thin wives and freckled daughters. Lured by King
Arthur they came, Victorian romantics, to that holy island with its
Celtic cells and chapel – a sort of Lindisfarne of Cornwall: Tintagel.

Cornwall is milder on its Southern coast
Which has a holy island too: St Michael's Mount.
What Mont St. Michel is to Britanny,

---

* Public Relations Officer.
† Refers to waterskiers.

This is to Cornwall. A monastic fort,
Later a fortress reached by a spit of land.
Covered by water when the tide is high.

Celtic saints came here and, later, Norman barons.
Then King's men and Cromwell's men.
Shrine, chapel, castle – later private house.
A hundred years ago J. P. St Aubyn
Very well restored its outer walls and turrets.
Victorians liked it. So do we,
Who gaze across its battlements today.

In best positions all along the coast
Rose the new castles of the newly rich.
The well-appointed family hotels:
The Headland, Newquay, 1891.
Lifts to all floors. Electrically lit.
Views of the sea from all the suites of rooms.

The gaps between the large hotels were filled
With boarding houses, tea places and shops,
Electric palaces and bright arcades.
Newquay became indeed the kind of place
Romantics avoided. Cornwall's holiday town.
But once below the level of the cliff,
And on the lovely beaches, what a wealth
Of rocks and sand and long Atlantic surf.

What people really came to Cornwall for
Was picturesque villages like this.
That's Port Isaac.

Do you remember those Royal Academy paintings of King
Edward's reign? –

Sturdy fishermen pulling the lifeboat out,
The Methodists on a Sunday after chapel,
The red-cheeked fishergirl with sea-green eyes,
The quayside chat,
The widow in a whitewashed room,

'A Hopeless Dawn', an angry sea outside,
The little climbing lanes of slate-built cots,
The wharves and sagging rooftops,
The seaweed-slippery quay.
Cornwall became an artists' paradise
And the amateur photographer's as well.
Those camera studies of weather-beaten skin
Those sepia slightly out-of-focus views
Of bollards on the quay . . .
Posing for artists here in famed St Ives
Became quite an industry.

There's something in most of us that wants to be what we aren't:
a Cornish fisherman, a Cornish boatbuilder or sailmaker. We wear
navy-blue jerseys and sou'westers if we can. We want to be taken as
natives. That's because we feel the need of solitude and roots.

We listen guilelessly to sailors' yarns
Oft told to tourists while the seagulls scream.

The shrewd Cornish – independent, proud – cash in on the foreigners: and small blame to them.

Look at Polperro down there. Plenty of car parks on the way to
the quay and plenty of gift shops on the way to the car parks. It's economics, see. The Mermaid's Ditty Box, the Witch's Boutique,
another car park and then Davy Jones's Diner with a nice smell of
fish and chips. The Delinquent Piskey, home-made teas and Cornish
clotted cream and then we're at the harbour. There's not much
money in fishing now. Ferrying visitors – there's that.

The Cornish have always been actors and singers – Henry Irving
for one – so there's the literary side and very popular it is with tourists
on warm evenings.

But bring your rugs and hot drinks just in case.

Minack Theatre, Porthcurno, rehearsing *The Thracian Horses*, a witty
comedy set in classical Greece. I know no better-sited theatre.

Nature has made the Minack Theatre famed.
Let's go to Minehead and see Nature tamed.

'This is Radio Butlin's calling.
The time is a quarter to twelve.
And lunch for first sitting campers
Is available.'

I floated over Butlin's between luncheon time and tea
And wished that I was young again and as I used to be,
When anticipated pleasure was as boundless as the sea.

When Peter came from Peterborough, my goodness he
                                         was shy.
When Wendy came from Wendover she felt she'd like to cry.
But now they've formed a friendship that will lead to Lovers'
                                          Lane
For they hold each other by the hand when travelling on the
                                          train.

Shirl and Sheila just are friends, for boys they do not care.
They tell each other secrets in the safety of the air
Regardless of what's going on in chalets over there.

The twins inveigled Grandpa on the switchback by a trick,
But Grandpa had the laugh on them, for both the twins were
                                          sick.

'Hard luck, Norman!
Never mind!
I think there's a consolation prize –
Now next, all of you . . .'

Look at this competition. We've all come here to seek
The most cheerful, charming, chubby lass, Miss Venus of the
                                          week.
Which of them do you think it is? Then use your eyes and
                                          brains,
Miss Harringay, Miss Stoke-on-Trent, Miss Widnes or Miss
                                          Staines?

I'm glad I came to Butlin's – I hope you liked the fun.
There's some of it in all of us – or almost everyone.

We don't all want to be organised but if we aren't we seem to sprawl everywhere. Look what's happened at Westward Hoe, North Devon. We find a lovely bit of country and methodically we start to spoil it. It's not just true here, it's so along many miles of coast: too many, I'd say.

Where yonder villa hogs the sea
Was open cliff to you and me.
The many-coloured caras★ fill
The salty marsh to Shilla Mill,
And, foreground to the hanging wood,
Are 'toilets' where the cattle stood.
Now, as we near the ocean roar,
A smell of deep-fry haunts the shore.
In pools beyond the reach of tide
The Senior Service packets glide,
And on the sand the surf-line lisps
With wrappings of potato crisps.
The breakers bring, with merry noise,
Tribute of broken plastic toys,
And lichened spears of blackthorn glitter
With harvest of the August litter.

One day a tidal wave will break
Before the breakfasters awake,
And sweep the caras out to sea,
The oil, the tar, and you and me,
And leave, in windy criss-cross motion,
A waste of undulating ocean.[†]

Out there it's solitude: they can't build on the sea.

'They've taken our wind!
Oh no, she's going about!
Stand by to gybe!

★ Caravans.
[†] This is a version of 'The Delectable Duchy' by Betjeman. A slightly longer version of this poem appeared in the *Cornish Review* in 1967.

Ready about!
Lee O!

Starboard!'

Can the sea be solitude? No, it's being developed.

Hark to the song of the water hogs
As they charge at us over the waves.
Executive chases executive,
    Mercury, Volvo and Ford.
'Steady, old man, with the steering –
    Your company chairman's aboard!'
The water's as still as a mill pond
    We'll open it up like a flower,
We'll drive and we'll thrust as competitors must
And the prize of our driving is power.

I'm glad that it's quiet again and I'm on foot. You know that sort
of holy hush there is in the land on Christmas morning? The roads
fairly empty, the sky almost free of aeroplanes and you begin to hear
and see and smell once more. The Seaside can be like this if you
find an unspoiled stretch of it like this one in North Cornwall. An
enlightened landlord has saved this part; other bits have been saved
by the National Trust and local authorities. The developers have
taken more than their fair share of the coast. A third of it is already
completely built up. We must keep the rest of it for the good of our
souls.

George III took the seaside cure for biliousness; we need the
seaside cure for relief from stress and tension, we need it to realise
that there's something greater than ourselves – even if it only comes
in little things: turf, scented with thyme and mushrooms; the feel of
firm sand underfoot; the ripple of an incoming tide; a salt breeze; the
smell of seaweed – that's where the cure is: at the sea's edge.

And all the time the waves, the waves, the waves
Chase, intersect and flatten on the sand
As they have done for centuries, as they will
For centuries to come, when not a soul

Is left to picnic on the blazing rocks,
When seaside is forgotten. Still the tides,
Consolingly disastrous, will return
While the strange starfish, hugely magnified,
Waits in the jewelled basin of a pool.★

★ This is a version of the last ten lines of Betjeman's poem 'Beside the Seaside' (opening line: 'Green Shutters, shut your shutters! Windyridge'), first published in the *Strand*, 1947. The line 'When England is not England, when mankind / Has blown himself to pieces. Still the sea' has been replaced by the single line 'When seaside is forgotten. Still the tides'.

15
FUN PALACES
High-wire and Hoop-la

Wembley's Empire Swimming Pool (1934)
The Festival of Britain South Bank Exhibition (1951)
Pleasures and Palaces (1950)
The Music-Hall (1964)
To The Crazy Gang (1962)

WEMBLEY'S EMPIRE SWIMMING POOL

Evening Standard
23 July 1934

•   •   •

In six months there has risen up on that disconsolate rubbish heap that was once Wembley Exhibition a building as large and in its way as beautiful as St Paul's Cathedral.

When you see the new Empire Swimming Pool, gleaming white, terrifyingly simple and utilitarian, with its great concrete ribs elbowing out of the landscape, you will at first find it difficult to believe that it has anything in common with the swelling majesty of St Paul's. There are no classical columns on it, no little bits of decoration with which so many modern buildings are adorned. This is because the new swimming pool is an honest building. In the days when wood and brick and stone were the only building materials, classical columns added proportion and dignity; they even fulfilled their purpose of support.

Now that concrete reinforced with steel has given us different proportions, classical columns are lost in the vast new dimensions. They are not only unnecessary but harmful to the general design. The new pool is a modern cathedral to the modern god of sport.

Sir Owen Williams, who designed it, was oddly enough the engineer for the Wembley Exhibition by which his masterpiece is surrounded. He designed the *real* architecture in the Wembley Exhibition – that is to say, the simple, light buildings to house the exhibits. It was left to architects to complete the effect by putting on the 'architecture' afterwards. And this 'architecture' already looks out of date.

It is with relief that you turn to the startling simplicity of Sir Owen Williams's swimming pool.

There are some people who like to have pieces of information of this nature – that 12,500 people can be accommodated in the seats, which is twice the capacity of the Albert Hall; that 250 miles of steel scaffolding were used to put the building up; that the roof is 83 feet from the ground; that the highest diving board is 36 feet; that waves four feet high can be made to smash against the terraced sides of the pool; that in winter this pool can be covered over with ice for skating or with boards for boxing and that the seating capacity can be nearly doubled on these occasions.

All such information is for those who mistake facts for knowledge. I do not want to seem priggish but what interests *me* about the Empire Swimming Pool is none of these things. I like the construction.

Sir Owen might well have prayed before his pool was finished. Six thousand tons of concrete, 2,000 people and the buffets and dressing rooms are balanced on a razor edge of concrete 22 feet long and 6 inches wide. This feat of construction accounts for the curious shape of the building. When you look at it from the side you see a row of fourteen ribs, thin and angular, projecting from each side of the building and looking rather like playing cards sticking out of a pack that has not been neatly shuffled. These projections are the muscles of the building and hold together the roof, walls and floor.

Imagine an athlete balanced on his hands with his legs kicked up in the air. Now imagine another athlete with his back to the first athlete. He, too, is balancing on his hands with his legs in the air. Next imagine that they both bend their legs back so that their toes touch and they are in this position. In that case all the weight will be equally divided between their hands and their touching toes. Of such is the Swimming Pool at Wembley. It consists of fourteen pairs of athletes pressed together at either end by two low, heavy buildings containing the entrance hall at one end and the kitchens at the other. The hands of the athletes are each that razor edge of concrete 22 feet long and 6 inches wide. The toes are the middle of the roof. The concave curve of their bodies between the head and the stomach contains all the seats. The arms have steps down them leading to the exits.

This simple construction is the covering of the Swimming Pool at Wembley. It is as simple as the guillotine – once you know how it is done.

There is only one puzzling feature about the outside and that is the presence of four tall pillars, one at each corner, with a box on top. They are water towers.

When you go into the building the effect is overwhelming. You see why these athletes are so kindly performing for you. On the plot of ground that they are sheltering is an enormous pool. Sir Owen Williams becomes a beneficent but distant creator. He drills us about like insects. Women to the left, men to the right; food and looking-on upstairs; swimming downstairs. You can't come out of the swimming pool without walking through a compulsory foot-bath.

Sir Owen has carried the insect metaphor even further. He has dispensed with notices by using colour as a guide. Just as insects are attracted by highly coloured flowers so the inhabitants of Metroland will be attracted by highly coloured doors. Orange for attraction, green for distraction, red for danger. Thus a door that only opens one way is painted orange on the side it opens and green on the other side. A door into an electric switchboard or an irate manager's office is painted red for danger. Public bars will be neatly edged with orange.

Nothing exists in the Empire Swimming Pool without a purpose unless it be some of the people who will come to swim.

Sir Christopher Wren built St Paul's: he obviously built it for God and it was a truly modern building. Doubtless it came as a shock to the citizens of London but it stood for what they stood for: urbanity, craftsmanship, scholarship and thoroughness. The Empire Summing Pool is a permanent memorial to our civilisation. It stands for what we stand for: machinery, mass production, physical health. It makes Sir Owen Williams the modern Christopher Wren.

THE FESTIVAL OF BRITAIN SOUTH BANK EXHIBITION

BBC Home Service
7 May 1951
Producer: Arthur Langford

• • •

Like you, I was not mad keen on the Festival at first. The word itself stood in my mind for the very reverse of feasting – discussion groups, processions, scaffolding, youth parliaments, some extra geraniums outside the town hall and that sort of thing. Had the money been spent on giving us half a dozen oysters each – and I would have had yours if you didn't like shellfish – then that would at least have been the beginning of the feast a festival ought to be.

But now the Festival is here I like it very much. The sun has come out just as though we had emerged from a tunnel. After all that rain, to have constructed something at all was a bit of a feat. The Festival of Britain on the South Bank is a visible sign of British endurance, through months of mud and anxiety. I hope the late opening of the Festival Gardens in Battersea is not a sign that we cannot always nowadays stay the course.

The greatest thing the Festival has done for London is to reintroduce the Thames into a life of pleasure. Most Londoners have long thought of the Thames as brown, sliding water hidden away below high stone walls. The South Bank exhibition has brought it back to what it used to be in the days before the Embankment was made nearly a century ago. In those days, the Lord Mayor's procession was a stream of many-coloured barges pulled down the river by liveried oarsmen. The new procession will be of passenger steamers up and down stream to Battersea and Poplar. The restaurants of the Festival hang over the water, palaces of glass and plants from which you can see the outline of the Royal Palace of Westminster, the fine chimney stacks of Scotland Yard and the domes and towers of the North Bank, until finally the great dome of St Paul's is seen riding over Waterloo Bridge.

There's no doubt that the Festival – the South Bank, the serious part of it – makes one feel balmy and gay. There are a great many things that have been put there just for the fun of the thing and not for some economic reason and not just because they're 'cheap and efficient', which is the excuse all the brutes used to give us for the hideous concrete lamp-posts, wire-mesh fences and poles and wire with which they have been destroying our delicate and varied landscape. They will have to think up another excuse. The Festival has introduced the useless and beautiful, thank goodness. It is as pleasant and unlikely as a glasshouse full of tropical plants built on a government office.

I am supposing you haven't seen the South Bank in London. I am even supposing you don't realise how important it is as a site. If you were to take a piece of cardboard and cut it out in the shape of the County of London and then balance it on your finger in order to find out the exact centre of London, the true central spinning point of London would not be Piccadilly nor the City nor Oxford Street but the South Bank, the very site of the exhibition, here where the Thames takes a loop to the north before sliding on eastwards again to the sea. If all those delightful warring railways of Queen Victoria's reign – the South Eastern, the London Chatham and Dover, the London and Brighton and the London and South Western – had only agreed to have one huge terminus in common, south of the river, then the South Bank would have come into its own years ago. As it is, I have an idea that the site was cleared and chosen by the promoters of the Festival with the object of extending the centre of London south of the river and eventually demolishing those charming stations Charing Cross, Holborn Viaduct, St Paul's and Cannon Street. It would be efficient but not, thank goodness, cheap.

And now for the exhibition itself. We will cross by the Bailey bridge from Charing Cross. Up the steps and along and along and along, over reverberating planks with steam and electric trains on one side painted the hideous Southern Green, or the too-ubiquitous red and green of the expresses. Hiss and thunder, roar and rumble. We cannot hear ourselves speak. On the other side, through the girders of this endless bridge, we can see the Thames and the white masts that decorate this bridge we're on. There are golden diamonds upon them that turn round in the wind. Will this corridor of girders never end? There are times when we wish we had come round by one of the other entrances – one, for instance, by the ponderous County Hall, where the administrative offices of the Festival are slung in little glass boxes above the turnstiles. That's the way to deal with administrative officers: hang them out as exhibits so that we can see them plotting and scheming. But I've taken you this duller way by the Bailey bridge from Charing Cross for a special purpose and now that we have reached the end of it – there it is, the purpose: that, you will admit, is the best view of the exhibition and it's reached with the fewest number of stairs, here at what is called Embankment Gate.

Here is the Skylon below you, shooting hundreds of feet to heaven, resting on nothing and ready to rocket to the moon. What's it for, this steel cigar? Goodness knows. Can I go up it, Mummy? No, Cedric, if you could it would be at Battersea. The child in me says, 'I wish it worked'; the man in me says, 'All the same, I like the look of it.'

And I'm afraid I can't say that for the Royal Festival Hall, which is there beyond the railway. I know it works but I don't like the look of it, for outside it looks incomplete. What seems a drab cement extension in the distance turns out to be marble now we are near. And what's the meaning of all those squares and holes on the side? Is that the Tote, mummy? No, Cedric, it's art. And why is the roof such an ugly shape? I expect all the holes and lumps can be explained and have to be there so that we can get the best out of Sir Malcolm Sargent's baton. But it is not a pleasing outline. Glance across the river to St Paul's or to the many pinnacles and towers and spires of the Houses of Parliament and then back at Royal Festival Hall and you see what a good outline means. But inside the hall – and I'm going to go into some of these buildings while we're still standing here looking at them – inside there is a colour scheme of grey and cedar and you can't help realising that this is the best concert hall in the world. It is enormous and efficient. True, the decoration does remind one a bit of the Stratford Memorial Theatre but the eye is led to the orchestra. The hall is always a background and is, I'm told, perfect for sound. It is also perfect for silence.

I was sitting in the front row of the empty auditorium and the doors were open. Through them I could see across to the Southern Railway not a hundred yards away. An express train went past and I never heard a rumble of it. It was like watching a silent film in colour. And that brings me to the most imaginative part of the hall – its shell as seen from the inside. I mean the hall is really built inside another building. Between the inner building and the outer there are promenades with huge glass walls from which you can look out across the Thames, with a foreground of exhibition gaiety, or out into the exhibition. Criss-crossing this vast glass promenade are the structured ribs of the concert hall itself. And very good and strong they look and the walks and stairs are so arranged that you do not fall over them.

Back again to where, beyond the Skylon, is the low non-flying saucer of the Dome of Discovery. It is a lovely silver colour outside and a happy outline on the sky, as smooth and soft as the Skylon is sharp and pointed. Nearer to, it is like a saucer put on top of a huge breakfast cup. Inside, the Dome was rather a disappointment for me – too many exhibits and those all about the Darwinian Theory, nuclear fission and South Sea Islanders – which took away from the vastness of the building and gave it an air of the science room at a 'progressive' school.

And there by the water's edge is the Sea and Ships pavilion which is not so severely educational, thank heaven, but a varied walk through the mahogany, brass, paint, scrubbed decks, ropes and steel gangways of a liner, with views of the hulls and sterns of various types of craft.

Down here, also by the river, is another triumph of the exhibition: the seaside section, which is a model seaside town under an awning hung with nets and buoys and boathooks and the like and with huge peep-shows of 'What the Butler Saw' such as you see on the pier for a penny. But the peep-shows here are free.

The old Shot Tower is still there. From the top of it they used to pour molten lead which separated into bullets by the time it had reached the bottom. Now the top has paraphernalia on it, which looks like a Sussex windmill made of wire. It is for receiving messages from the moon. I wonder if there's anyone there who speaks English?

At the foot of the Shot Tower is one of my favourite things – Hugh Casson's 1851 Centenary Pavilion, a little conservatory that commemorates the dear old Crystal Palace and is the prettiest thing in the exhibition. It is made of cast iron and reminds one of England, though it comes from Glasgow and is compiled out of items in Macfarlane's catalogue of castings in stock.

Far over from here on the Waterloo side of the ground, away from the river, is a wall of coloured balls, red and blue and daffodil yellow. Through them you can see the chimney-pots of London and those chimney-pots look like a forgotten age, here in this dream world of the Festival. And near that wall, squashed in beside a railway arch, is a Telecinema by Wells Coates. It is all blue inside and chaste and cool and quiet. And then suddenly the strangeness starts. Sound runs all over the theatre, behind you down the walls and into the screen. You are given special spectacles and you see films in three dimensions. Circles loop above the head of the lady in front. They writhe away through blue stars and disappear deeper and deeper into the screen. A travelogue of the Thames shows water spilling over into your nose. A sea lion's dive at the Zoo seems to splash you. And then I saw Television. And the remarkable thing about it in this cinema is that although the screen is as big as in any news theatre, those awful horizontal lines of Television are not magnified. Indeed it is clearer than most Television I have seen – and just about as interesting.

After all that, let's descend into the Regatta Restaurant here below the bridge. Do you see the doorhandles? A brass hand with fingers curled round for you to pull. The back of a hand for you to push. And do you feel we are stepping down into the water? There through the glass are the Houses of Parliament, Scotland Yard and the domes and minarets of Whitehall Court across the river. There is so much to see, there cannot be too many restaurants and chairs. And this is the best of them, I think: so light and airy like most of the exhibition – yes, even the Transport Pavilion with its heavy great railway engines is light and airy.

There were many other things I would have shown you. But the eye and the ear can't stand more than a certain amount. And there are days of things to look at here. Some of them are ugly, like the cluster of concrete lamp-posts mercifully hidden behind the Transport building, the absurd kiosks and the coarse and wrongly pointed walls on the Homes and Gardens Pavilion, meant to be

British traditional walling but looking like the vulgarest part of the South of France.

But nearly everything is beautiful, gaily coloured, light and fantastic. Light and airy buildings and new and modest, like a well-cut suit. But chiefly I enjoy the fantasy, whether it's that flight of doves suspended from the roof of the Lion and Unicorn Pavilion, the Skylon or a tea set made of fishbones by an old lady in Winchester; whether it's the Dome of Discovery or the machine for grinding smoke in the inventions section, the fountains with the gas flares roaring among them here at our feet or that mandolin made of matchsticks by a Brighton locksmith. Whatever it is, there's fantasy, lightness, gaiety and uselessness, thank goodness – uselessness after all this crashing utility, sunlight after rain. Instead of moral maxims and schoolmarm facts and figures – yes, even here in the serious part of the exhibition – we can enjoy ourselves. All honour to Hugh Casson and his team for these buildings and the paintings and the poetry of it all.

PLEASURES AND PALACES

Contribution to *Diversion: Twenty-Two Authors on the Lively Arts*
Edited by John Sutro
Max Parrish, 1950

• • •

If there is one word that can safely be applied to almost all the constructions for entertainment, it is the adjective 'impermanent'. Fire consumes and fashion changes; new and more hideous structures arise on the sites of older and less hideous, as we continue to slide into deeper depths of barbarism. One day, no doubt, something more blatant than the tower of the Odeon Cinema in Leicester Square will challenge comparison with the steeple of St Martin-in-the-Fields. For the present we must gaze at the pseudo-functional monument of the 'serious thirties', watching it grow more and more dated every week, while the steeple of St Martin's glows in its white Portland stone perfection, a dateless memorial of more settled days.

The architecture of entertainment, of fairs, exhibitions, concert halls and theatres may be considered alongside church building. Like churches, places of entertainment are where people go for short spells only – that is to say, all except the cleaners and permanent staff who may be compared to the nuns and priests of churches (and very heartily they may laugh at the comparison). But the difference is this: churches are built to last, places of entertainment are not.

Nothing is more empty than a deserted fairground. A walk through the White City with no one about, the Baroque sculpture collapsing, the plaster façades damp-stained, the halls echoing and dusty, the railway lines – for special trains that carried long-dead merrymakers – rusty and grass-grown, is macabre even in broad daylight; and empty race-courses seem emptier than that. But an empty church is full, especially one in which the Consecrated Host is reserved in a tabernacle or cupboard in the wall with a light before it. Such a building may be alarming. One may feel oneself elbowed out by angels but the emptiness is awe-inspiring, not desolate.

For the truth is that in England and Scotland and Wales fairs and entertainments are the cast-offs of the church. Their ancestors were hurled out of churches when the religious plays acted in naves were considered too secular. They waltzed away into the churchyard and then into a field near the church. And on the date of the patronal feast of the church in many an English village today, a fair is held in a neighbouring field. When I look at the roundabouts and swings and hoop-la canopies gaily coloured in King's Lynn in the same style as barges are coloured at Braunston and as some old-fashioned wagons are still painted, when I see these traditional colours of red and blue and gold and green twisting round the flashing mirrors that hide the steam organ, when I catch sight of flares or electric bulbs reflected in barley-sugar rods of polished brass, I think how near the church these really are. I remember they must be derived from the trappings of images carried with a mixture of reverence and guffaws centuries ago in English sunlight. And I wish that this people's art would come back to churches – a little more vulgarity of painted wood; a little less of the church furnisher and the art expert and a little more of the fairground. For this colour decoration of old-fashioned fairs is the oldest and most permanent feature of the architecture of entertainment.

English visitors are often shocked by the garishness of patronal feasts and processions in the towns and villages of Italy and Spain. There, fair and church, entertainment and worship, are undivided. We are shocked because we have still such a Puritan sense of sin about pleasure that we drive it out into the open fields of the world. From these outcast fairs, from strolling players and booths and competitions, grew up the entertainment business whose structures are the subject of this article.

Churches are built on reality in the mystical sense of that word. Fairs, exhibitions, theatres and cinemas are built for daydreams of personal wish-fulfilment, which is a phrase for pride. No wonder then that, unlike churches, impermanence pervades them.

Architecturally, the most impermanent, the most quickly dated of entertainment buildings, are exhibitions and cinemas. The first Great Exhibition of 1851 was undoubtedly beautiful within its limits. I have a peep-show perspective of it. Under a bright light the eye looks down long glass avenues whose cast-iron columns are painted with bright reds and blues under the direction of Mr Owen Jones (the same man who later designed the pleasant colours of Paddington Station roof that have recently been changed for the worse). The eye is stayed by crystal fountains, statues and hangings, flags of all nations, the great elm trees of the Park that the palace enclosed, statuary, ormolu lamp standards and hundreds of ladies walking about in coloured crinolines. All seem bathed in old sunlight. One does really, in this Victorian perspective, recapture the idea current at the time that everything was getting better and better and that this exhibition of the flowers of Industrial Art was the beginning of a material millennium of peace on earth and goodwill towards men. But Ruskin, who saw through most things, was suspicious: 'We used to have a fair in our neighbourhood and a very fine one we thought it,' he writes in *The Ethics of the Dust*. 'You never saw such a one; but if you look at the engraving of Turner's "St Catherine's Hill" you will see what it was like. There were curious booths, carried on poles; and peep-shows; and music, with plenty of drums and cymbals; and much barley sugar and gingerbread and the like; and in the alleys of this fair the London populace would enjoy themselves, after their fashion, very thoroughly. Well, the little Pthah set to work on it one day; he made the wooden poles into iron ones, and put them across, like his own crooked legs, so that you always fall over them if you don't look where you are going; and he turned all the canvas into panes of glass, and put it up on his iron cross-poles; and made all the little booths into one great booth; – and people said it was very fine, and a new style of architecture, and Mr Dickens said nothing was ever like it in Fairyland, which was very true.' And he then proceeds to pour scorn on the exhibits. The Crystal Palace was indeed a new style of architecture. It was the first prefab, brought in numbered pieces in carts from the factories and erected swiftly in a public park. There is something ironic in the way this impermanent architecture, so well suited to an exhibition of lifeless industrial products, should have been resurrected in this century to make buildings which of all should be most permanent – homes for families.

The impermanent, utilitarian style of the Crystal Palace was, despite Ruskin's strictures, just the thing if industrial exhibitions were to continue. Yet later exhibitions – the Alexandra Palace, Earl's Court, the White City, Wembley, to cite London alone – seem to have been inspired by an over-confidence in material success. They are permanent buildings without that flimsy semi-rurality that must have been the charm of pleasure gardens like Vauxhall, Cremorne and Rosherville that preceded them. Not that I would condemn them. All lovers of the useless – and they must be increasing in Britain hourly with each 'utility' object that comes on the market – could hardly have failed to delight in the Alexandra Palace before the war. What a pleasure it was to tread acres of echoing boards past disused slot machines in search of the roller-skating rink where the huge steam-organ would be playing to a few swirling couples; what a pleasure to open a wrong door, as I once did, to find Gracie Fields with a full chorus behind her, singing to an empty theatre. Gas, brickwork, silent, dark towers, wet and windy amusement parks, bandstands where no silver band has played for twenty years, all these are associated with deserted exhibitions. What terrible crimes, hinted at by Denton Welch or invented by Graham Greene, may not be perpetrated in the dark, deserted refreshment rooms or cloakrooms where water drips everlastingly into stained, cracked and no longer hygienic porcelain. That is part of the romance of decay.

As soon as exhibitions become permanent buildings like those I have mentioned, they quickly look out of date. Their appeal is in being in the very latest style when they are erected. Decoration, to convey the latest style, even if it is a coating of chromium pseudo-simplicity as at the Glasgow Exhibition of the 1930s, must predominate. Hence the sad wilderness of the White City, hence that mysterious area of inner Metroland around the Wembley Stadium where, for all I know, those concrete temples of Empire may still be standing among thin poplars and rusty railway lines.

Cinemas too have their origin in fairs. They were, in living memory, booths where people paid a few pence to see the phenomenon of moving photographs. The exaggerated language of the huckster ('the most daring, stupendous, thrilling spectacle ever staged in the history of the Universe') applies as much to the architecture of the cinema as it does to the language of the play-bills, trailers and advertisements of films in the daily prints. However much the film, as far as producers and directors are concerned, may progress towards an art, the exhibiting side is still in the hands of those who have the mentality of the old fairs. There is hardly a cinema in Britain, except for a high-brow exception like the Curzon, that is not architecturally on its outside a showy attempt to be up to date. The interiors, whether designed to look like the Garden of Allah, a Moorish mosque, a Spanish palace, Stockholm Town Hall or Imperial Rome, are designed as an exotic daydream. That daydream looks still more pitiful in daylight when the place is being swept of old cigarette ends and cartons and the manager has not yet assumed his boiled shirt. The earliest cinemas to be erected as permanent buildings may still be seen in some suburban and provincial high roads, the words ELECTRIC PALACE done in plaster among baroque twirls reminiscent of the White City and a little pay-box in mahogany protruding out below the colossal entrance arch. They are survivals of the days when the cinema needed to attract people to go in. There is no need for a flashy entrance now, for the cinemas are the chapels of most of our people who feel it a sin not to attend each change of programme. The chief problem is to hold their increasingly sophisticated attention once they are inside. Slap-up-to-date decoration may help to hold it. There seems to be more sense in the comparatively modest façades of the Granada cinemas whose wildly fantastic interior decoration may, possibly, be changed as different styles come in to suit another popular mood.

Music-halls come halfway between the cinema and the theatre. Their origin is older and more homely and permanent than the first. They started as entertainments in public houses and they ended as theatres, with the single difference that the bar opened straight into the auditorium as at dear old Collins's on Islington Green.

Theatres themselves are an older and more respectable form of architecture, Renaissance in origin: it would be absurd to connect them with the theatres of ancient Greece and Rome since, in this country at any rate, theatres did not exist until after the Reformation. Nor do many of the older ones survive. The round and open wooden theatres of Shakespeare's time, Wren's Drury Lane, the magic effects created by de Loutherbourg with real waterfalls at Sadler's Wells, not all the water in the New River has saved. They were destroyed by fire or fashion. The most complete survival is the Theatre Royal at Bristol and even that is mostly 1800 in date. Mr John Summerson, that most learned and caustically entertaining of architectural writers, says, 'The theatres of this country have never been much studied as architecture, though many books have been written on their owners, lessees and managers and the men and women whom their audiences have applauded.' And this is surprising, for when great dramatists were alive and actors like Garrick were known to all the world of intellect, the best architects were proud to design theatres. James Wyatt and Henry Holland both built Drury Lane theatres, Nash designed the Haymarket, Smirke did Covent Garden and Foulston designed Plymouth's Theatre Royal. All these buildings, except Covent Garden, have been destroyed or altered out of recognition 'by successive generations of profit-eager lessees', once again to quote Mr Summerson.

Many fine Victorian theatres survive, of which the best is the Theatre Royal at Newcastle (John and Benjamin Green architects).*

---

* In the original text Betjeman credited only Benjamin Green, who carried out the interior.

It is almost a Georgian building and mercifully preserved from successive generations of fashion. In London the noblest surviving building – in my opinion more impressive within and without than Covent Garden – is the Royal English Opera House (1892; Thomas Collcutt architect), now called the Palace Theatre. This is on an irregularly shaped island site. Its main façade on Cambridge Circus is concave and the awkwardness of the corners of such a façade is overcome by graceful octagonal turrets. The dressing rooms are all along the Shaftesbury Avenue side of the building and serve as a buffer against the noise of that main thoroughfare, just as the entrance-hall stairs keep out the sound of Cambridge Circus. The building slopes inwards from the auditorium and is acoustically a great success, though it is built on opposite principles to those generally employed in theatre design. The three tiers of galleries are cantilevered out – a revolution at the time – so that no columns obstruct the view of the audience. The decoration throughout is scholarly Flemish Renaissance. Nothing is skimped on the entrance hall and staircase, which are rich in those contrasting marbles Collcutt delighted to use and which he employed so effectively in the Holborn Restaurant. The Palace is the only theatre architecture in London – or for that matter in the provinces – of the last sixty years that climbs into the regions of a work of art. But many have a splendid richness, as do those by Charles John Phipps (1835–97), notably His Majesty's, which was completed in the year of his death. Phipps designed some elegant, exuberant provincial theatres of which the Gaiety, Dublin, is a still unspoiled example.

Some of London's smaller theatres preserved a charming quality of an Edwardian or late-Victorian drawing-room with their white-wood or mahogany, plush seats, watered-silk panels and electroliers. In the cheaper parts of these houses Dickensian fishtail gaslights in wire cages lit long stone staircases and passages. But most little theatres, of which the Criterion and the Comedy were outstanding examples, have been stripped, pickled, shaved, sprayed, chromiumed or simplified according to DIA* rules of good taste so as to have lost

---

* The Design and Industries Association, founded in 1915 by designers, businessmen and industrialists, under the slogan 'Nothing Need be Ugly'.

most of their original character. The St James's survives as a charming period piece.

It would have been fun to have traced the architecture of cast-iron bandstands, of piers and their pavilions, of tea-rooms and restaurants and other phases of the architecture of entertainment.

Fire is, until the next war, better controlled than before. The enemy of old-fashioned theatres today is fashion. Fashion has about it that impermanence that suits the impermanent architecture of entertainment. But if ever a man wants to study a popular style exaggerated to its vulgarest, let him look at the decoration of the buildings of entertainment. Cherubs will have chubbier cheeks and bottoms, caryatids have more protuberant breasts, *art nouveau* water-lilies will be more attenuated, cubes and triangles outstrip the ugliest followers of the worst of the imitators of Picasso's Cubist period; and if the word goes round 'be functional', wall spaces will be plainer, chromium shinier, off-white be more off-white in or upon the theatres, cinemas, music-halls, exhibition buildings, bandstands, piers and restaurants of the Kingdom. Only the fairs survive.

THE MUSIC-HALL

Foreword to *Red Plush and Grease Paint: A Memory of the Music-Hall and Life and Times from the Nineties to the Sixties* By Clarkson Rose
Museum Press, 1964

• • •

I feel honoured to be asked to write a foreword to this book by my friend, Clarkson Rose. It is on a subject after all our hearts – music-halls, from the nineties to the present day, and it embodies glimpses of the times, customs, manners and way of life in the background.

Many of us can remember those gilded halls of variety that the title of this book suggests. We can hear the swish of the bar doors as people come out of the auditorium during the first turn – which is acrobats, or the dancing girls doing a can-can; we look up at the boxes and the plaster cherubs holding electric lights; we hear the crackle of peanuts in the pit; the stage is darkened, except for a standard lamp that illumines the grand piano, and then a single flood spotlights the artist (it is a serious turn and we see tears run down old cheeks in the audience); excitement mounts as we reach the big names on the bill who appear just before the interval and last but one after it; the whole house rocks with laughter or waits in breathless suspense for a well-timed joke: that rapport is established between the artist and audience – an intimacy and understanding that we remember all our lives. It is the true genius of music-hall and something that television can never give us and it differs from legitimate theatre in this way: in a play, it is the actors as a team who triumph or fail; and if there is a failure, the author and the producer can be blamed. A variety artist is his own producer and, more often than not, his own author. If the variety artist cannot put his or her personality across in a couple of minutes, all is up.

Music-hall, which, from the time of Sir Oswald Stoll, was renamed variety, is a hard school. It breeds a self-sufficient, clever and warm-hearted people. If its members were not all these things, they would never have made their names. Clarkson Rose and Olive Fox have kept the flag of variety flying for many years with their show *Twinkle*, from which, incidentally, many sterling variety artists have emerged – the most recent being Norman Vaughan. How many millions of waves must have thundered among the iron struts of piers below the seaside theatres of our coasts since the first production of *Twinkle*! Clarkie has known all the 'greats' of variety this century and he is among them himself. He has the additional advantage – which is rare in his profession – of being a writer of readable and enjoyable prose.

TO THE CRAZY GANG

Written to commemorate the last performance of the Crazy Gang
May 1962

• • •

One Saturday night I sat in The London –
     The London Shoreditch – as peanuts cracked
With my tie askew and my waistcoat undone
     And sweating a lot as the house was packed.

The bar door swished when the bell was ringing
     And pipe smoke curled to the golden dome,
And Leo Dryden himself was singing
     Once more 'The Miner's Dream of Home'.

Oh, Saturday nights I've seen in plenty
     At Bedford, Collins's, South London, Met,
And I've laughed and wept since 1920
     At brilliant talent I can't forget.

But this is *the* Saturday night tremendous,
     This is the night with a parting pang,
This is the Saturday night to end us –
     We say goodbye to the Crazy Gang.

Goodbye old friends of the great tradition!
     From the serious thirties of slumps and tears
Into this age of nuclear fission
     You kept us laughing for thirty years.

Bud and Jimmy and Teddy you've done it,
     Monsewer, Charles Naughton and you, James Gold –

You've ridden a race and you've all of you won it
    And you've ended fresh as a two year old.

Goodbye old friends! and in skies above you
    Harry Tate, George Robey and Wilkie Bard
Are with us and watching – like us they love you –
    If there's clapping in heaven they're clapping hard.

Goodbye old friends! and now, Jack Hylton,
    I give you the greatest toast of all –
The toast of a rhymer, for I'm no Milton –
    But here's to London and Music Hall!

16

LONDON

Tunnels and Termini

Gas and Speed (1938)
Parliament Hill Fields (1940)
The Steam Trains of London (1954)
Coffee, Port and Cigars on the Inner Circle (1963)
The Metropolitan Railway (1953)

GAS AND SPEED

Spectator
28 January 1938

• • •

It is still possible to recapture the experience of Victorian locomotion in London. A nice long wait at Highbury Station on the North London Railway on a dark, empty evening will cause you soon to people the gaslit platforms with tall-hatted City men; to see bustled women in the deserted Ladies' Room, Sir Georgius Midas in the First Class Waiting Room and Mr Pooter in the Third. The gas shines on the green walls. The coal fires, economically laid in the tall cast-iron grates, warm few people now, the boarded floor of the huge Booking Hall (probably designed by Philip Charles Hardwick) resounds only to your own footsteps. Similar thrills may be enjoyed at Camden Town, Canonbury, and Hackney and Bow Stations on the same line. Indeed the rolling stock of the Poplar Branch of this line is, much of it, Victorian. I hope these fine stations will never be destroyed. They were built in the good, early railway tradition in 1850.

Those who do not want to go so far for their pleasure can have a last sausage-roll in the street-level Buffet at Sloane Square (1869) and see a huge iron chimneypiece, the gas standards and the bar fittings before Progress has destroyed them.

The experience of the old steam underground railway can still be enjoyed by anyone entering an up train at King's Cross (York Road Station) and travelling to, let us say, Aldersgate Street, in one of those unaccountable steam trains. He can make an even longer underground journey from Kentish Town (Midland) to the same station.

Mr Sekon's book *Locomotion in Victorian London* is for Londoners who know the Metropolis fairly well, for it will dazzle those without a clear sense of London's topography. Mr Sekon is clearly a Londoner and brings in some pleasant personal reminiscence — pickpockets at work on an open-deck bus, water supply brought in pails to his father's house. He edited the *Railway Magazine* from 1897 to 1910 and the *Railway and Travel Monthly* from 1910 until 1922, so that he may be said to know his subject thoroughly. The chapters include ones on pedestrianism, omnibuses, steamboats, cabs, bicycling and trade vehicles and a long section on railways.

The book jacket says that this book contains information for the statistician. With the aid of a good index he will find it but the book will give most pleasure to the other person whom the publisher recommends to read it: 'the amiable student of periods and manners'. Mr Sekon does not write like a don, tracing developments to the bitter end. He has no bibliography. His is the fact-collecting mind of a paragraphist and his book reads like a series of entertaining footnotes. I found it stimulating and readable. His little tricks of style seem to suit his subject:

> Rowboats . . . were also hired by the London apprentices *et hoc genus*, workmen on the spree and industrial Londoners generally on holiday, to a not inconsiderable extent — the state of the weather and of the personal exchequer permitting!

Since this book is one of facts, I have extracted a few that may please the general reader. The London General Omnibus Company was French in origin and finance. The average speed of a bus in the 1860s was five-and-a-half miles per hour. Short cuts on foot had a toll of a halfpenny on them and were called 'Halfpenny Hatches'. A horse bus ran down Farringdon Street till 1916. The original name of the *Daily News* was the *Daily Chronicle and Clerkenwell News*. *The Times* had a personal grudge against the SE Railway because a relation of one of its owners had been sacked from the London and Greenwich Railway. The grudge lasted sixty years. The London and Blackwall started as a cable railway. Many SE London lines were atmospheric.* The first cab shelter was erected in 1875 in St John's Wood. The first hansom appeared in 1834. The first bicycle of the type we see today appeared in the 1880s. The first oil-driven bus appeared in 1899. Dogs were forbidden to draw carts in 1839. The GWR (Great Western Railway), which ran the first underground trains (Paddington to Farringdon Street), introduced gaslight in the carriages and block telegraph signal control. Early coaches on the NLR (North London Railway) were of papier mâché. 'Tubes' were called such because the tunnels were made out of tubular iron segments. The first tube was the City and South London (King William Street to Stockwell), opened in 1890. It was also the first electric train.

I only regret that Lady Halberton's bold move in first wearing bloomers for bicycling is not mentioned, nor is my great-great-uncle, who invented the contraption whereby a cabby was able to open the doors of his hansom without getting down from the box.†

PARLIAMENT HILL FIELDS

New Statesman and Nation
24 February 1940

• • •

Rumbling under blackened girders, Midland, bound for
Cricklewood,
Puffed its sulphur to the sunset where that Land of Laundries
stood.

---

* See p. 216.
† The Alexandra Palace patent lock, referred to in Betjeman's *Summoned by Bells*.

Rumble under, thunder over, train and tram alternate go,
Shake the floor and smudge the ledger, Charrington, Sells,
                                         Dale and Co.,
Nuts and nuggets in the window, trucks along the lines below.

When the Bon Marché was shuttered, when the feet were
                                         hot and tired,
Outside Charrington's we waited, by the 'STOP HERE IF
                                         REQUIRED',
Launched aboard the shopping basket, sat precipitately down,
Rocked past Zwanziger the baker's, and the terrace blackish
                                         brown,
And the curious Anglo-Norman parish church of Kentish
                                         Town.

Till the tram went over thirty, sighting terminus again,
Past municipal lawn tennis and the bobble-hanging plane;
Soft the light suburban evening caught our ashlar-speckled
                                         spire,
Eighteen-sixty Early English, as the mighty elms retire
Either side of Brookfield Mansions flashing fine French-
                                         window fire.

Oh the after-tram-ride quiet, when we heard a mile beyond,
Silver music from the bandstand, barking dogs by Highgate
                                         Pond;
Up the hill where stucco houses in Virginia creeper drown –
And my childish waves of pity, seeing children carrying down
Sheaves of drooping dandelions to the courts of Kentish Town.

THE STEAM TRAINS OF LONDON

Punch
25 August 1954

• • •

It is my delight to travel by suburban steam trains in London. I have waited half an hour in the echoing and unfrequented half of Aldersgate Station for the rare and nearly empty steam trains to grind up the slope from Moorgate on their way to the Midland and Great Northern suburbs. I have sat in the gaslit compartment of a Great Northern train here with the ghosts of Carrie and Charles Pooter, Murray Posh, Mr Padge and Eliza's husband and Jerome K. Jerome's Harris and seen from the window mysterious arcades of sidings that are something to do with that goods line the Great Western runs to Smithfield.

I have gone by steam from Liverpool Street to Chingford and from Liverpool Street to Palace Gates, changing at Seven Sisters in order to do so. And at that high-up wooden junction I have crossed the little bridge to the lonely platform where the train from North Woolwich awaits to take me through West Green and Noel Park to its countrified forgotten terminus. And walking thence over municipal grass I have climbed the slope to Ally Pally and there seen the summer evening sunlight catch the steeples and water towers of North London.

Who are the passengers on such unfrequented lines? Who are they who for so long, to quote E. V. Lucas, have

> peered from a third class 'smoker'
> Over the grimy waste of roofs
> Into the yellow ochre?

They are certainly not those who must use steam because they have to, living in Tilbury or Southend and feeling obliged to arrive at Fenchurch Street. The people who use the lines I mention could perfectly well take the dull Tubes or duller buses. Looking at them, I think they must be seekers of peace and creatures of habit loyal to the glorious pre-grouping days* and aware that the personalities of the old railways still survive in suburban stations that have been spared rebuilding in concrete. 'I've always used the line and my father did before me. Now that there's not so much for me to do in the office I find I can comfortably catch the 5.11 from Moorgate to Cricklewood.'

All this is a prelude to the most exciting and unknown of London's steam suburban lines to survive – the West London Extension Railway. It is not mentioned in *Bradshaw*. But it *is* mentioned at the end of the green Southern timetable and is printed in different type from the rest of the tables so as to show it is independent. This line runs from Clapham Junction to Addison Road (for Olympia). The trains are few and irregular and they start at different times on different days of the week, like times of services when the vicar is without a curate, except that on the WLER there are no Sunday services. A porter at Waterloo told me that two old ladies own the line and that they have refused to sell out to British Railways and that they receive one shilling and sixpence for every train that crosses their bridge over the Thames from Battersea to Lots Road. So glorious a story cannot be true – but I like to believe it.

Let me recommend a visit to the most northerly and the least used of all the platforms on Clapham Junction, that flimsy collection of cast iron, glass, wood and brick set among so many shining rails. Let it be where the rails are least shiny, on a weekday when the WLER is working at about 4.30. Not a soul will be on the platform. Suddenly an antique engine will be seen riding over brick arches among the Battersea chimney-pots and then curving in towards the platform, dragging a trail of London and South Western rolling stock. Surprisingly the train is crowded. Perhaps they are people who work

---

* Before the independent train companies were amalgamated into British Railways.

at Cadby Hall,* perhaps civil servants from that hideous new barrack near Olympia. They dismount slowly and are let out one at a time by the ticket collector down dark stairs into Clapham.

The train that goes back through Battersea, over the Thames (with the best possible view of Battersea Reach) and downstream to Westminster, is empty except for you and me. The interior wood-work is grained to look like oak; sepia photographs of Parkstone and Sidmouth adorn the walls. The seating arrangements are rather like the top of a tram. We hurtle through a land of docks and canals at great speed. Willow herb rises on the ruins of Chelsea and Fulham Station as we flash past its dismantled platforms. Soon West Brompton is upon us in a brown brick cutting and here we are, slowing down into that neglected waste of platforms that was once to be the great station of West London, the Paddington, St Pancras, Victoria and Willesden of all first- and second-class passengers: KENSINGTON (Addison Road), more recently named Olympia. The whole journey took eight minutes. Never did man move so far in London so fast in recent years. There is no one to collect our tickets. Two late typists board our train for the last journey of the day back to Clapham.

In one of those tall Italianate streets that are not quite Kensington and not quite Fulham, I can picture a tall four-storey semi-detached house. All the other houses in the road have been turned into flats. The district has 'gone down'. But this house alone retains its privacy, though the windows are dusty and some of the blinds have stuck. Here live the two old ladies, the proprietors of the West London Extension Railway. Now as we leave Addison Road they will be having tea and it is pleasant to think that as our train crossed the bridge from Battersea they received one-and-six towards their cakes and jam.

---

* The headquarters of J. Lyons in Hammersmith, demolished in 1983.

COFFEE, PORT AND CIGARS ON THE INNER CIRCLE

The Times
24 May 1963

• • •

Each line on the Underground system had a distinct personality. From about 1916 until 1921 I used the holidays for travelling over the system so that there was not a station at which I had not alighted. The result is that the Underground map of London is firmly imprinted in my mind and from Golders Green to Clapham Common, from New Cross to Ealing Broadway, from Finsbury Park to Hammersmith, I know the stations by heart.

I remember Park Royal as a little wooden platform, high above the football ground of the Queen's Park Rangers, and what a pleasant walk one could take by the leafy lanes and elmy fields of Middlesex between Preston Road Station on the Metropolitan to the newly electrified Kenton Station on the extension beyond Queen's Park of the Bakerloo. It is surprising how little the map has changed and even the colours used to denote the different lines have in many cases continued until the present day. During the First World War these colours were: red for the Metropolitan, green for the District, grey for the City and South London, blue for the Central London, orange for the Great Northern and City, and brown, yellow and violet for the Bakerloo, Piccadilly and Hampstead lines respectively of the London Electric Railway Company.

Electricity was in the air and gas was on the way out. Electricity stood for cleanliness, quietness, hygiene, swiftness and progress. By electricity the City clerk could glide, when he had left the Underground at the bottom of Highgate Hill at a station euphemistically called Highgate, by electric tram to North Finchley and from Edgware Road he could take another electric tram to Harlesden, while at Shepherd's Bush and Hammersmith there was a choice of tramway routes out into the flat hay fields and market gardens that still held out in West Middlesex against the oncoming villas.

The line with the dominating personality in the system was the Metropolitan. Since it had started in the age of steam as the first Underground and had a nasty reputation for sulphur and soot, it was most anxious to live down its past. The Inner Circle, which it shared with the District Railway, was electrified and so was its line from Baker Street to Swiss Cottage and beyond. Only the smoke-blackened brown bricks of its stations in the tunnels and the shapely round glass globes enclosing gaslights – illuminating such stations as Bayswater, Praed Street, Notting Hill Gate, Portland Road, Euston Square, Marlborough Road and Swiss Cottage – reminded one that this line had once been steam. Under that great general manager Mr R. H. Selbie, the Metropolitan invented Metroland and the phrase 'Beechy Bucks'; and by means of enticing sepia photographs in its carriages, brochures and refreshment rooms – 'Cottage at Prestwood', 'Near Great Missenden', 'Haydon Hall, Eastcote', 'At Ickenham' – tempted the Londoner out on to new estates far beyond the Wembley Exhibition. The line affected a white-tiled Classical style just after the First World War, as may be seen still at Farringdon Street; and below the Portland stone cliffs of Chiltern Court and Edgware Road it tried to forget the steamy origins of huge echoing, iron-roofed stations like Aldersgate Street where, until the Second World War, there used to be a notice in white china letters on the windows of the refreshment room: 'Afternoon Teas a Speciality'. The Metropolitan stretched its tentacles round the Inner Circle to Mansion House and South Kensington, over the Great Western to Hammersmith, eastward to Whitechapel and even had running powers over the London and South Western to Richmond. There was an inexplicable branch to Addison Road, while the District, never a line with as much personality, ran its red carriages up to Uxbridge Road and west to the Ealings and Actons and Uxbridge. The poor relation of these lines was the East London, from Shoreditch, with two stations at New Cross and green diamonds behind the names of the stations and very few advertisements on the platforms because the people who used the line were so poor that they were not considered worth advertisements.

There was one mysterious line that differed from the rest in having larger tunnels and rolling stock and this was the Great Northern and City, from Finchley Park to Moorgate, which had been opened in 1904. The line still seems to be out on a limb and Drayton Park has always seemed to me the remotest of the older Underground stations, just as Essex Road is the least used now that City Road, South Kentish Town, York Road, Brompton Road and Down Street have been shut.

The City and South London was the first real 'tube' electric railway and it still had when I first knew it the atmosphere of 1890, the year of its opening. Little orange engines carried rolling stock with basket seats and cut-glass electric lights. Many of the platforms, as still to be seen at Angel, King's Cross and south of the river, were central and narrow with trains running either side of them so that there was a temptation to fling oneself on to the live line. The whole railway had a strong smell of wet feet or a changing room after games and the line was delightfully uneven so that one could look down the length of the carriages and see them switchbacking up and down, behind or before one. The Waterloo and City, which belonged to the London and South Western, never really counted in my mind as part of the system any more than 'the elevated electric' from Victoria to London Bridge; but the Waterloo and City was allowed to appear on the Underground maps and it had a smell, with engines and rolling stock slightly similar to the City and South London.

The Central London from Bank to Wood Lane, extended to Liverpool Street in 1912, was the highest-class line because it went by Bond Street to the City. It was also regarded as a sort of health resort because it was ventilated by the Ozonair system, which was meant to smell like the sea and certainly did smell of something. Air came out of grilles at the ends of huge aluminium pipes and sent a health-giving breeze down the platforms, causing the crinkly glass shades that hung over the white-tiled stations to move slightly. The carriages had basket seats and were, as on all Underground lines, operated by men who pulled open the gates between the carriages at the stations. The Central London went in for terracotta above ground and one may still see the outside of the old British Museum Station where High Holborn and New Oxford Street join.

The Bakerloo was one of the enterprises of the share pusher and art connoisseur Whitaker Wright but he died in 1904 and the line was not opened until 1906. I've often thought that his artistic taste may however have pervaded the three railways of the London Electric Railway Company: the Bakerloo, the Piccadilly and Brompton, and the Hampstead and Highgate. All these lines had and still have stations above ground of red and shiny tiles in the Classical style; and it is noticeable at Leicester Square Station how to this very day the name of Wisden is commemorated in the red tiles on the Cranborne Street façade where the celebrated firm, presumably, had a shop and refused to move to make way for the station. The doors of the lifts had an *art nouveau* pierced pattern in their ironwork and the stations below were – and still are, where they have not been renewed – built with bands of different coloured tiles: for instance, Covent Garden, orange; Dover Street (now Green Park), duff grey; Goodge Street, green; York Road, yellow; so that the traveller who came to a halt not opposite the station name could tell where he was by the colour. The colours seem to have been chosen on some principle of alliteration and association. These stations do not seem to have been designed originally for advertisements for here and there along the tiles are little *art nouveau* notice spaces, made of tiles, presumably for timetables and rules and regulations.

The herald of the new age came first with the Crowing Crock by E. McKnight Kauffer in the Eno's advertisements and then the Gill Sans and the posters of the era of Frank Pick and the new Underground stations by Holden. Rolling stock ceased to have its differences. Lines, except on the maps, ceased to be differently coloured. Only in the refreshment rooms on the Metropolitan and in those long-distance trains from Moorgate Street to Harrow and beyond, where the door handles were engraved 'Live in Metroland', did the individuality survive until the sixties.

The chief difference between the London Underground of today and that of 1918 is in the number of passengers. Far fewer people travelled by Underground. Not only was London much smaller and the system less extensive but people preferred travelling on the open

tops of buses and the half-protected tops of trams. They could see
the streets and buildings for road traffic was less congested. Down
below the earth, as one sat on those basket seats, there used to be a
silence like deep country after the man between the carriages had
opened the trelliswork gates and footsteps of the few passengers could
be heard walking towards draughty passage and shuddering lift.
Lancaster Gate Station still has some of this atmosphere.

The District Railway, in an effort to eclipse the Metropolitan, was
ahead of its time when it made that desperate liaison with the London
Tilbury and Southend. For a time it ran express trains stopping at most
stations from Ealing Broadway to Southend and I can recall Pullman
carriages passing through Sloane Square Station.

Now that the main roads of London are so much less attractive
than the tunnels underneath, ventures such as these might well be
revived. I have long wished to travel round the Inner Circle in a
dining car: hors d'oeuvres at South Kensington, fish at the
Monument, joint at Baker Street, cheese at Notting Hill Gate and
perhaps once round again with the coffee, port and cigars.

THE METROPOLITAN RAILWAY

BAKER STREET STATION BUFFET

Punch
28 January 1953

• • •

Early Electric! With what radiant hope
        Men formed this many-branched electrolier,
Twisted the flex around the iron rope
    And let the dazzling vacuum globes hang clear,

And then with hearts the rich contrivance fill'd
Of copper, beaten by the Bromsgrove Guild.

Early Electric! Sit you down and see,
   'Mid this fine woodwork and a smell of dinner,
A stained-glass windmill and a pot of tea,
   And sepia views of leafy lanes in PINNER, –
Then visualise, far down the shining lines,
Your parents' homestead set in murmuring pines.

Smoothly from HARROW, passing PRESTON ROAD,
   They saw the last green fields and misty sky,
At NEASDEN watched a workmen's train unload,
   And, with the morning villas sliding by,
They felt so sure on their electric trip
That Youth and Progress were in partnership.

And all that day in murky London Wall
   The thought of RUISLIP kept him warm inside;
At FARRINGDON that lunch hour at a stall
   He bought a dozen plants of London Pride;
While she, in arc-lit Oxford Street adrift,
Soared through the sales by safe hydraulic lift.

Early Electric! Maybe even here
   They met that evening at six-fifteen
Beneath the hearts of this electrolier
   And caught the first non-stop to WILLESDEN GREEN,
Then out and on, through rural RAYNER'S LANE
To autumn-scented Middlesex again.

Cancer has killed him. Heart is killing her.
   The trees are down. An Odeon flashes fire
Where stood their villa by the murmuring fir
   When 'they would for their children's good conspire'.
Of their loves and hopes on hurrying feet
Thou art the worn memorial, Baker Street.

17

SUNDAYS

Pews and Punts

Thank God it's Sunday (1972)
The Victorian Sunday (1951)

THANK GOD IT'S SUNDAY

Second of two films

BBC 1 Television
17 December 1972
Producer: Jonathan Stedall

• • •

What do most Londoners do on Sunday? They leave it.

Most comfortably of all of course by rail
From Fenchurch Street
Over brick arches.

Who would want to stay behind in an inhuman slab of council flats, built in the priggish 1960s, when sea and country call? We leave by every means we can. Swift, swiftly eastwards through Stepney, Barking, Dagenham, Upminster. Electric railway, diesel, coach and bus. Car and motorbike, bypass and high road. Eastward and further east until the last brick is out of sight and then we see the wide, enormous marsh of Essex, London's nearest real countryside, and join the others speeding to Southend.

Hold on, what's that? A different sort of noise.
And now we're in a different sort of train.
We're travelling down Southend Pier by tram,
For a mile and a third towards the coast of France.
The longest pier in the world.
Was it perhaps a mid–Victorian dream
Of bringing England close to France at last,
And getting there on foot?

Or was it to build an elongated jetty for vessels making the Thames's mouth? At any rate,

Today upon the pier they sell a map
That shows you where to find the different kinds
Of fish the estuary yields
And what's done with them.

Southward from Southend across the Thames
You faintly see along the Kentish coast
The oil refineries that work on Sunday:
Give me Sunday here,
Sniffing the salt sea air and salt sea water.
Sundays of patience waiting for a bite.
Sunday the day when fathers push the pram.
Sunday for lovers walking in the wind.
Sunday for running to catch a lunchtime tram.
And missing it.
It doesn't matter here,
Time's of no consequence in kind Southend.
An unpretentious breezy friendly place.
I like Southend. East-London-on-the-Sea.
Southend where Charlie Chaplin as a child
Saw the real sea and thought it was a wall
Of sky-blue water.

I can't like motor traffic on the Sunday struggle out of London south through the Sussex Downs to the sea. Motor traffic. It smells nasty; it looks nasty. It's out of place in a human-scale village street, it's like a poisonous snake – a killer too. Not even a bit of nonsense like a nodding dog in the back window makes a motorcar agreeable and driving a car makes the mildest man competitive and turns him into a fiend. All this for a first sight of the sea.

Early-morning Brighton waits in Sunday early-morning calm. Waits for the inflow of the human tide.

Seaside people are a friendly race because their job is looking after strangers and trying to make them happy – for a fee. I think that clever patron of the Arts, the spendthrift Prince Regent, later

George IV, with his pavilion, parties, mistresses, gave Brighton the cheerful smile that has never left its face. 'Old ocean's bauble' it once was called and the name still suits it. It's a toyshop for London, open on Sunday – a place to lie back in and to look around and wonder who is who.

> Of all the things this toyshop has to show,
> The favourite's the most dangerous toy of all:
> The English Channel.
> Oh, friendly and luxurious at the edge,
> Delightful to the lazy and the tired.

Look at it, breathe it, listen to it, but do not try to cross it. How comfortable the roar that rakes the shingle, the feel of rounded pebbles underfoot.

> The Brighton English Channel seems a friend.

And most people have come down for the day: swell bookies, shorthand typists, acrobats from Reigate, Purley Oaks and Thornton Heath.

> 'Old ocean's bauble!' Yes, indeed she is.
> Confectionery Brighton in the sun.

> Regardless of the sunlight on the sea,
> The businessman discusses stocks and shares.
> Regardless of the whisper of the waves,
> Ladies compare the prices at the sales.
> And some are old but still cling on to life★
> And some are young and wonder what it's for.†
> For some this is the first time they've been down.
> For others, perhaps the last. For more and more,
> It's a first view of England and its coast.

> I wonder what that lady used to do,

★ An old lady being pushed in a wheelchair.
† Close-up of twins in a pram.

So unattracted to the sleeping youth.*
A cook? A missionary? A woman don?
And is she self-sufficient or afraid?

The joyous time of Sunday lunch is near:
Theirs is a set one in a private hotel.

From this point we can survey the whole field of seaside sociology.
Its income brackets and that sort of jargon. These can't have come far
in that uncomfortable position† or, if they've come from London, she
must be absolutely mad about him.

And all of us would rather go by bus
Than sit frustrated in a stuffy car,
And all of us will want to view the sea.
What are the girlfriends talking of?
Men or starfish? What the palmist said?
Madam Gymkhana and her crystal ball?
How different this than the bus to work –
The 19, for instance, or the 22.

A day of recreation and of rest.
But oh, it is still travelling along.

On Sunday morning, Matins or Morning Prayer, the Mass or the
Eucharist, whichever they like to call it, is over in Bosham Church.
But still she paints,‡ forgetful of the time and food and other people.
Absorbed in what she sees. She puts it down. Happy, contented,
quiet, competent.

Under those stones the local farmers lie.
Their old brick houses mostly have been bought
By businessmen who mess about with boats.
The old church looks forlornly from the shore.
And a very curious thing it seems to see.

---

* Close-up of an old lady sitting in a deck chair next to a young man.
† A young couple on an easy-rider motorbike.
‡ A woman painting a watercolour.

What explanation can there be of this?★
I wonder why that man is wearing tails.

That's going to leave a trail of misery behind it in the country lanes.† Those two rugged workers may well be retired admirals, such is the camaraderie of the sea. Just to anticipate any trouble – 'Take a letter: from Wheelhouse Grange, Albatross Lane, Havant, to the Chairman of the Governors, BBC, London. Sir, I was disgusted to find the BBC had the effrontery to turn its cameras on to the private marine activities of the English coast and, what is more, on a Sunday morning when they should all have been in church. My aunt, who is not an expert oarswoman, was shown on the screen without her permission. My own picnic party, with my niece and daughter, was also filmed without permission, as was the party of my staff who were on holiday at Burnham-on-Crouch. How would you like to have the private moments of your family life shown to millions and commented on facetiously by a man with an unpronounceable name? Is nothing sacred? There are many good sailors at the Yacht Club: why did you only select shots of incompetent amateurs? And why this emphasis on food and drink? Are you in the pay of the breweries, sir? What will foreigners think if this film is shown abroad as depicting the English way of life? Do we only live for pleasure? Surely on Sunday at least a reverent expression might have been shown somewhere. And I have one final and very serious complaint to make. The wife of my managing director kindly came down to the shore to meet me and your cameraman took the unpardonable liberty of filming her as she was getting ready for the bridge party to which we were going. Yours, etc.'

A happy Sunday slowness haunts the Thames
Between its Buckingham and Berkshire banks.
The river of our contemplative youth,
River for family parties, Cockney salts.
Who with such skill can push the boat away
And moor her safely into Boulters Lock?

★ A man in a wet suit launches a boat.
† A boat trailer being pulled up a beach.

For Londoners are faithful to the Thames
As the Thames has been to them for centuries.
'Sweet Thames run softly till I end my song.'
So Spenser said it and we say it still.
River and London mingle into one –
Riparian rights and lock-keepers and locks,
Sluices and weirs, punts and fishing permits.
Sweet Thames, the sliding wonder of our youth.
Fish on, fish on, until you find yourself
Or find yourself again, in years to come,
Alone among the strangers in the boat,
Or in the bosom of your family
Who don't quite seem to know what they should do,
With all those awkward bits of coiling rope.
Bear us along the river of our youth*
Into the long-remembered world of steam
Down here in Sussex, where from Sheffield Park
The Bluebell Railway runs to Horsted Keynes.
Here middle-age remembers joys of youth
And youth can share the joys of middle-age.†

Deep down in Sussex listen for it here –
The sound the poets hated makes by now
A melancholy music in the hills.

Whiter than the daisies are the flannels on the field. It's an heraldic
game and cricket is the heraldry of Sussex.

And cricketers are large, large-hearted men
And boundaries are waiting to be saved.
(Thank God it isn't I who have to do it.)
I like to watch the calculated bowl,
The subtle curve along the cherished grass,
The hushed awaiting till the final kiss
Of wood on wood, directed from afar.

---

* A pleasure boat passing the camera.
† Little boys watch steam trains.

Some Londoners most unwisely make for home,
Thinking they ought to make an early start.
Now we can take the dog out for a bark
And Alfriston becomes itself again
Under the shadow of the Sussex Downs.
If I may quote two lines of Thomas Gray
And leaving out the one that's in between:

> The lowing herd winds slowly o'er the lea
> And leaves the world to darkness and to me.

Except for some late last Londoners who still savour the country quiet. At half-past six some villagers will go to Evensong. For evening is a time when some of us are thinking of the evening of our lives and of the vastness into which we go, or nothingness, or of eternal bliss.

Whatever it is, for sure we've got to go
Alone, alone, and time will part us all
And somehow, somewhere, waits the love of God.

Sunday is sad. But Monday's so much worse
For those of us who haven't any hope.
Faith, hope and charity. Oh, give me hope.

Her brief accomplishment is somewhere there,★
The painting that she did and tucked away.

The match is over and the game they played
Was much more fun than work will be tomorrow.

Oh dear, oh dear, the agonies of youth.
Oh dear, oh dear, the trials of middle-age.
But do they matter? There's the mystery.

★ The lady watercolourist walks home with her easel and her dog.

THE VICTORIAN SUNDAY

From the radio series 'The Faith in the West'

BBC West of England Home Service
10 July 1951

• • •

I went for a walk on the Berkshire Downs with Bishop Sheddon, the Vicar of Wantage. I am not a Victorian myself. He says he is. What I tell you now are largely his impressions.

I think the first thing we would have noticed would have been the quiet. No wireless on, neither this nor any other programme. No motor-bicycles, no aeroplanes nor motorcars. Silence so deep on a Sunday morning that you can hear the sheep nibbling if you live in the country and you can hear the church clocks three parishes away if you live in a town.

Now let us suppose you or I were children of the lower-middle, middle or upper-middle classes – that is to say, anything from trades-men upwards – and that it is a Sunday morning seventy years ago: 1881. We are a very respectable family and, like almost all Victorian families, a large one: eight of us including Papa and Mama.

The first thing is that we get up a little later on Sunday and outside it is unnaturally quiet: no carts and jingle of harness, no street cries, no noise of gravel being raked on the drive or of hedges being clipped. The world seems asleep under the Sunday sun. The cart horses are turned loose in the fields, the farm implements are glittering undisturbed, even the dogs are not barking.

We put on our best clothes. An elder sister today will wear that new dress, for church is the place to show it. Younger brothers will be in Eton jackets, elder brothers in tails. And as we all assemble for morning prayers in the dining room and Papa opens the Bible and the servants in clean black dresses and new caps sit in the chairs against the wall – as we assemble for our first worship, there is a crackle of new starch and slight smell of moth-ball.

The urn has been boiling for breakfast coffee all through prayers. After the meal comes almost the nastiest part of the day for the children. The younger have to learn their catechism; the elder have to learn the collect for the day from the prayer book. Half an hour before church they are assembled in front of Papa. Oh what heart-burnings! Oh what stammerings! Oh what bitter words or beatings or punishments are meted out in various Italianate villas, sham castles and stucco terraces all England over in that fatal after-breakfast hour on Sunday morning!

And now, tears wiped away and a clean Eton collar on – to replace the one Papa seized in his wrath when for the third time you stumbled in the fourth commandment – you are ranged in your place with the rest of the family and you walk to church. From far and wide come other processions. Top hats are doffed and smiles exchanged. Or people look the other way, for in the genteeler suburbs of our towns there is much class distinction and people in the wholesale way of business are distant with those in the retail trade and professional classes, apothecaries, attorneys and the like look down on any form of trade whatever.

Over chimney-pots and billowing smoke where servants cook the Sunday lunch, over trees and hedgerows call the bells, beautifully rung by teams of six or eight men whose delight it is to practise the old English art of change-ringing.

As for the church itself, the family will have its own pew with a visiting card slipped into a brass frame on it to show the pew rent has been paid if we live in a town or its pew established by custom if we live in the country. And woe betide a stranger who sits in a private pew. 'Excuse me, this is OUR pew.'

The service will be Morning Prayer, although at St Michael's, the High Church in the poor part of the town, there are all sorts of bowings and scrapings of which Papa does not approve. Respectable families like Morning Prayer. The parson's black trousers show under his long white surplice. He wears an Oxford MA hood, slipping over one shoulder, and a very broad black scarf. And my word! – he preaches for a long time.

Every now and then it is Sacrament Sunday. Flagons and a silver cup appear on the Holy Table and the children are chased out halfway through the service, thankful to escape home without all the grown-up chatter that goes on during the walk back from church on an ordinary Sunday.

Wet or fine, winter or summer, Sunday lunch is always hot and it always consists of a large sirloin of beef and Yorkshire pudding followed by a fruit tart.

In the afternoon the boys go out for a walk. On rainy days the children must stay indoors. But no games are allowed. They may read *The Pilgrim's Progress* or that more thrilling allegory *The Holy War.*★ Perhaps in kindly disposed households with Tractarian leanings they may read the novels of Charlotte M. Yonge – *The Daisy Chain*, *The Little Duke*, *The Heir of Redclyffe* – for although she is an entertaining and brilliant novelist, she makes up for those defects by being a Christian. Did I say no games are allowed? There are a few Sunday games: a spelling game with Bible texts and a sort of Happy Families with cards depicting famous missionaries.

There is also at some time in the afternoon Sunday School for the children. And oh what pretty girls teach in the Sunday School. And oh how much more the gentler side of our faith was learned in Sunday School than from the harsh admonitions of Papa or the wearisome sermons of the rector.

The evening meal is cold to enable the servants to go to church. Evensong or Evening Prayer was always, as it still is in some of the more old-fashioned places, the popular service. Young couples went there together and courted on the way back in the lanes of a summer evening. In country districts fifty years ago the farm workers usually went to Evensong only, even though they had been confirmed. In some parishes it was believed that only squire and farmers were fit to take the Sacrament. 'Sacrament ain't for the likes of us.'

Those days are gone. The Victorian Sunday is gone. The chapels that did so much to bring a faith in Christ as the Son of God to the people are less well attended than they were in those days. Then the

---

★ Bunyan published *The Holy War* in 1682, four years after Book One of *The Pilgrim's Progress* and two years before Book Two.

Church of England was 'respectable' and the other places of worship, whether Methodist, Congregational, Roman Catholic or Baptist, were thought not quite the right thing socially. This respectability very nearly killed the Church of England. But its great Victorians – Catholic, Liberal and Evangelical alike: Pusey, Kingsley, Simeon and later those martyrs for the Faith like Charles Lowden, Robert Dolling and Arthur Mackonachin – helped to make the Church of our country what it is today: a place where you go to worship your Creator and not for social convention.

Oh dear. I seem to have given the impression that most Victorian church-going was hypocrisy and that the Victorian Sunday was a miserable affair. Of course it was not. It was part of the life of our land. Its origin was Puritan, dating from those Reformers whom Queen Mary burned at the stake. It was their attempt to revive the Jewish Sabbath on a day when the people had leisure for recreation; to impose discipline on the fun and games of Catholic England's holy days which were getting somewhat out of hand. It was, as it were, the nationalisation of leisure.

It survived, the Victorian Sunday, till lately. I can still remember when the old North London Railway did not run during church time. And to this day Sunday services of trains and buses are different, shops are shut, licensing hours vary, cinemas do not open till churches shut and there is an atmosphere of partial peace. Sunday is, thank goodness, *different* and we must have one day in seven different or our nerves collapse, our way of living goes too fast and there is no escape from the machines that all but control us.

The Victorian Sunday was not just different. Those who remember it look back on it not wholly with loathing; some of them even look back on it with affection. Sunday then brought religion into life, even if it was only for one day a week and then rather boringly: Victorian children at least learned what the Christian Faith was, even if they rejected it or ceased to practise it afterwards. Today most of us don't even know what it is we say we don't believe.

18

OPTIMISM

Vistas and Visionaries

The Ten-Storey Town (1935)
All-Steel Homes (1938)
The Culture of Cities (1939)

THE TEN-STOREY TOWN*

The New Statesman and Nation
24 August 1935

• • •

'The full consciousness of my responsibility . . .' 'the immensity of the mission of the architects of my own generation . . .' These are two expressions from the mild logical statement of what is meant by architecture that Professor Gropius makes. For he thinks of an architect 'as a co-ordinator – whose business it is to unify the various formal, technical, social and economic problems that arise in connection with building'.

You have only to read the eighty pages of large type to be convinced that he is right.

After outlining the constructional possibilities given to architecture by glass and steel, Professor Gropius turns to the subject of standardisation. At the Bauhaus, which is now no more, pupils were taught by designers and craftsmen to produce standard designs of everyday objects such as lamp fixtures, teacups, fabrics and chairs. These were made with an eye to mass production. German manufacturers bought Bauhaus designs and the result is that the most modern flats and houses in Germany have nothing so repulsively pretentious to show as the various modernistic designs that glisten in many a British parlour, the smartistic inspiration of some purely commercial workshop.

Would that Professor Gropius would refound the Bauhaus in England! But I think it highly unlikely that the individualism of

---

* Review of *The New Architecture and the Bauhaus* by Walter Gropius (Faber & Faber, 1935).

British industry could be broken down by such an excellent institution.

This book is full of important suggestions. The author advocates prefabricated houses. Prefabrication is obviously essential in any industrial country where populations are removed and rehoused at a moment's notice regardless of the time of year. Pleasant-looking houses that can be transported anywhere, put up and taken down again and removed to a more useful site are illustrated in this book. Yet in England we still go on building rows of only too substantial villas in districts where, for all we know, they will no longer be needed in ten years' time.

All architects, in the wide sense that Professor Gropius is an archi-tect, have some theory about town planning. It is all too easy to plan out a town on an unbuilt piece of ground, with its industrial, domes-tic and official sections neatly spaced among belts of sunny greenery. Professor Gropius offers one important suggestion that can apply directly to the present chaos of a town like London. He says: 'The height limit imposed by regulations is an irrational restriction which has hampered evolution in design.'

He explains why. Tenements (and, for that matter, New York sky-scrapers) have fallen into disrepute because the intervals between the blocks are too narrow and the lower storeys remain in darkness all day. But Professor Gropius regards the flat system as the only solution to 'that most burning and baffling problem of all – town planning'. He publishes some remarkable facts about the spacing of blocks of flats on a circumscribed area:

> Given an equal angle of light between the blocks (say 30 degrees), the amount of utilisable area *increases* with the number of storeys. In comparison with two-storied [blocks], ten-storied blocks have over 60 percent more utilisable superficial area; and this in spite of the fact that they enjoy the same amount of light and air.

He considers eleven storeys the ideal height for office blocks com-pared with ten storeys for domestic ones. This presupposes, of course, that there is a correct minimum distance between the blocks.

There is not space here to elaborate on the admirably clear case Professor Gropius makes for ten- and eleven-storey blocks in town planning. Obviously it is the only solution for as small an island as Britain if any greenery is to be left.

The New Architecture is not only a book for architects. It is a book that everyone can read and I am sorry that it has not been produced in a cheap popular edition, possibly with only one or two of the illustrations.

Mr P. Morton Shand's translation has made a book that might have been oppressively technical clear and easy reading. There is none of the jargon of architectural journalism. I spotted that silly word 'architectonic' only twice. Once it was in Mr Frank Pick's introduction.

This book is a change from the comic anger of Sir Reginald Blomfield and the delicate aesthetic shiverings of Mr Goodhart-Rendel because it has something to say that will make even an architectural student sit up. It tells us about something more important than 'the battle of the styles' and that is the battle we must fight for an ordered existence.

ALL-STEEL HOMES

The Times
14 June 1938

• • •

Bodywork of motorcars has changed rapidly since the war. Saloon cars, long-distance coaches and motor caravans are, like the comfortable armchair, among the few important contributions of this country to architecture.

It is extraordinary that when we have experimented so successfully with steel architecture where the architecture is on wheels, we have not until lately used it to any extent for domestic and office building.

True, large steel girders are hoisted into place on the site of many an honest Georgian terrace but no sooner are the girders erected than the architects, as though ashamed of themselves and their material and in compliance with Building Acts, hide them under some huge and usually sham-Georgian façade of Portland stone.

Steel certainly made architects shy when the Weir and similar houses were built. They had a temporary look and character. That day is over. A steel house may now be erected even in the Tudor style – though heaven defend us from it – and may look as hideous or as handsome as the designer likes to make it. Spot-welding of sheet steel and the pressing and rolling of sheet and strip have been so developed since the days of the Weir houses that this important change has come about.

Whenever a new material is extensively used for building it creates a style of its own. The timber-framed cottages of Hereford and Cheshire, the stone-built cottages of limestone districts, the weather-boarding of Essex, the brick of eighteenth- and early nineteenth-century London – each method created a style of its own. The fearful hideousness of architecture today is largely due to an unfortunate eclecticism that makes an architect think he can use the best of each style. The effect is not that of a complete poem but of a dictionary of quotations.

A certain restraint is essential in all decent building. That restraint will come as steel for housing is increasingly used. A steel building may now be given almost any finish. Well-designed units are already here, capable of limitless mass-production – steel doors, floors, sinks, baths, ceilings, window frames and partitions. Such standardisation of units for house-building does not mean harsh restraint. It means only the elimination of fussiness and pretentiousness. For this reason among many others, we must be grateful to those who have been experimenting in steel for housing.

For some years experiments in steel housing have been carried on abroad. The most interesting of these have been made in the United States. Though some of the American systems of steel house con-struction are older, several companies were floated in 1932 and the number has steadily increased until there are now seventeen different types of steel-constructed houses in America.

The actual number of houses constructed is not yet great, in fact little more than a thousand. Some of the systems, however, are remarkable. A house may be packed ready for construction at the factory, rolled out from a sort of hangar on to a trailer and delivered by road to the site. The house is then erected in a matter of days. It is ready for habitation as soon as drainage and plumbing have been connected.

In appearance American steel houses are at their best simple, good-looking dwellings of one storey and two storeys high, rather than after the manner of our own Regency lodges and small farm-houses. At their worst they are not as ugly as the average seaside English bungalow.

But the Americans have used different methods from our own of evolving a steel house. They have experimented in the construction of whole houses. In Britain we have given attention chiefly to finding suitable building units. We have worked from the inside of the house outwards.

British experiments seem to have borne the Crystal Palace in mind. The Crystal Palace was the first modern building not because it was of glass and cast-iron but because it was prefabricated, brought in carts to Hyde Park and erected silently and swiftly in numbered parts. British steel houses are designed to be built with similar ease and celerity. The units of building arrive from the factory. The only work that need be done on the spot is the laying the foundations, plumbing and the external and internal finishing of the steel structure.

The result of British experiments may be seen in a block of two-storey demonstration flats, comprising four flats in all, near King's Cross, London. The steel flats may be erected up to any height but two storeys is considered an adequate height for a demonstration block and research unit.

It is necessary to describe the flats in a semi-technical manner because only in fairly detailed descriptions does their importance become apparent. The outside half of the cavity wall is a half-built wall of Rustic Fletton bricks. The steel framework is arranged in rectangular bays of standard sizes. Sheet steel is the structural material for the whole of the staircase, landing and intermediate floors and the roof. These floor units are the outcome of research into the application of spot-welding to light dovetail-corrugated sheet. No fixing connections are required and sound-deadening asbestos strips can therefore be interposed.

In the flats a 'floating' over-floor has been added, consisting of a single layer of dovetail-corrugated steel sheeting screed-covered. The floating floor rests on wooden battens laid on asbestos strips that cover the screed surface of the structural floor. Further asbestos strips isolate the floating floor in every room from the partitions.

A hollow sheet-steel unit has been used for the roof. The units are jointed into each other at the sides and stiffened internally by vertical and diagonal members. No concrete ribs are required. Such a roof withstands extremes of temperature because of a continuous 4½ inch unit airspace thus provided. The roof may be finished with almost any type of flat-roof finish.

There is no doubt that the steel partitions and floors are effectively soundproof. A loudspeaker on at full blast on the ground floor is inaudible in the floor above.

The window frames are so constructed that the pressing that forms them also forms the internal sill, jams and soffit of the window opening so that there is not the danger from damp and heat to be found at points where plaster and wood are normally used. The doors are composed of two flush steel surfaces on a core of light-steel framing and provide a consistently smooth and undamageable surface for paint. There is no risk of warping or cracking. Sanitary fittings, baths and sinks are of pressed steel.

The constructional problems of strength, heat and sound insulation have been solved. There is not space to mention many important innovations. But a reference must be made to standardisation. Clearly in a steel house full use must be made of the opportunities offered for mass production and prefabrication, rapid assembly and simplified organisation. Standardisation should not impose too harsh a restraint on design and flexibility. But it should eliminate fussiness and needless variation. The experimental flats show effectively enough how good the standardisation of the components of a steel building can be. As soon as the site is cleared and the steel framework erected the roof can be fixed and work can proceed unhampered by bad weather. Construction is rapid and simple and can proceed simultaneously over a large working space.

A visit to the flats will prove that the steel house – in many parts the *pressed* steel house – is ready for the attention of architects and builders. At present the cost is about the same as that of a brick-built house. With the extended use of steel in building, the cost is bound to go down as soon as production gets going. It would be ridiculous to suppose that the steel house could ever be erected as cheaply as the body of a motorcar. But it is far from ridiculous to suppose that the King's Cross demonstration flats have inaugurated a new era of building.

The surface advantages of a building in steel are obvious. Weather and time need no longer delay the builder.

The situation of the demonstration flats is gloomy, hedged in by gasometers and railway lines. But the flats themselves are quiet and airy. Their appearance externally and internally is modest and satisfactory. They form a contrast with their surroundings that may almost be taken as symbolic.

Out of industrialism a new simple style has emerged as worthy of this century as was English architecture up to the last of the four Georges. Like the brick, stone and wooden architecture of the past that we are now so busily destroying, the architecture of steel is an honest expression of its age. Before 1850 England must have been the most beautiful country in the world; when the steel built house comes into its own, there should be some hope for the future. The most pretentious designer will find it difficult to make a steel house ugly.

THE CULTURE OF CITIES*

Decoration
Spring 1939

•   •   •

W hat the Sunday critics do when they come up against a book
of the substance, range and erudition of Lewis Mumford's
recently published study, *The Culture of Cities*, is an interesting speculation. Having used up all the latest superlatives on a novel with an
outside chance of a six-months' life, it must be difficult to cope with
this book which is likely to be a standard work for the next half-
century.

Here surely is one of the profoundest contributions ever made to
the history of man's endeavour to understand himself and the wayward
means by which he lives. From Plato to Le Corbusier the visionaries
have dreamed and talked and written of the way that man should live.
They have seen a vision and have given that vision words. Sometimes,
however, the more difficult task is to be more prosaic: instead of
showing how man *should* live, to show how he *could* live. The first is
more exciting, the second, Mumford's way, more exacting.

In his previous book, *Technics and Civilisation*, Mumford traced the
history of the impact of the machine upon society. In *The Culture of
Cities* he traces the effect of urban development upon society. The
two books give a picture of the history of the modern world that is
unequalled for close and scholarly attention to historical, mechanical
and architectural detail.

Despite this scholarship there is nothing of the pedant about
Mr Mumford. His prose is quick, vital and contemporary. The captions
to his wide choice of engravings, plans, drawings and photographs,

---

* Review of *The Culture of Cities* by Lewis Mumford (Secker & Warburg, 1939).

for example, provide in themselves an incisive and colloquial commentary upon the history of the city. These illustrations are completely engrossing, ranging from engravings of the medieval city to aerial photographs of the modern metropolis.

It is manifestly impossible to attempt to convey any idea of the scope of this book by quotation, however long. Perhaps the most satisfactory method would be to give a list of the chapters. The book opens with a study of the medieval city. Such political issues as the domination of the church and such technical considerations as hygiene and sanitation are fully discussed. From the medieval city we turn to what Mumford terms 'the afterglow of the Middle Ages'. Now we come to the analysis of vaster problems in their relationship with the city. 'War as City Builder', 'The Shopping Parade' and 'The Position of the Palace' are specimen sub-divisions of this second section of the book.

Then we are brought face to face with the full horror of the insensate industrial town, with its factories and slums. Mumford deals with this mechanisation of human lives with a vitriolic but still objective pen. His is not the mad fervour of the communist agitator (although even the most objective critic can see scarcely anything but evil in this nineteenth-century agglomeration of squalid industrial cities) but the dispassionate probing of the inquiring scientist. Then we are introduced to the main part of Mumford's examination: the growth of Megalopolis, a coinage that needs no further explanation. From this point Mumford becomes almost a twentieth-century Dante, but this inferno is certainly not one of the author's imaginings. It is here in real life and, indeed, one of the sub-divisions of the section 'Rise and Fall of Megalopolis' is entitled 'A Brief Outline of Hell'.

Mumford sees hope for mankind in the first signs of regional development and devotes the final sections of his work to an examination of regionalism as the planned basis of the new urban order. In these chapters, written by a scientist with the pen of a visionary, there is the beginning of a new hope for society – until one looks again to the daily newspaper. But Mumford has more and more contemporary architects on his side and it is to these men that Mumford looks. Such men have to a great extent the future of this new social order in their hands. The later photographs in the book show various attempts to evolve an urban background that is not the haphazard offshoot of twentieth-century industrialisation. Starting with Radburn,* the first town that 'consistently abandoned the corridor avenue lined with houses', Mumford passes to Greenbelt in Maryland, a first-class example of this regional planning, and to Romerstadt, a suburb of Frankfurt, which the author regards as the best of the modern approaches to the question of zoning.

One gives up the attempt to do justice to this book. It is quite impossible in a review of less than 10,000 words to begin to review the innumerable aspects of *urbisme* that Mumford tackles so ably in this book. Some indication of the sound, solid research that has gone into this book is given us by the publishers: the author has been twenty years collecting his material and eight years assembling it for this book.

Mumford's articles in the *New Yorker* have long been known to architects in this country for their keen criticism of contemporary architecture in New York. This book shows on what deep knowledge those lightly written articles are based. Every architect will want to read the book, want to study it, want to own it. For any reader of this journal *The Culture of Cities* is a five-starred choice. While all the book clubs are busy choosing their Book of the Month, step round to the bookseller and put down a guinea for this book of the decade. It will be a wise investment for some intensive (yet never wearying) reading.

---

* Radburn, New Jersey, was founded in 1929 as 'the town for the modern age'.

19

WAR

Pacifists and Propaganda

FOR ENGLAND

Extract from Chapter 5, 'Private School'
Summoned by Bells
1960

• • •

Before the hymn the Skipper would announce
The latest names of those who'd lost their lives
For King and Country and the Dragon School.
Sometimes his gruff old voice was full of tears
When a particular favourite had been killed.
Then we would hear the nickname of the boy,
'Pongo' or 'Podge', and how he'd played 3Q
For Oxford and, if only he had lived,
He might have played for England – which he did,
But in a grimmer game against the Hun.
And then we'd all look solemn, knowing well
There'd be no extra holiday today.
And we were told we each must do our bit,
And so we knitted shapeless gloves from string
For men in mine-sweepers, and on the map
We stuck the Allied flags along the Somme;
Visited wounded soldiers; learned by heart
Those patriotic lines of Oxenham

> What can a little chap do
> For his country and for you –

'He can boil his head in the stew,'
We added, for the trenches and the guns

Meant less to us than bicycles and gangs
And marzipan and what there was for prep.

THE STORM CLOUDS APPROACH
Letters to Patrick Balfour and Camilla Russell (1931)

• • •

Letter to Patrick Balfour
16 August 1931

I am counting on the break-up of capitalism for a chance of marry-ing. The Oxford economists are giving it another six months. Germany and America have another two months. Poor old Maurice Hastings.* Neither you nor I have anything to lose and I think it is rather pleasing than not and we are living in the most important times since the Reformation. I wonder whether we will survive to see the changes that are rapidly approaching.

Letter to Camilla Russell
21 December 31

I am no longer worth knowing with this doom impending. I am now utterly convinced that capitalism is going to crash and here in England we will be caught like rats in a trap as there is insufficient food, and transport to other countries will be affected. If you want to remain alive I should not come back to your native isle. Send back that horrid Dorothea† and she will starve to death.

---

* A friend of Maurice Bowra who had married an heiress and lived in rented country houses.
† Camilla Russell's mother, Lady Russell.

IN WESTMINSTER ABBEY

New Statesman and Nation
30 September 1939

• • •

Let me take this other glove off
    As the *vox humana* swells,
And the beauteous fields of Eden
    Bask beneath the Abbey bells.
Here, where England's statesmen lie,
Listen to a lady's cry.

Gracious Lord, oh bomb the Germans
    Spare their women for Thy Sake,
And if that is not too easy
    We will pardon Thy Mistake.
But, gracious Lord, whate'er shall be,
Don't let anyone bomb me.

Keep our Empire undismembered
    Guide our Forces by Thy Hand,
Gallant blacks from far Jamaica,
    Honduras and Togoland;
Protect them Lord in all their fights,
And, even more, protect the whites.

Think of what our Nation stands for,
    Books from Boots' and country lanes,
Free speech, free passes, class distinction,
    Democracy and proper drains.
Lord, put beneath Thy special care
One-eighty-nine Cadogan Square.

Although dear Lord I am a sinner,
  I have done no major crime;
Now I'll come to Evening Service
  Whensoever I have the time.
So, Lord, reserve for me a crown,
And do not let my shares go down.

I will labour for Thy Kingdom,
  Help our lads to win the war,
Send white feathers to the cowards,
  Join the Women's Army Corps,
Then wash the Steps around Thy Throne
In the Eternal Safety Zone.

Now I feel a little better,
  What a treat to hear Thy Word,
Where the bones of leading statesmen,
  Have so often been interr'd.
And now, dear Lord, I cannot wait
Because I have a luncheon date.

ON THE OUTBREAK OF WAR

Letters to Ninian Comper and Cyril Connolly (1939)

• • •

Letter to Ninian Comper
12 October 1939

I am here in a silly old thing called the Observer Corps, and hope
to get into the RAF. But only if I can persuade myself that it is
right to fight at all. At present fighting in a war seems to me to be
committing a new sin in defence of an old one. But I am not bother-

ing. I feel that when my conscience is clear on the point and my mind made up, I shall know what to do and have no qualms about doing it.

Letter to Cyril Connolly
19 October 1939

Well, old man, – It was good to see how this spot of bother is affecting you. *Horizon*, eh?★ Some sort of highbrow journal, eh? Well, chaps, it's going to give Jerry what for. Teach him to take a slosh at the British lion by giving him as good as he gives, gets, gives, gets – which is it?

My missus is a Red Cross Nanny brave little woman and I hope your missus is doing something equally daring. We must all do our bit. *There's a war on, you know.* But if the best you can find to do is some highbrow paper with a communist-poet fellow, then take my advice and chuck it up and get a job in the Sussex Light. And tell Peter Watson[†] to strip off his 'artistic' poses and get down to real work. Has he ever emptied latrines from the C/O into the GHO, I wonder, with the Quartermaster Sergeant bellowing at him every five minutes? Till he's done that, he's not a man. *There's a war on, you know.* Tell him that.

Of course I understand your kindness in asking me to write for your journal. I appreciate it. But we are fighting for LIBERTY to make the world fit to live in for Democracy, to keep our splendid system of Local Government going, to make the world safe for Slough to go on and to see that every John Citizen gets a square deal so he can pay up his instalments into the Building Society without having to go without his Ovaltine. Am I justified, then, in taking up the pen when so many gallant lads like Lord David Cecil are doing their mightiest to take up the anti-aircraft gun? I enclose a poem, to hearten our lads 'somewhere in France'. Of course none of us wanted a scrap, but now it's here let's keep smilin' through. *There's a war on, you know.* I shouldn't be surprised if that fellow Schurhoff you mention isn't a German spy. Look out. WRITE SOON again. God bless you. Jolly, all this, isn't it?

★ Connolly had just got the job of co-editor as the war began.
† A friend of Betjeman who had inherited a fortune from his father's dairy business.

THE NEWPORT 'RISING', 1939

To Stuart Piggott*
Christmas 1939

•   •   •

Left Wing! Left Wing! Again I say, Left Wing.
To Peggy and poor old Stuart let me sing.
Uffington Workers from their sloth arise,
A light of Marxist frenzy in their eyes:
Send MARXIST GREETINGS to the Captain too
And Communistic grunts and groans to you,
Bold Mrs Piggott. Now no Malvern Lays
Shall charm away the Workers' Day of Days.
Miss Butler's barns are blazing! Wheeler's ricks
Crackle and sport; and see the bright flame licks
The Vicarage! The Church! The School! The Pubs!
The Institute! The Fellowship! The Clubs!
Workers arise: throw off your servile chains
And smash the Piggotts as you smashed the Danes.
And crush the Betjemans and kill their maids.
Burn the McIvors, send to Hell's red shades
The motley bourgeoisie. The Day is bright
With Revolution. Uffington Unite!

---

* A neighbour of the Betjemans at Garrards Farm in Uffington, on the borders of
Oxfordshire and Berkshire, which they moved into in February 1934.

LIFE IN WARTIME

Letters to John Lehmann, John and Myfanwy Piper,
Oliver Stonor, Douglas Goldring, John Arlott, Cecil Beaton,
John Murray, Geoffrey Taylor and Alan Pryce-Jones
(1941-5)

• • •

Letter to John Lehmann
27 January 1941

My address in future (Hitler permitting) will be The Office of the UK Representative to EIRE, 50 Upper Mount Street, Dublin. I would be pleased to look out for any good Irish authors for you: if you will let me know any you would like me to see, tell me. It all helps, don't cher know, the great cause of Anglo-Irish amity.

Letter to John Lehmann
12 February 1941

I enclose a copy of *The Bell* in which there may be stories or articles to interest you for *New Writing*. If there are, I should write direct to Sean O'Faolain, the Editor. There is no need to mention that I put you on to the idea or I will be accused of doing propaganda and I do not think that the accusation would be justified . . . They are all very fearful of British propaganda here. I don't blame them.

Letter to John and Myfanwy Piper★
2 March 1941

Oh God! I miss you both. Do both pour out your hearts to me at the above address and you will miss the censor for the letter will go in the bag.

I wish I cared more about the war, then I would care more about my job. All able-bodied pro-British have left Ireland for the English services and we are at the mercy of people who are either anti-British, anti-German and pro-Irish (faintly a majority) and there are pro-Irish and pro-German (about 48 per cent) and 2 per cent pro-German about everything. The Irish papers are all anti-British and the best-selling writers are pro-German. I am beginning to hate Ireland and the Irish . . .

The British Legation here is a great joke. No contact with the Irish at all. I don't blame 'em. If only I had more time I could write at greater length on the subject of Ireland and the Legation. But do write to me in the bag. God bless England. God Save the King. Up the British Empire. The C. of E. (High) for Ever!

Letter to John Piper
17 March 1941

I miss you very much. There's no one else to fire one with enthusiasm. Here it is giving out all the time and then the fear that one is doing propaganda and then one remembers one is British and feels an itch for a decent transept with a Mowbray side chapel.

A woman who is pro-Nazi and thinks she is a spy has made a pass at me and I have been through embarrassing scenes in motorcars. I didn't know beech trees could shade one, brown streams rush and cattle have foot and mouth disease in neighbouring fields and yet one could be in hell. I am in hell. A hell of my own choosing . . .

★ John Piper (1903–92) was an artist and one of Betjeman's closest friends. His wife, Myfanwy, inspired at least three of Betjeman's more 'amatory' poems.

Letter to Oliver Stonor
19 April 1941

Just over two months ago I got the job of Press Attaché here.* I did
not want it, as I was just beginning to enjoy myself at the Ministry
of Information† and had made many friends and was actually making
films. I made great friends, by the way, with 'Bartimeus', author of
A Tall Ship, Naval Occasions etc; then this job came along. I now move
in diplomatic circles and have moved Propeller and the child‡ over to
here, where I find myself very pro-British and absolutely longing for
the darn old blitzes. It is most surprising. I would give £10 to see a
nice over-restored church in England and would embrace the first
piece of polychromatic brickwork I could clap eyes on. I have to see
pro-Germans, pro-Italians, pro-British and, most of all, anti-British
people. The German Legation here is pretty dim and repulsive. I have
to see journalists, writers, artists, poets. I have to go about saying
'Britain will win in the end' and I have to be charming to everyone
and I am getting eaten up with hate of my fellow beings as a result.
The strain is far greater than was that of living in London during the
blitz . . .

Letter to John and Myfanwy Piper
20 April 1941

My mother was bombed at West Kington but not damaged. Hope to
God the Bum is intact.

I am afraid I often think of Goldilox's§ figure, hair and face and it
compares very favourably with all colleens.

Martin Travers' daughter Sally who acts over here with a repertory
company is pro-German and sleeps with my opposite number. He is
so unpopular here except among politically minded tarts and stockbroking and lawyer place-hunters that he does his cause more harm
than good. I am a little sunbeam and very pure in contrast.

---

* In Dublin.
† In London.
‡ Betjeman's wife Penelope and their son Paul.
§ Myfanwy Piper.

Letter to John and Myfanwy Piper
26 May 1941

What a blessed relief it was to hear from you and what a relief it is to be able to write to you. Good food and no bombs are poor compensation for no friends and intangible balderdash. Yet if conscription is introduced into the Six Counties area, which it probably will be, I shall resign this job with a clear conscience. I cannot go into it now, the subject will be too boring. But believe me, if it is done and if it means that our government is so damn silly over Ireland, then God help its tactics in the rest of the world . . .

It is our *job* to know *everyone* – to go to dinner and to supper parties with them, to have tea in suburban houses with reproductions of Van Gogh and have the law laid down to us on Milton, to listen to sycophants, to talk about the war, to minimise defeats, to magnify victories, to give the official line, to be attached, and never to be thought of as a poet, or writer, or man of any sensibility at all. It is like being in a cartoon . . .

Most of all we miss any church life. We have to bicycle three miles to a N side eight o'clock HC★ and no church life at all surrounds us and the Protestant church identifies with politics and class and the Catholics are incomprehensible to such as us, used to the cold, pure English liturgy . . .

Conscription may settle things for me – unless they make some sort of compromise in which case I will have to go on – for given any *chance* of friendly relations between Eire and England they must be promoted, and I can help and it is a nice positive kind of war work.

Letter to Douglas Goldring
14 July 1941

I would to heaven I were in England. One feels very exiled here at times. The glory seems to have gone off the old and the new glory is so small in the bud, it is hard to see it – but it must be there.

★ Holy Communion.

Anyhow it is so bloody political, dividing itself into these categories in descending order of magnitude:

1) pro-British with relations fighting, but above everything pro-Irish
2) pro-Irish and not caring who wins, so long as Ireland survives as a united nation
3) pro-Irish and anti-British, but also anti-German
4) pro-Irish and pro-German.

But it doesn't really matter what they think. One friend gained for England is one enemy for Germany and that is my job.

Letter to John Arlott
27 December 1943

I am back home but being KILLED by the Min of Inf in London. A sadist in charge of the Films Division is trying to do me in. I am under him. Oh God! I have not time to do anything. That is part of his system of torture.

Letter to Cecil Beaton
13 November 1943

I have discussed this question of your movie camera (which would have to be 35mm) with the Director here and he has seen Francis.

There is no possibility of getting a camera from a British unit, desirable though that would be. There simply aren't any to spare and they are all turning round madly, the cameras I mean. But a large American film unit is going out to Lord Louis Mountbatten's command for the express purpose of filming China and I think it would be best for you to approach Major Irving Asher of the US Army at Denham Studio to see if you could get one from him.

Letter to John Murray
21 June 1944

The war will never end.

To Geoffrey Taylor
18 September 1944

I don't think I have ever been more miserable in my life as I am now.
I have not had the *time* to write one line of poetry since May. I have
had the urge time and time again but not the time and now all my
perceptions are blunted. We are in a slave state* here and I am beginning to think I would sooner be in prison or dead. Everything one
loves threatened by post-war plansters of different types. Satire
impossible owing to the law of libel. No redress, just arrogant
destruction by keen young careerists left and right. I don't see any
end to the war — not for two years at least in Europe and another
three for Japan on top of that.

Letter to Geoffrey Taylor
24 November 1944

I have left the Admiralty. I got guilty about my unsuitability for that
sort of work. I was able to do it all right and the people were charming and so was Bath. But I got a sense of futility. I dare say I shall have
it more, looking after a hundred quarrelling women in the British
Council, which I do next week probably.

To Alan Pryce-Jones
11 January 1945

At last I am for a month or two the most fortunate man in the war.
I have been put in charge of 112 quarrelling women (and a few Qs)
situated in the Rhodes Building Quad of Oriel (St Mary Hall) and I
am staying with the Colonel.

---

* A phrase that Betjeman enjoyed using and which he attributed to Evelyn Waugh.

20

PESSIMISM

Civics and Vita-Glass

The Passing of the Village (1932)
Councillor Bloggins (1936)
The Planster's Vision (1945)
The Dear Old Village (1947)
The Town Clerk's Views (1948)
Love is Dead (1952)

THE PASSING OF THE VILLAGE

Architectural Review
September 1932

• • •

Last Saturday I was driving in a dogcart through a remote part of Hampshire: not in the New Forest where sanatoria by Sir Aston Webb and half-timbered bungalows peep about among the pines but in the northern part of the county near Alton, in an unvisited tract of land between two main roads from the Metropolis – the one to Winchester and the other to the West of England.

Nor was the country defaced by fir trees and larches which, because they grow fast and can quickest afford shelter to a generation that must do everything in a hurry, are planted on downs and in districts that have formerly rolled with beeches, regardless of future generations and regardless of the appearance and general character of the surroundings. And this part of Hampshire undulated gently with hills that grew broader and barer as they neared the Plain. On the slopes were beech plantations and in the valleys unfenced roads ran like streams between fields of oats and barley. And on the one-inch Ordnance Map I found the remotest village to drive to: it was called Wield. Many roads led to it; nearly all of them were marked white on the map – not available for motor traffic. But from Bentworth, from Burkham, from Alton, from Preston Candover, from Astley's Farm, from Church Bradley and Herriard all roads led to Wield. But now it seemed that no one wanted to go to Wield for nearly all the roads were white on the map, which meant that as we jolted down them in the dogcart there was the high grass of a wet August beneath us for a surface and hawthorn bushes and dripping hazel made a thick, low arch above us.

Through a farmyard and past an overgrown pond that spread from the village green out on to the road and we were in Wield. The village may have been of importance once but it was not so now. There was not even a cottage with orange curtains behind which an artistic person was making etchings of picturesque bits, nor was there a hand-painted board announcing the presence of gentlefolk making hand-made cakes. The brewers had not seen fit to erect a Tudor public house. Instead there was a deep green surrounded by rows of brick cottages, thatched. Interspersed between them were elms and round the gardens were clipped yews. Little footpaths led to the church and around the church the cottages centred. Even the church had escaped many repulsive efforts of restorers. It was a small Norman building, aisleless, with Perpendicular windows with clear glass in them, a cool whitewashed interior containing a Norman chancel arch and alongside the Holy Table a vast early seventeenth-century canopied tomb to a family that had long ceased to exist. In the churchyard again, the grass was long, over square unpretentious gravestones and from the sunny walls of the church, plaster had fallen to disclose patches of flint and, in one place, mellow red brick that had blocked up a chancel window.

We stood in silence while the earth ticked as it absorbed the moisture. It seemed as though all life had left Wield. A motorbike roared away from some cottage quite near us. The Primitive Methodist Chapel, a humble and decent building for 1867, had grass on what was once a well-kept path and on the blistered, grained oak door was an old torn notice about an electoral roll. The windows were grey with a furry fungus. The cottages that skirted the chief road to the village had uncared-for gardens high with cow parsley whose trunks were as thick as young trees and the hawthorn hedge was out of shape and choked with bindweed. The place looked as though everyone had gone away.

Round the corner we came upon a telegraph pole. Someone had pasted a notice on it [*See opposite*].

Of course, everyone had gone there, unable to resist so attractive an entertainment. At that moment an old car shook itself out of the farmyard. Beyond the telegraph pole was a shed: 'LYONS' TEA: HEPWORTH WILL MAKE YOU A MAN OF FASHION FOR

ELECTRIC PALACE
BASINGSTOKE

!! HOOP-LA !!

An all-talking, all fun-making, romantic, roaring, all-star, elevating, enervating, gorgeous, rollicking, pageant of mirth, passion and melody, featuring your old friend

CLARA BOW

POPULAR PRICES   8.30

FORTY-FIVE SHILLINGS: WILLS' GOLD FLAKE: Oyez! Oyez! Steppe in to Ye Olde Tudor Restaurante, Basingstoke. BARGAINS IN HARDWARE! BARGAINS IN UNDERWEAR! HAVE YOU BEEN TO ASTON'S ARCADE?' Of course, the villagers had gone to be made men of fashion by Hepworth, to drink Lyons' tea in Ye Olde Tudor Restaurant and smoke Gold Flake and to obtain those bargains to the sound of the wireless in Aston's Arcade. A motorbus marked 'Basingstoke' brushed the hedges and drew up to take away some waiting villagers. Wield was empty. It seemed that it was no longer needed.

Nor is Wield needed. Village communities, except for somewhat arty collections of weavers and spinners in the Cotswolds, have practically ceased to exist. Not all the desperate munificence that erects village halls and arranges local concerts will preserve them. The inhabitants will remain in their houses listening to the wireless – and this is a typical remark you will hear: 'No, I don't go about in Wield much.' When they are not listening to the wireless they spend their leisure in the Electric Palace and Timothy White's. The centre of interest has moved from Wield to Basingstoke.

Not that Basingstoke was until recently of no importance. It was, in the past, a market town with its own occupations and attractions for the villages around it. But Basingstoke is no longer Basingstoke

321

but London. To Timothy White's comes toothpaste from London, the cloth for the fifty-shilling tailors is not made anywhere near Basingstoke, the films at the Electric Palace come from Hollywood, the tea in Ye Olde Tudor Restaurant comes from Cadby Hall. Basingstoke is no longer a country market town but a suburb of the Metropolis. And the same may be said of every other provincial town in England.

It is useless to deplore this change – as useless as it is to deplore unalterable economic facts. Industrialism has changed the whole social order and that is surely a trite enough remark. Only an escapist who has not the courage to face the creations of the machine age in which he lives will fly to the country to find rural peace. But the tentacles of motorcar, motorbike, telephone and motorbus will get him there. Even the lamp is shattered and the pylons stride across the field he views, all for the sake of a glaring electric bulb. It is useless to blame Wield for going to Basingstoke or to blame Basingstoke, vile as the main road in that town is, for attracting Wield.

All one can do is to blame Basingstoke for being so hideous when it need not have been. A main road is a main road and a petrol station is a petrol station and there's an end of it. But there is no disguising a main road to look like a Stratford-on-Avon street with half-timbered hideosities decorated with the art of Stratford-atte-Bow and there is no disguising a petrol station to look like a Swiss chalet; fortunately no one yet has tried to disguise a pylon as a Northamptonshire steeple. There are some heights to which even commercial imagination cannot stretch. In a little while, when it is too late and when every provincial main street has become a replica of that blatant mile of pretentiousness, Oxford Street, a few people will realise that something is wrong. This will probably not happen until commercial Tudor and bank and post-office fancy Queen Anne cease to be paying propositions. But when that glorious day comes – and it may take a revolution to bring it – perhaps the house will show its grace of construction in steel and concrete, the petrol station its useful function and the main road will soar straight and unbothered as a Roman road, a monument to a civilisation that has been brave enough to master the machine.

For the machine age is in its way a beautiful age but it is not the way of a bygone agricultural civilisation. So much misdirected energy is put nowadays into 'preserving the countryside'. Such energy would be far better spent in preserving the towns by disciplining the jazz-modern of cheap tailors, the vulgarity of co-operative stores and the haphazard planning of self-important local councils.

The Machine has won and England seems to be the last country to realise the fact. Those little spaces between the main roads, war memorials to defunct agricultural labourers, should where possible be preserved but the stateliness of pylons and the clear-cut lines of a new unostentatious factory will not detract from their beauty.

On the day of writing this article I came upon this significant notice in *The Times* (4 August):

The Estate Market

SELLING VILLAGES

" WEEK-END " BIDDERS

Next Wednesday the little Bedfordshire village of Tingrith, 12 miles from the county town, will almost all come under the hammer. There are 42 lots, with a total area of 914 acres, including four farms of from 145 to 250 acres, the village hall, the school, and many cottages. The agents are Messrs. John D. Wood and Co. (Berkeley Square) and Messrs. J. R. Eve and Son (Bedford).

A liberal outlay has been made in the upkeep of the estate for a long period, and management as an entirety has provided safeguards which will be lacking if the offer of the whole in one lot is not taken. It may he hoped that some, at any rate, of the villagers will be able to buy the freeholds that they live in and probably love. If they cannot, the emphasis that

is laid on the value of country cottages for
" week-end " use may have an unwelcome
meaning for them. There is not much time to
make arrangements.

This should prove that we are no longer able to afford to retain the relics
of an agricultural civilisation to any considerable extent. We have
created a machine age and we should not be afraid of it but rather
become accustomed to it and control it. The machine age may be a
roaring lion in the land but the lamb of agriculture can lie down beside
it. It is such a shorn and shivering lamb that it is hardly worth the eating.

Two hundred years ago England was a park dotted here and there
with mellow towns; now it is a town dotted here and there with
derelict parks. After all, I am not very brave to exchange my dogcart
for a motorcar.

COUNCILLOR BLOGGINS

Daily Express
15 July 1936

• • •

We all have a favourite village. The townsman thinks of some
place he manages to see at the most once a year. When the
noise and the strain of town life beat him down, he looks out of his
office window and visualises the elms, the quiet street, the cottages,
the local pub with its blistered sign and the church tower of his
favourite village. Perhaps he idealises it a little.

The countryman feels his village is part of himself. He knows
everybody in it and everybody's movements. In that village his

mother died, over there he lived with his parents, in that corner Ted Goodman broke his leg falling off a rick. This garden in which he is standing has given him and his wife vegetables year in, year out. It is looking well today, with the peas coming on and the borders white with 'snow on the mountain'.

But all that is an England of the past. New people have moved into many houses – 'week-end' people who are only there a month or so in the year all told. The cottage where his mother died was condemned as insanitary. His parents' cottage is turned into a garage and the garden is occupied by a tin shed. Ted Goodman's son keeps him and his wife awake at night by charging round and round the village on a motorbike with a girl from a town on the pillion. His own garden is not what it was. The electric-light people cut down his hazel bush and put up a wooden pole with a 'transformer' on it. It looks like a monkey-up-a-stick. Creosote from the pole pours down into the earth and poisons his vegetable bed. Electric light (installed free) is ninepence a unit. This is a lot when you have ten shillings a week old-age pension. 'We must move with the times,' says the local councillor. But he has more than ten shillings a week to live on.

Even the townsman notices the difference. His favourite village has become a 'beauty spot'. The old pub has gone and a sham Elizabethan one has been put up in its place, with palms and little tables in the 'Tudor lounge' and an electric sign in place of the old painted one. The old gated roads have become tarred highways. Posts and wires stretch across everything. The elms have been felled because the county council decided that all elms are 'dangerous'. On a Saturday or Sunday the village is as noisy as Oxford Street. The field through which a footpath wound to the church has been covered with council houses built in a style alien to the district. Worse still, the squire has sold his estate and the edges of the parts all along the road are lined with new villas. The manor house has become a country club.

But considerations like this of 'beauty' are of less importance than the hard fate of thousands of old country people. Some of the great electioneering cries of the Labour Government were 'There are worse slums in the country than ever there were in the towns' and

'Pull down the old, insanitary cottages.' The cry was taken up by the noisier and stupider members of the local council. The Ministry of Health made a regulation that windows in all houses must equal one-tenth of the floor space and half of each window must open. Such a by-law is very sensible in a London slum where light and air are precious. In the country, where light and air are sometimes too much of a good thing, it is ridiculous. You cannot enlarge most cottage windows without pulling down the whole structure.

As a result of the regulation many local councils rushed round condemning cottage after cottage. In the small village where I lived then thatched cottages were condemned. Several, but not all of them, should have been condemned. One old man who can neither read nor write came to me in tears with his notice to quit. 'But you will have a lovely new council house; they must give you one in place of your old cottage,' I offered as consolation. But what consolation is it to an old man with ten shillings a week old-age pension to be offered a five-room council house at five shillings a week (parlour type with bathroom) or at the lowest three shillings and sixpence a week (non-parlour type, no bathroom)? Two shillings a week is the average rent for a cottage. And what will become of the old man's peas and beans and apple trees and 'snow on the mountain'? He would have to make a new garden on unprepared soil when there is no strength left in him. Our old cottages are excellent as almshouses for old people who cannot afford a council house. Our council houses are probably excellent for large families of young, vigorous people who can afford to pay the rent.

There are two sorts of 'progress': one for the towns and one for the country. At present town laws are applied to country districts. That is why England is becoming one big suburb. Electric light should be put underground in villages; new houses should be grouped in a separate place and built in a style suited to the district. If they are of concrete, for reasons of economy, they should be washed the same colour as the old cottages in the village. Old cottages must be preserved in good condition for old people. Meadows and fields should be preserved by the Government, not subscribed for against the avarice or penury of landlords by larger-hearted members of the public.

There are all sorts of preservation societies – unfortunately associated with crankiness. Believe me, they are the only people who are going to save rural England unless the Government does its duty and turns them into state departments.

Rural England must be planned: you *can* build here; you *cannot* build there. Local councils cannot do this on their own. Here is the sort of thing that occurs at council meetings:

Member of the council: I propose we pay a guinea subscription to the Council for the Preservation of Rural England.

Councillor Bloggins (Self-styled Socialist. Speaks at every meeting. Objects to everything): What's the address of this society?

Member of the council: Great Marlborough Street, London.

Councillor Bloggins: There you are, gentlemen – a London address. What do London people know about us? I object to subscribing.

Objection sustained.

I'm only a zig-zagging lane, with wild rose borders
And a few little birds in the bushes. I'm waiting for orders.*

Orders from whom? From Councillor Bloggins, I fear.

---

* From 'Country Conversation' by Edmund Blunden (*Choice or Chance*, 1934).

THE PLANSTER'S VISION

The New English Review
June 1945

• • •

Cut down that timber! Bells, too many and strong,
   Pouring their music through the branches bare,
   From moon-white church-towers down the windy air
Have pealed the centuries out with Evensong.
Remove those cottages, a huddled throng!
   Too many babies have been born in there,
   Too many coffins, bumping down the stair,
Carried the old their garden paths along.

I have a Vision of The Future, chum,
   The workers' flats in fields of soya beans
      Tower up like silver pencils, score on score:
And Surging Millions hear the Challenge come
   From microphones in communal canteens
      'No Right! No Wrong! All's perfect, evermore.'

THE DEAR OLD VILLAGE

Harper's Bazaar
July/August 1947

• • •

The dear old village! *Lin-lan-lone* the bells*
  (Which should be six) ring over the hills and dells,
But since the row about the ringers' tea
It's *lin-lan-lone*. They're only ringing three.
The elm leaves patter like a summer shower
As *lin-lan-lone* pours through them from the tower.
From that embattled, lichen-crusted fane
Which scoops the sun into each western pane,
The bells ring over hills and dells in vain.
For we are free today. No need to praise
The Unseen Author of our nights and days;
No need to hymn the rich uncurling spring
For DYKES is nowhere half so good as BING.†
Nature is out of date and GOD is too;
Think what atomic energy can do!
   Farmers have wired the public rights-of-way
Should any wish to walk to church to pray.
Along the village street the sunset strikes
On young men tuning up their motorbikes,

---

* The expression '*Lin-lan-lone*' comes from Tennyson's poem 'Far-far-away' ('The mellow lin-lan-lone of evening bells'). Betjeman was so taken with it that he used it frequently in his poetry and prose to convey the sound of distant church bells.
† John Bacchus Dykes was a Victorian composer of hymn tunes, much admired by Betjeman; Bing is Bing Crosby.

And country girls with lips and nails vermilion
Wait, nylon-legged, to straddle on the pillion.
Off to the roadhouse and the Tudor Bar
And then the Sunday-opened cinema.
While to the church's iron-studded door
Go two old ladies and a child of four.

    This is the age of progress. Let us meet
The new progressives of the village street.
Hear not the water lapsing down the rills,
Lift not your eyes to the surrounding hills,
While spring recalls the miracle of birth
Let us, for heaven's sake, keep down to earth.

    See that square house, late Georgian and smart,
Two fields away it proudly stands apart,
Dutch barn and concrete cow-sheds have replaced
The old thatched roofs which once the yard disgraced.
Here wallows Farmer WHISTLE* in his riches,
His ample stomach heaved above his breeches.
You'd never think that in such honest beef
Lurk'd an adulterous braggart, liar and thief.
His wife brought with her thirty-thousand down:
He keeps his doxy in the nearest town.
No man more anxious on the R.D.C.†
For better rural cottages than he,
Especially when he had some land to sell
Which, as a site, would suit the Council well.
So three times what he gave for it he got,
For one undrainable and useless plot
Where now the hideous Council houses stand.
Unworked on and unworkable their land,
The wind blows under each unseason'd door,
The floods pour over every kitchen floor,
And country wit, which likes to laugh at sin,
Christens the Council houses 'Whistle's Win'.

---

* A caricature of Farmer John Wheeler, the Betjemans' landlord at Uffington.
† Rural District Council.

Woe to some lesser farmer who may try
To call his bluff or to expose his lie.
Remorseless as a shark in London's City,
He gets at them through the War Ag. Committee.★
    He takes no part in village life beyond
Throwing his refuse in a neighbour's pond
And closing footpaths, not repairing walls,
Leaving a cottage till at last it falls.
People protest. A law-suit then begins,
But as he's on the Bench, he always wins.
    Behind rank elders, shadowing a pool,
And near the Church, behold the Village School,
Its gable rising out of ivy thick
Shows 'Eighteen-Sixty' worked in coloured brick.
By nineteen-forty-seven, hurrah! hooray
This institution has outlived its day.
In the bad times of old feudality
The villagers were ruled by masters three –
Squire, parson, schoolmaster. Of these, the last
Knew best the village present and its past.
Now, I am glad to say, the man is dead,
The children have a motor-bus instead,
And in a town eleven miles away
We train them to be 'Citizens of Today'.
And many a cultivated hour they pass
In a fine school with walls of vita-glass.
Civics, eurhythmics, economics, Marx,
How-to-respect-wild-life-in-National-Parks;
Plastics, gymnastics – thus they learn to scorn
The old thatch'd cottages where they were born.
The girls, ambitious to begin their lives
Serving in WOOLWORTH'S, rather than as wives;
The boys, who cannot yet escape the land,

★ 'Ag' was a wartime abbreviation for agriculture. War Ag committees were formed in rural areas to advise farmers what to grow during hostilities, as advised by the Min of Ag (the Ministry of Agriculture).

At driving tractors lend a clumsy hand.
An eight-hour day for all, and more than three
Of these are occupied in making tea
And talking over what we all agree –
Though 'Music while you work'★ is now our wont,
It's not so nice as 'Music while you don't'.
Squire, parson, schoolmaster turn in their graves.
And *let* them turn. We are no longer slaves.
    So much for youth. I fear we older folk
Must be dash'd off with a more hurried stroke.
Old Mrs SPEAK has cut, for fifteen years,
Her husband's widowed sister Mrs. SHEARS,
Though how she's managed it, I cannot say,
Sharing a cottage with her night and day.
What caused the quarrel fifteen years ago
And how BERT SPEAK gets on, I do not know.
There the three live in that old dwelling quaint
Which water-colourists delight to paint.
Of the large brood round Mrs COKER'S door,
Coker has definitely fathered four
And two are Farmer Whistle's: two they say
Have coloured fathers in the U.S.A.
I learn'd all this and more from Mrs FREE,
Pride of the Women's Institute is she,
Says 'Sir' or 'Madam' to you, knows her station
And how to make a quiet insinuation.
The unrespectable must well know why
They fear her lantern jaw and leaden eye.
    There is no space to tell about the chaps –
Which pinch, which don't, which beat their wives with

straps.

Go to the Inn on any Friday night
And listen to them while they're getting tight
At the expense of him who stands them drinks,

★ *Music While You Work* was a twice-daily radio programme first put out by the BBC in 1940 to encourage workforce morale in factories.

The Mass-Observer★ with the Hillman Minx.†
(Unwitting he of all the knowing winks)
The more he circulates the bitter ales
The longer and the taller grow the tales.
'Ah! this is England,' thinks he, 'rich and pure
As tilth and loam and wains and horse-manure,
Slow – yes. But sociologically sound.'
'Landlord!' he cries, 'the same again all round!'

TIIE TOWN CLERK'S VIEWS

Selected Poems
1948

• • •

'Yes, the Town Clerk will see you.' In I went.
    He was, like all Town Clerks, from north of Trent;
A man with bye-laws busy in his head
Whose Mayor and Council followed where he led.
His most capacious brain will make us cower,
His only weakness is a lust for power –
And that is not a weakness, people think,
When unaccompanied by bribes or drink.
So let us hear this cool careerist tell
His plans to turn our country into hell.
'I cannot say how shock'd I am to see

★ Mass-Observation was a programme of sociological fieldwork begun in 1937.
† The first 'Minx' in the range of Hillman cars came out in 1932.

The *variations* in our scenery.
Just take for instance, at a casual glance,
Our muddled coastline opposite to France;
Dickensian houses by the Channel tides
With old hipp'd roofs and weather-boarded sides.
I blush to think one corner of our isle
Lacks concrete villas in the modern style.
Straight lines of hops in pale brown earth of Kent,
Yeoman's square houses once, no doubt, content
With willow-bordered horse-pond, oast-house, shed,
Wide orchard, garden walls of browny-red –
All useless now, but what fine sites they'd be
For workers' flats and some light industry.
Those lumpy church towers, unadorned with spires,
And wavy roofs that burn like smouldering fires
In sharp spring sunlight over ashen flint
Are out of date as some old aquatint.
Then glance below the line of Sussex downs
To stucco terraces of seaside towns
Turn'd into flats and residential clubs
Above the wind-slashed Corporation shrubs.
Such Georgian relics should by now, I feel,
Be all rebuilt in glass and polished steel.
Bournemouth is looking up. I'm glad to say
That modernistic there has come to stay.
I walk the asphalt paths of Branksome Chine
In resin-scented air like strong Greek wine
And dream of cliffs of flats along those heights,
Floodlit at night with green electric lights.
But as for Dorset's flint and Purbeck stone,
Its old thatched farms in dips of down alone –
It should be merged with Hants and made to be
A self-contained and plann'd community.
Like Flint and Rutland, it is much too small
And has no reason to exist at all.
Of Devon one can hardly say the same,
But "South-West Area One"'s a better name

For those red sandstone cliffs that stain the sea
By mid-Victoria's Italy – Torquay.
And "South-West Area Two" could well include
The whole of Cornwall from Land's End to Bude.
Need I retrace my steps through other shires?
Pinnacled Somerset? Northampton's spires?
Burford's broad High Street is descending still
Stone-roofed and golden-walled her elmy hill
To meet the river Windrush. What a shame
Her houses are not brick and all the same.
Oxford is growing up to date at last.
Cambridge, I fear, is living in the past.
She needs more factories, not useless things
Like that great chapel which they keep at King's.
As for remote East Anglia, he who searches
Finds only thatch and vast, redundant churches.
But that's the dark side. I can safely say
A beauteous England's really on the way.
Already our hotels are pretty good
For those who're fond of *very simple food* –
Cod and two veg., free pepper, salt and mustard,
Followed by nice hard plums and lumpy custard,
A pint of bitter beer for one-and-four,
Then coffee in the lounge a shilling more.
In a few years this country will be looking
As uniform and tasty as its cooking.
Hamlets which fail to pass the planners' test
Will be demolished. We'll rebuild the rest.
To look like Welwyn mixed with Middle West.
All fields we'll turn to sports grounds, lit at night
From concrete standards by fluorescent light:
And over all the land, instead of trees,
Clean poles and wire will whisper in the breeze.
We'll keep one ancient village just to show
What England once was when the times were slow –
Broadway for me. But here I know I must
Ask the opinion of the National Trust.

And ev'ry old cathedral that you enter
By then will be an Area Culture Centre.
Instead of nonsense about Death and Heaven
Lectures on civic duty will be given;
Eurhythmic classes dancing round the spire,
And economics courses in the choir.
So don't encourage tourists. Stay your hand
Until we've really got the country plann'd.'

LOVE IS DEAD

First and Last Loves
1952

• • •

England though not yet so ugly as Northern France and Belgium is very nearly so. The suburbs, which once seemed to me so lovely with their freckled tennis girls and their youths in club blazers, have spread so far in the wake of the motorcar that there is little but suburb left. We are told that we live in the age of the common man. He would be better described as the suburban man. There is a refinement about him that pervades everything he touches and sees. His books are chosen for him by the librarians, his arguing is done for him by Brains Trusts, his dreams are realised for him in the cinema, his records are played for him by the BBC; the walls of his rooms are in quiet pastel shades, he has cereals for breakfast and he likes everything in moderation, be it beer, religion or tobacco. He has a wife, a motorcar and a child. He is the Borough Engineer, the Listener, the Civil Servant, the Town Clerk, the Librarian, the Art Historian, the Income Tax Inspector. So long as he is not any sort of creative artist he can be assured of an income and a pension at the end. He collects facts as some collect stamps and he abhors excess in colour, speech or decoration. He is not vulgar. He is not the common man but the average man, which is far worse.

He is our ruler and he rules by committees. He gives us what most people want and he believes that what is popular is what is best. He is the explanation of such phenomena as plastic tea-cups, Tizer, light ale, quizzes, mystery tours, cafeterias, discussion groups, Chapels of Unity, station announcers. At his best he is as lovable as Mr Pooter but he is no leader. He is the Lowest Common Multiple; not even the Highest Common Factor. And we have put him in charge of us, whatever his political party at the moment.

His indifference to the look of things is catching. We discover it in our attitude to the horrors with which the delicate variety of our landscape has been afflicted. We accept without murmur the poles and wires with which the Ministry of Fuel and Power has strangled every village, because they bring electric light and telephones to those who have been without these inestimable benefits. We put up with the foully hideous concrete lamp-standards for which the Borough Engineer and the Ministry of Transport are jointly responsible – each playing off the other – because the corpse-light they spew over road and pavement makes it safer for kiddies to cross and easier for lorries to overtake one another round dangerous corners. We slice off old buildings, fell healthy trees and replace hedges with concrete posts and chain-link fencing, all in the name of 'safety first' which is another phrase for 'hurry past'. We accept the collapse of the fabrics of our old churches, the thieving of lead and objects from them, the commandeering and butchering of our scenery by the services, the despoiling of landscaped parks and the abandonment to a fate worse than the workhouse of our country houses, because we are convinced we must save money. Money is even more important than health or road-widening, so it is obviously infinitely more important than something so indeterminate as beauty. He is a foolish man who in a letter to a paper or at a local council meeting or in Parliament dares to plead for something because it is good to look at or well made. He is not merely a conservative: he is a crank. He is unpatriotic and prepared to sell the country for an invisible asset. We have ceased to use our eyes because we are so worried about money and illness. Beauty is invisible to us. We live in a right little, tight little clinic.

Oh come, come, Mr Betjeman, aren't you allowing your eloquence to run away with you? Things are not as bad as you imagine; I doubt if there has ever been a time when the desire for culture has been so wide-spread among our menfolk and womenkind. The interest in ballet, in opera, in chamber music and documentary film is something phenom-enal. Museums have never had better seasons and even picture galleries are widely patronised. Then you must admit that in your field of archi-tecture the government housing schemes, particularly for our dwellers, have shown a taste and reticence unknown in the evil days of private speculation by the jerry builder.

I doubt whether this interest in culture is more than an expression of restlessness. It is reaching for something that cannot be explained in terms of economics. It is a desire for the unworldly. It is a search for religion and it is far smarter than Christianity. As for the taste and reticence of government control, it is certainly easier on the eye than the brutalities of the speculator. By looking only at well-laid muni-cipal estates and averting one's eyes from the acres of unimaginative modern housing, by forgetting those terrible pipedreams come true of thick-necked brutes with flashy cars, elderly blondes and televi-sion sets – those modernistic, Egyptian, Beaux-Arts and other façades of the new factories outside every large town, by ignoring all these and much more, it is possible to live in a fool's paradise of imagined culture, a sort of Welwyn Garden City of the mind.

But look for a moment at what is really there and the suburban man is before us again. The old High Street just peeps above the shop façades. The well-known chromium and black gloss, Burton the Tailor of Taste, Hepworth, Halford, Stone, Woolworth & Co., Samuel, Bata, The Fifty Shilling Tailor, the Co-op, have transformed what was once a country town with the characteristics of its county into a home from home for the suburbanite, the concrete standards adding the final touch. When the suburbanite leaves Wembley for Wells he finds that the High Street there is just like home, provided that he does not raise his eyes from the pavement to see the old windows and uneven roofs or go so far off the beaten track as to wander down a side-alley and see the backs of the houses and their neglected Somerset craftsmanship. Enterprising brewers, backing culture for all they are worth, have turned the old inns into 'pubs' and 'locals'. They have made a virtue of the solemn drinking of their chemicals. They have had Izal and porcelain put in the gents and made the bar similar to it, save that they have added little tables and a counter. Sawdust and oil lamp or engraved glass and gaslight, all the subtle distinction between private, jug and bottle, public and saloon, are being merged into the cleanly classlessness of the road-house. The local crudely painted inn sign is replaced by the standardised sign with the big brewer's name. And inside, the old photographs of local teams and the framed picture from *Pears' Annual* are put in the dustbin, the walls are painted a light biscuit colour and reproductions of favourite artists of a brewers' publicity board are hung in their place. Nationalised or not yet nationalised, the gradual suburbanisation of enterprise continues, the killing of local communities, the stamping out of local rivalries and the supplying of everything by lorry from industrial towns. By luxury coach and local bus the villages are drained of life. Jealous of the misery created by too much road transport, the railways are trying to standardise themselves too. Those colours by which we were wont to know the part of England we were in – red for Midland, brown for Great Western, grained oak for East Anglia, green for Southern – have disappeared. For the convenience of suburbanites who like everything uniform and call it Administration, the trains are one of two colours.

Oh prams on concrete balconies, what will your children see? Oh white and antiseptic life in school and home and clinic, oh soul-destroying job with handy pension, oh loveless life of safe monotony, why were you created?

I see the woman with a scarf twisted round her hair and a cigarette in her mouth. She has put the tea tray down upon the file on which my future depends. I see the man on the chain-belt feeling tired, not screwing the final nuts. In a few months I see the engine falling out of the motorcar. I see eight porters, two postmen and an inspector standing dazed for forty minutes on a provincial station, staring into space and waiting for what was once the Great Western which is now forty minutes late. I see those sharp-faced girls behind the buffet and the counter insulting the crowds who come to buy. Too bored to think, too proud to pray, too timid to leave what we are used to doing, we have shut ourselves behind our standard roses; we love ourselves only and our neighbours no longer. As for the Incarnation, that is a fairy story for the children, if we think it healthy for children to be told fairy stories. We prefer facts. They are presented to us by the thousand and we can choose those we like. History must not be written with bias and both sides must be given, even if there is only one side. We know how many tons of coal are produced per week, how many man-hours there are in a pair of nylons, the exact date and the name of the architect and the style of a building. The Herr-Professor-Doktors* are writing everything down for us, sometimes throwing in a little hurried pontificating too, so we need never bother to feel or think or see again. We can eat our Weetabix, catch the 8.48, read the sports column and die; for love is dead.

> *O Lord, who hast taught us that all our doings without charity are nothing worth: Send thy Holy Ghost and pour into our hearts that most excellent gift of charity, the very bond of peace and of all virtues, without which whosoever liveth is counted dead before thee. Grant this for thine only Son Jesus Christ's sake.*†

---

* This refers to Nikolaus Pevsner and other Central European architectural historians who came to England to escape Nazi persecution and whose academic methods Betjeman derided.
† *Book of Common Prayer.*

21

HOUSES

Towers and Tower Blocks

The Englishman's Home (1969)

THE ENGLISHMAN'S HOME

Third in the thirteen-part television series 'Bird's Eye View'

BBC 2 Television
5 April 1969
Producer and director: Edward Mirzoeff

• • •

There is a saying – you've heard it before: 'The Englishman's home is his castle'. Well I suppose, in a way, it is.

The Celts in coracs crossed to Anglesey
Pre-Christians. Early Christians. Irish Celts.
What were they like who dug these holes for huts,
Roofed them with boughs to keep the winter out?
What were they like, who lived in such a place?

  The Ancient Romans too
Who settled here at Rockbourne on the downs
Before the Saxons called them Hampshire, Dorset, Wilts.
Patterned floors,
Remains of hypocausts, luxurious life,
Where never luxury was seen again.

Why did the Normans choose an Iron-Age fort
To build the castle of Old Sarum here?
Why did the clerics – outlined in the turf;
You see their old cathedral over there –
Why did they go away?
Was it a water shortage or a feud
That drove them down to build in Salisbury?
We do not know.

    But when across the waves
From Ireland and the west, the shores of Wales,
Rise mountainous along those mountains' feet
We see the castle of an English king –
Edward the First – oh, then the answer's clear –
Attack, defence; after defence, attack.
Conquer, subdue and dominate the Welsh
With arrow, shot and battering ram and lead.
Harlech and Conway and Caernarvon, three
Grey bastions guard the northern coast of Wales.

Peaceful today.
A poet of the Welsh
Has thus translated from his native tongue:

        One night of tempest I arose and went
            Along the Menai shore on dreaming bent.
        The wind was strong and savage swung the tide
            And the waves blustered on Caernarvon side.

        But on the morrow, when I passed that way
            On Menai shore the peace of heaven lay.
        The wind was gentle and the sea a flower
            And the sun slumbered on Caernarvon tower.

Far over in England, how peaceful are names
Like Deeping St Nicholas, Deeping St James,
Long strings of rich soil and low houses of men
Where slow flows the Welland through Lincolnshire fen.

Villages, once Saxon or Danish, grew rich on ploughland.

The earth is the Lord's and all that therein is: the compass of the
world and they that dwell therein. [*Psalm 24:1*]

Here at Chipping Camden in the Cotswolds
The people prospered on the wool from sheep.

They built themselves small substantial houses all along the market street. And at Nun Monkton, in the flat West Riding of Yorkshire, where roads and rivers meet at the village pond and green, is the picture people have of Merrie England, with dancing round the maypole on the grass.

But life could be nasty, brutish and short, even for people at the top who lived in castles. Berkeley Castle, Gloucestershire, where the Berkeleys still live. Here on the night of 21 September 1327 Edward II was barbarously murdered. You'll remember how Thomas Gray describes that fearful fate of the first Prince of Wales:

> Weave the warp, and weave the roof,
> The winding-sheet of Edward's race
> Give ample room, and verge enough
> The characters of hell to trace.
>
> Mark the year and mark the night
> When Severn shall re-echo with affright
> The shrieks of death thro' Berkeley's roof that ring
> Shrieks of an agonising King.*

A castle then. A castle still. But its walls are breached with windows that look at the world outside. A castle turning into a house: Stokesay, Shropshire – the timbered gate lodge is almost ornamental. Around the yard the wall is only a curtain wall. In that hall the Lord of the Manor eats at a high table above the salt. In that overhung bit, he and his family sleep.

> Across the hills, the borders of Wales are quiet
> And over everybody is the King.

Compton Wynyates in Warwickshire. It was rebuilt by Sir William Compton, First Gentleman of the Bedchamber and favourite of the King. He dedicated that porch to 'my lord, King Henry the Eighth'.

> Yet if His Majesty, our sovereign lord,
> Should of his own accord

---

* From 'The Bard' by Thomas Gray, 1716–71. This extract is also known as 'The Curse upon Edward'.

Friendly himself invite
And say 'I'll be your guest tomorrow night'
How should we stir ourselves, call and command
All hands to work! 'Let no man idle stand.'*

Compton hid his house in a Warwickshire hollow – to be out of the weather and not to hide from enemies. Thomas Wolsey, a mightier man, Cardinal of England, built *his* palace at Hampton.

Set me fine Spanish tables in the hall;
See they be fitted all;
Let there be room to eat
And order taken that there want no meat.
See every sconce and candlestick made bright,
That without tapers they may give a light.

Thus, if a king were coming, would we do
And 'twere good reason too,
For 'tis a duteous thing
To show all honour to an earthly king.†

It was not enough for Henry VIII, who deposed Wolsey and took the palace for himself.

The rich Elizabethans built to please themselves. Longleat in Wiltshire. Longleat is not a castle except in its square plan. Look: its outside walls are mostly glass and stone. The formal gardens are patterned like tapestries that hang on the gallery walls inside. On the roof, the rediscovered gods and goddesses of ancient Rome –

Elizabethan fancy carved again.

Pleasure on the roof,
Pleasure in the garden,
Pleasure in the park,
Mythical beasts from tapestries

---

* Anonymous, 16th century (*The Oxford Book of English Verse*: 1250–1900) but attributed by other to Thomas Ford (1580?–1648).
† Ibid.

Inhabit the waters and woods.
Cars £1, with children free, no dogs.

Harlaxton Manor, near Grantham, Lincolnshire, the grandest
Elizabethan house of all. But look at the date: 1837. Victorian
Elizabethan. But just as genuine-looking as the real thing and, I
think, as impressive. This was about the last time that a private
unenobled citizen, Mr George Gregory, a landowner, would be rich
enough to build himself a palace. He and his architect Salvin were
inspired by the Elizabethans.

To earlier ages, earlier inspiration.

Stay traveller! With no irreverent haste
Approach the mansion of a man of taste.
Hail Castle Howard! Hail Vanbrugh's noble dome
Where Yorkshire in her splendour rivals Rome!

Here the proud footman to the butler bows
But kisses Lucy when she milks the cows.
Here a proud butler on the steward waits
But shares his mistress at the Castle gates.
Here fifty damsels list my lady's bells
And a whole parish in one mansion dwells.
Chef, Housekeeper and humblest Houseboy, all
In due gradation of the servants' hall.
Dependent on the slightest frown or smile
Of him who holds the Earldom of Carlisle.

But what of wealth and pomp of Worldly state?
To yonder Mausoleum soon or late,
Up those broad steps will go great Howard's dust –
A journey no man makes before he must.

By now the garden becomes more than a tapestry –

It's a place to walk in when the weather's fair.

The ingenious Monsieur Grillet in 1694, at Chatsworth in
Derbyshire, with the aid of the first Duke of Devonshire, turned the
garden there into something as remarkable as the house. High on the

moors was stored the water and he trained it to cascade downhill, through planted woodlands, down to lesser ponds, and thence to burst from a temple. Step by step,

Formal and straight, it charged with rushing force
And burst as fountains in the vale below.
High to the heavens, behold the silvery shower,
A dancing tribute to hydraulic power.

Big houses set the fashion. First, formality was all the rage: from the garden front at Melbourne Hall in Derbyshire

Windows looked out to straight and formal lines
A vista made of shrubs and ordered beds.

The fashion had come from France.

Here at the Fountain's sliding foot,
    Or at some Fruit-tree's mossy root,
Casting the Body's vest aside,
    My Soul into the boughs does glide . . .
. . .
How could such sweet and wholesome Hours
Be reckon'd but with herbs and flow'rs!*

Belton, Lincolnshire. Formal on this side,

And conscious wildness in the park beyond.

Too much formality? 'Nature abhors a straight line,' said the eighteenth-century landscape gardener Capability Brown. 'I will make the Thames look like a small stream.' And so he did when he dammed the little river Glyme in a Cotswold valley and turned it into a mighty winding lake at Blenheim, Oxfordshire. It was given by a grateful nation to the Duke of Marlborough for his victories over the French in 1704. As for Vanbrugh's splendid palace, I think of the lines of Alexander Pope:

'Thanks Sir,' I cried, ''tis very fine,
    But where d'ye sleep, and where d'ye dine?

---

* From 'The Garden' by Andrew Marvell.

> I find by all you have been telling
>> That 'tis a house but not a dwelling.'

A country house is nothing without its setting. In later Georgian days that setting had to be wild or changed to look wild. 'Nature abhors a straight line.'

> Curve of land, and curve of groups of trees,
> Curves on the surface of a landscaped lake,
> In Bedfordshire, Woburn.

> The sun shines out, no Mediterranean sun,
> For this is Stourhead where a chalky vale
> Planted with trees is turned into a scene
> Of temples, bridges, obelisks and rocks
> Commanded by the eighteenth-century taste
> Of a rich London banker, Henry Hoare.

> Instead of Claude or Poussin on his walls
> Showing a ruin dark against the light
> His garden walks became his gallery –
> The Temple of the Sun, the Pantheon,
> Reflected in the water, seen through trees,
> A Wiltshire valley changed to Italy.

On the shores of North Wales, overlooking Cardigan Bay, what fair Mediterranean port is this that stumbles to the sea? The port of Merioneth: Portmeirion. It's the work of a living architect, Clough Williams-Ellis, who has brought Italy and English eye-catchers to his native Wales. An architectural antique shop of the open air. The charm's deliberately plaster deep; colours are shown up by the grey Welsh skies yet it looks no more strange or out of place than must another such Italian dream have looked two centuries ago when first it rose. This – Chiswick House: an Italian villa from the banks of the Veneto, built by Lord Burlington and his architect William Kent,

> Copying much-admired Palladio
> In what was orchard land of Middlesex.

Country houses joined together
To make the Royal Crescent, Bath:
Ancient Rome in Somerset,

built in the mid-eighteenth century by a father and son, both called
John Wood.

The Royal Crescent was a good address.

Façade only. You built your rooms behind – as many as you could. It
didn't matter about the back. The front counted. You and your family
had to be in Bath for the season, to attend assemblies and Routs, to take
the waters and fall in love, when the city of Bath was as smart as
London, but all for a season – only a season.

Façades, façades along the Somerset hills. And the smartest of all
was the Circus. Bath led – but Bath seems to me to be in the crater
of an extinct volcano. I prefer a part of Bristol that copied Bath:
Clifton. High up upon the downs, built in the 1790s: a place to live
in, not just to stay in for a season. Where East Indiamen returned
from voyages. In some of the vaults below these Clifton terraces and
crescents that hang above the Avon Gorge, the Bristol merchants
stored their pipes of port. Bristol, the second city of England;
Clifton, the fairest suburb of the West; Brunel's Suspension Bridge
poised like an insect across the Gorge.

And there along the Gorge,
The Avon winds by Woods to Severn sea.

Seaside brings out the best in all of us.
When England left her inland spas for sea

following royal fashion (not able to travel to Europe because of the
wars with Napoleon), Brighton became what still it is: the best-
looking seaside resort we've got.

Those cheerful stucco squares and promenades
Those winding paths, romantic clumps of shrub,
All in the curving Georgian landscape style
An intended contrast with straight seaside fronts,
They were all the work of speculative builders

Before spec. building got its dirty name.
Spec. building of the Thirties – 1830s.

The pleasure-loving Regent, George the Fourth,
Liked Brighton better than his palaces.

His favourite architect, John Nash, built for the King at Brighton an Oriental pavilion. 'It is as though St Paul's Cathedral had gone down to the sea and pupped,' said the Reverend Sidney Smith.

Outside Bristol John Nash tried the cottage style with Blaise Hamlet, a model village on the big estate of Blaise Castle, so designed

That every step you take when on the ground
Gives another subject for a watercolour.

On the great estate of Chatsworth, the sixth Duke of Devonshire in the 1830s wanted to improve the rolling vistas of his park –

And glorious those rolling vistas are.
He was a sovereign lord in his domain.
He cleared away th'old village that spoiled the view
And only left a single house of it.

But he built for his tenants a better-looking village further up the hill, a model village done in various styles, spelt Edensor and pronounced Ensa. And I can't see why this sort of thing is any more inhuman than what a council does today.

And in the Sixties, in the midst of it,
Sir Gilbert Scott rebuilt the village church:
Uncompromising middle-pointed Gothic.

And so's North Oxford. Cradle of individualism, where professors – freed at last from the university statutes that forbade them to marry –

Bred families of first-class brains in all
That gabled brick.

So many rectories and not too close together.
Each house is slightly different from its neighbour.
A pleasant place of wide and shady roads,
Humane, High Church and Liberal.

It gave birth to these swim-pool suburbs, far from industry.
The sort of house that everybody wants:
An acre and a garden and no cow.
The Keston Park Estate, near Bromley, Kent.

'We'll house our workers not in flats but farms
And cottages their forebears might have lived in.'

So thought the Lever Brothers, who made soap
And built Port Sunlight outside Birkenhead.
A protest against Northern back-to-backs.
They housed their workers in the Eighties here.
This was a very early garden village,
With each house different.
Work for each for weal of all
And the Non-Conformist conscience turned to Art.

New Anzac-on-Sea. Just after the First World War.
Eventually they called it 'Peacehaven':
A garden suburb on the Sussex coast.
We were told to laugh at it in days gone by
As a dreadful example of urban sprawl
And bungaloids and all that sort of thing,
But where you can still call your house your own
And plant your garden with the plants you choose.
The downland air is laced with a scent of sea.
Your house detached.
Others mayn't like it but it's what you like.

Harlow in Essex, just after the Second World War. A new New
Town. And as the guidebook says: 'You've come to live in a newly
developed area of Harlow which incorporates the most up-to-date
ideas and layout.'

Indeed it does, with sports facilities,
Pubs, community centres, play areas
And shopping precincts and a string quartet
And public works of art
And public woods and a church

And houses designed by the Corporation architects,
Privately owned or rented from the Town.
Do you think this is the way we ought to live?
Perhaps we should and do as we are told.

Or do you prefer to live a country life
With built-in urban joy?

If you're in plastics or an account executive, handling quality
consumer durables for the foreseeable future – New Ash Green, a
neighbourhood unit development in Kent, is maybe what you need.

The terrace houses with car courts, patios,
And no loneliness
Can be obtained for about £6,000 each.

A dream for some; for others *this* is home –
In Dockland, Germans bombed the little streets
That had been homes for thousands. After that,
Partly to keep the rates up, partly to get
As many as possible in a minimum space,
Out of this devastation slabs arose.
Sometimes they called them towers
And these replaced the liveliness of streets.

Now new high densities in open space
High Rise and Low Rise, towers and terraces.
The planners did their best,
Oh yes, they gave it all a lot of thought,
Putting in trees and keeping grassy rides
And splendid views across to Richmond Park
And landscaped streets and abstract sculptures – oh,
Roehampton won the prize.
It was all so well laid out.
Just so much space from one block to the next.
Perhaps this is the way we ought to live?

Where can be the heart that sends a family
To the twentieth floor in such a slab as this?

It can't be right, however fine the view
Over to Greenwich and the Isle of Dogs.
It can't be right, caged halfway up the sky,
Not knowing your neighbour, frightened of the lift
And who'll be in it, and who's down below
And are the children safe?

What is housing if it's not a home?

Thamesmead is to be built on Plumstead Marsh.
    Another town – how human will it be?
New towns, new housing estates,
New homes, new streets, new neighbours,
New standards of living,
New financial commitments,
New jobs, new schools, new shops . . .
New loneliness, new restlessness, new pressure,
    New tension . . . and people,
People who have to cope with all this newness,
People who cannot afford old irrelevancies,
People who have to find
A God who fits in.

2 2

CHURCHES

Naves and Knaves

Hymn (1928)
Church-Building (1947)
Country Churchyards (1953)
Churchyards (1954)
The Lighting of Churches (1953)
Electric Light and Heating (1954)

HYMN

Isis
24 October 1928

• • •

The Church's Restoration
  In eighteen-eighty-three
Has left for contemplation
  Not what there used to be.
How well the ancient woodwork
  Looks round the Rect'ry hall,
Memorial of the good work
  Of him who plann'd it all.

He who took down the pew-ends
  And sold them anywhere
But kindly spared a few ends
  Work'd up into a chair.
O worthy persecution
  Of dust! O hue divine!
O cheerful substitution,
  Thou varnishéd pitch-pine!

Church furnishing! Church furnishing!
  Sing art and crafty praise!
He gave the brass for burnishing
  He gave the thick red baize,
He gave the new addition,
  Pull'd down the dull old aisle,

– To pave the sweet transition
  He gave th'encaustic tile.

Of marble brown and veinéd
  He did the pulpit make;
He order'd windows stainéd
  Light red and crimson lake.
Sing on, with hymns uproarious,
  Ye humble and aloof,
Look up! And oh how glorious
  He has restored the roof!

CHURCH-BUILDING*

Times Literary Supplement
6 December 1947

•   •   •

For a time so rich in materials as the decade before the recent war, English church design was remarkably poor. The Victorians, described so complacently by subsequent generations as materialists and hypocrites, gave of their most creative and costly to church architecture. Street, Butterfield, Burges, G. G. Scott, Jnr, J. D. Sedding and Bodley are only some of the names that come to mind at once of great Victorian architects whose best work was to be seen in new churches.

---

* A review of J. N. Comper, *Of the Atmosphere of a Church*, Sheldon Press; *Fifty Modern Churches: Photographs, Ground Plans and Information Regarding Thirty-Five Consecrated and Fifteen Dedicated Churches Erected during the Years 1930–1945*, Incorporated Church Building Society; E. Short (ed.), *Post-War Church Building*, Hollis & Carter.

Today, with the exception of Mr J. N. Comper, the late F. C. Eden and a very few others, there is none to compare with the Victorian masters.

Church design is at a low ebb but the subsidiary arts of church decoration appear to be at a lower ebb still. To take one example, the stained-glass windows shown in *Post-War Church Building* are almost all pale, dispirited affairs, designed, no doubt, with one eye on the cautious 'good taste' of diocesan advisory committees. If these and the new window in Henry VII's Chapel at Westminster Abbey are to be considered as representative of the best English stained-glass, then the art has declined indeed from the days of Victorian artists like Hedgeland and the early work of Wailes and the O'Connors, whose windows were both full-blooded and sensitive.

Perhaps the poverty of modern church design is a confirmation of the adage that every age gets the architecture it deserves. For without a doubt this age is not interested in new churches. Town planners, infected with twentieth-century unbelief, put churches below the cinema and a long way below the 'community centre' in their orders of priority. And it looks as though most of the architects whose work is illustrated in *Fifty Modern Churches*, if they do not share the current unbelief, are at any rate affected by it. Their buildings are often not so much churches as cinemas with ecclesiastical trappings or lecture halls with a reredos on the wall when normally there would be a blackboard. There is too much evidence of compromise with the world – cheapness in material, devices for turning the church into a community hall for youth discussion groups, jazzy symbolism borrowed from Scandinavia, Germany and the 1925 Paris youth discussion groups, jazzy decorative devices that are not even symbolic. Such decoration and planning is a composite of arrogance and ignorance. It is an understandable reaction from slavish copying of the old, which is not to be confused with tradition. Tradition is, as A. R. Powys once wrote, 'digested experience'. Jazz-modernism is a public display of indigestion. In *Of the Atmosphere of a Church* Mr Comper neatly summarises the difference between the arrogance of jazz-modern and the humility of tradition:

The man who sets to work to design an aeroplane or a motorcar has no self-conscious strivings to express himself or his age, like the pathetic architects and artists today. His one business is to make it go and, if possible, to go one better and he would not be so mad as to think he could do this without knowing the tradition of all that went before.

The churches with which these three books are concerned are all essentially traditional in purpose – that is to say, they are buildings whose function is to unite their users with what goes on at the altar as ordained by the long custom of Anglican and Roman liturgies. Though Mr Rothenstein in his introduction to *Post-War Church Building* pays a compliment to simple old Methodist chapels, there are none illustrated in any of these books. Indeed, we may dismiss them and the homely little Unitarian, Baptist and Independent conventicles still to be seen down side turnings of provincial towns by quoting Mr Comper once more:

> There is no such thing as a Protestant church. The church is of its very nature Catholic, embracing all things. There are Protestant Meeting Houses for preaching and for praying and hymn-singing in common and they are not to be despised; but if they are more than a plain room they have become a meaningless imitation of that from which set purpose they broke away.

Mr Comper's pamphlet is, like his architecture, an inspiration. It displays learning without pedantry and an originality that has regard for tradition.

Having defined what a church is, Mr Comper plans it from the altar outwards. An architect writing in *Fifty Modern Churches* says of a building, 'the form of roofing employed played an important part in the design and planning of the church'. This sounds rather as though the architect were being dictated to by his roof material. Mr Comper, on the other hand, receives his orders from the altar. The greater part, therefore, of his pamphlet is devoted to considering the altar. Anglican or Catholic, it should, he believes, be a throne for the Reserved Sacrament. Since he built St Cyprian's, Clarence Gate, London (1903), he shows how his theories about church planning have developed. He has discarded the four-posted English altar that he first introduced at Cantley, Doncaster, in 1893 and which has been badly copied, so that it looks like a box bed, in chancels old and new all over Britain. He now favours a ciborium, which is a four-pillared permanent structure with a flat or cross-vaulted ceiling from which the Reserved Sacrament is suspended in a pyx over the high altar. He cites medieval and even eighteenth-century precedents for this plan. By shifting the high altar and its ciborium westwards of the east wall, the congregation may thus, in an aisled or transeptal church, surround the altar on four sides. There are illustrations in the pamphlet of this arrangement as he has designed it at St Andrew's Cathedral, Aberdeen, and in the churches of St Mary, Wellingborough, and St Philip, Cosham. At Wellingborough the symbolism is complete for about the gold screen is a rood of the Suffering Christ, behind it the covenanted Presence over the altar and in the East Window, crowning all, a Majestas, our Lord Enthroned.

From the altar, Mr Comper passes to the two details that he considers most important in the atmosphere of the church: colour and lighting. And colour, he holds, depends on lighting.

> When the painted glass of our churches was smashed and the gold and colour of their altars and screen destroyed, the substituted clear glass and the plain oak and marble monuments, with slight touches of heroic colour, had an effect of simple beauty not inharmonious with the *Book of Common Prayer* in its severest interpretation . . . But directly the return is made to richly decorated altars and screens, all is out of gear and it becomes of first importance that the light should be qualified.

He cites King's College Chapel, Cambridge, as a surviving example in England of original lighting and remarks that there is in it not one pane of clear, transparent glass. He is opposed, as is anyone who values texture and colour in old buildings, to electric lighting and to floodlighting in any form. The writer on church lighting in *Post-War Church Building* would not agree with him. Nor does that writer mention the secret of electric lighting in churches (if it has to be) which is, as Mr Comper says, 'to have as many lights of as low power as possible and not to hide them'. He concludes with some sound strictures on the modern practice of touching up with over-bright colours old stonework, tombs and wall paintings.

Fifty Modern Churches is a varied selection of Anglican buildings from 1930–1945. Using the yardstick of Mr Comper's pamphlet, the reader will find only about half-a-dozen churches that look as though they might bring him to his knees. But the selection is judicious and ranges from jazz through the 'genteelism' of Mr Maufe to the sound work of such men as Harold Gibbons, Dykes Bower and Sir Charles Nicholson.

Post-War Church Building consists of several unrelated papers including three knowledgeable essays by Sir Charles Nicholson, some useful information on bells by a bell-founder and a stimulating introduction by Mr John Rothenstein. But in the main this is a mere piece of bookmaking and an incumbent who does not know his own mind will find less steadying sense for the thirty shillings he pays than he will for the one-and-ninepence expended on Mr Comper. Some of the illustrations are so ugly, by any but the trashiest commercial standards, that it is hard to believe the contributors can have approved the inclusion of them.

COUNTRY CHURCHYARDS

The Country Churchman
May 1953

• • •

Five hundred years ago there were no tombs in your graveyard. Bodies were under its ground but the souls that had lived in them were remembered at the altar in church. Sometimes after service the churchyard was used for sports. On feast days church wardens provided ale from the church ale house. In many old towns and villages there is an inn overlooking the churchyard, just as the Swan does at Wantage. It is probably a survival of a church ale house.

But after the Reformation people seem to have preferred to com-memorate themselves in stone. The rich had sculptured memorials inside the church, the less rich had stones in the churchyard and the poor had to be content with men's memory.

Many old customs survive connected with churchyards. No parson, for instance, can cut down the trees in his churchyards unless they are required for the repair of the chancel; and offending rectors can be heavily fined — and once they could be excommunicated. Then it is interesting to see how the old belief that the Devil haunted the north side of the church survived until the nineteenth century; in few old churchyards are there even any eighteenth-century tombs to the north of the church and only if the village happened to be on the north side was the north door used. All our parish churches in this district,* except Ardington, West Ilsley, West Challow and Sparsholt, are entered by the south door.

The great age of tombstones did not begin until the eighteenth century. I know of no headstones in our district earlier than 1740. But there are many fine ones of the Georgian period in every churchyard of Berkshire. The older they are, the thicker the stone and the more deeply carved the devices and the lettering. It seems as though the great tradition of English craftsmanship could not be killed. Do you remember, before the brewers standardised them all, how varied and attractive village inn signs were? And have you not noticed how on the few Berkshire wagons left the farmer's name with attendant flourishes and painting is a pleasure to see? Here and there, over shops, we can still sometimes see lettering skilfully done by modern sign writers in the old tradition.

But the best specimens of all of this local art of lettering and stone sculpture are to be found in the local churchyards. I think the best in the parishes served by this publication are to be found at Shrivenham, Shellingford, Lambourn, Chaddleworth, West Hanney, the Lettcombes, Childrey, Didcot, Wantage and the Hendreds. Yet every old churchyard in the area has a few stones with grandly carved let-tering and wreaths and urns. There are none, of course, as wonderful

---

* Betjeman was writing for the parishes around Uffington.

as those in the Cotswolds, in places like Burford where stone was plentiful and people were used to carving it. But in your own church-yard you will probably find a tomb with an hourglass carved on it or a cherub with a face like a Berkshire ploughboy with solid-looking wings or the scythe of Father Time or a skull and crossbones.

Notice too the shape of the tops of these old tombs. They are never crosses or Gothic arches (these are Victorian and later) but flat tops or sometimes gently curved or with curved ears at the sides and a hump in the middle. There are also table tombs, shaped like a stone altar. These were painted and there are fine specimens in Compton Beauchamp that have recently been restored.

The inscriptions almost always face west so that the early-afternoon sun catches the lettering, showing up all its depth and intricacy. These old tombs are often more weathered and beautiful than the walls of the church itself. They are softly coloured by lichens, which give a texture of time to the old stone. They are part of the history of the place and they should not be disturbed. The way they slope in all directions, rising out of the parson's hay, is in keeping with the haphazard look of all our old villages where houses are dotted here and there and not in trim rows as in modern streets and Council estates. I think it is a pity when these tombs are taken away from their original setting and ranged along the walls of a churchyard so that the sun does not catch them as it was intended to do. And I do not think that churchyards should be planted with standard roses and made to look too trim and suburban. Scythed or mown grass and old stone are enough.

The inscriptions on these stones do not mince matters. They are not afraid to say 'died'. And sometimes they have touching poems written by the parson or the village schoolmaster.

Too many of our old churchyards are spoiled by Victorian and modern tombs in bright Italian marble or in granite – alien materi-als to this district. The letters on them are prefabricated and not carved. But our monumental masons today are fine craftsmen and if you will employ a qualified architect he can produce for you a tomb-stone of local stone carved to fit in with a country churchyard and the carving will be done by a monumental mason under his instruction.

CHURCHYARDS

Poems in the Porch
1954

● ● ●

Now when the weather starts to clear
How fresh the primrose clumps appear,
Those shining pools of springtime flower
In our churchyard. And on the tower
We see the sharp spring sunlight thrown
On all its sparkling rainwashed stone,
That tower, so built to take the light
Of sun by day and moon by night,
That centuries of weather there
Have mellowed it to twice as fair
As when it first rose new and hard
Above the sports in our churchyard.
    For churchyards then, though hallowed ground,
Were not so grim as now they sound,
And horns of ale were handed round
For which churchwardens used to pay
On each especial vestry day.
'Twas thus the village drunk its beer
With its relations buried near,
And that is why we often see
Inns where the alehouse used to be
Close to the church when prayers were said
And Masses for the village dead.
    But in these latter days we've grown
To think that the memorial stone

Is quite enough for soul and clay
Until the Resurrection day.
Perhaps it is. It's not for me
To argue on theology.
    But this I know, you're sure to find
Some headstones of the Georgian kind
In each old churchyard near and far.
Just go and see how fine they are.
Notice the lettering of that age
Spaced like a noble title-page,
The parish names cut deep and strong
To hold the shades of evening long,
The quaint and sometimes touching rhymes
By parish poets of the times,
Bellows or reaping hook or spade
To show, perhaps, the dead man's trade,
And cherubs in the corner spaces
With wings and English ploughboy faces.
    Engraved on slate or carved in stone
These Georgian headstones hold their own
With craftsmanship of earlier days
Men gave in their Creator's praise.
More homely are they than the white
Italian marbles which were quite
The rage in Good Kind Edward's reign,
With ugly lettering, hard and plain.
    Our churches are our history shown
In wood and glass and iron and stone.
I hate to see in old churchyards
Tombstones stacked round like playing cards
Along the wall which then encloses
A trim new lawn and standard roses,
Bird-baths and objects such as fill a
Garden in some suburban villa.
The Bishop comes; the bird-bath's blessed,
Our churchyard's now 'a garden of rest'.
And so it may be, all the same

Graveyard's a much more honest name.
  Oh why do people waste their breath
Inventing dainty names for death?
On the old tombstones of the past
We do not read 'At peace at last'
But simply 'died' or plain 'departed'.
It's no good being chicken-hearted.
We die; that's that; our flesh decays
Or disappears in other ways.
But since we're Christians, we believe
That we new bodies will receive
To clothe our souls for us to meet
Our Maker at his Judgement Seat.
And this belief's a gift of faith
And, if it's true, no end is death.
  Mid-Lent is passed and Easter's near
The greatest day of all the year
When Jesus, who indeed had died,
Rose with his body glorified.
And if you find believing hard
The primroses in your churchyard
And modern science too will show
That all things change the while they grow,
And we, who change in Time will be
Still more changed in Eternity.

THE LIGHTING OF CHURCHES

The Country Churchman
July 1953

• • •

There are few things more beautiful than a candle-lit church and few things in modern England that are rarer. The supreme example is King's College Chapel, Cambridge. I know no more wonderful sight than to enter that chapel on an autumn evening when the time of Evensong synchronises with the end of day. The colours of the great stained-glass windows that line the walls fade away, the huge stone-vaulted roof disappears in misty darkness and warm and golden around us glow the candles, burnishing the white surplices of the choir. As the darkness grows the candles seem to burn brighter until dimly discerned high above us may be seen the vaulted roof, looking even more intricate and impressive than it does by daylight.

Oh it's all very well for you to rhapsodise about King's College Chapel, Mr Betjeman, but this isn't such a place. This is our parish church and we haven't got anyone to go messing around clearing up candle grease. We can't even keep the oil lamps trimmed as I remember seeing them done when I was a boy.

Ah, I'm glad you've still got oil lamps. Candles look best in an old church, of course – but next to them, oil lamps. The light is not too bright and suits the old walls and woodwork. Besides that, oil lamps help to warm a church.

Well you can come and clean 'em then. Nobody else will. That's why we're having the electric.

And I suppose the electricity board has sent a man along who has advised floodlights in the roof, floodlights in the chancel and a strip-light on the pulpit desk and lectern. You'll come into the church when it's all finished and as you come up the churchyard path you'll say to yourself, 'Hello, the Vicar's had the church connected to the telephone exchange,'* for there, clamped mercilessly into the old stonework of the tower, will be an iron thing with thick wires stretching to the nearest pole. Then when you go into the church you will see prom-inently placed on one of those old walls a switchbox, an array of meters† and yards of electric cable. Then when you've inspected that hideous mass, which no one would tolerate in their own best room but which is thought quite good enough for what ought to be the best room in the village – God's house, where you and your ancestors have worshipped for generations – when you've inspected that, I say, you'll go up the nave to see the other improvements. You'll look up at that glorious old roof and you'll see it has been stuck with huge pudding basins‡ with bulbs in the middle of them. You'll go into the chancel and you'll see more pudding basins there.

Ah, but you're talking about daytime. What about the night? We want to be able to see to read.

Well, first of all, a church is seen more in the daytime than at night – or it ought to be. But let's look at this precious night effect. You switch on the light and the church looks bare, cold, flat and half its size. The walls, whose patched and old appearance looks so well in daylight or in candlelight, are here submitted to a hard glare so that they merely look mean and dirty. You look up to the roof and your eyes are dazzled by a fearsomely powerful bulb burning goodness knows how much current. You look at the chancel and it seems small and tawdry and much meaner. How infinitely more restful to the eyes, more dignified and more mysterious was the altar when it was in comparative darkness except for the lit candles on it. The Vicar

---

* Betjeman's original form of wording – 'the Vicar's had the church put on the tele-phone' – is no longer immediately clear today.

† 'Metres', originally.

‡ Betjeman changed this from 'surgical basins'.

switches on the striplight on the pulpit desk and he looks like Grock, the French clown – to quote Frederick Etchells, the great architect. His chin – a bit bristly by the end of the day – is shown in all its unshavenness; the end of his nose is lit, and his eyebrows. The effect is heightened as the verger goes to the door and switches off all but the pulpit lights so that we may enjoy the Vicar's face during the sermon. And what will happen if one of those bulbs in the roof fuses? You will have to get a very long ladder to reach it and it will be an expensive bulb to replace. You have ruined the look of the church by over-lighting it, you have let yourself in for an enormous electricity bill and you have taken all the mystery and ancientness out of the church and made it look like a floodlit mausoleum.

Since you think you know such a lot about it, Mr Betjeman, what do you suggest? Go back to candles, I suppose, or farthing dips?

Please don't be angry. I won't suggest anything as old-fashioned and sensible as that. I know everyone is too busy now to look after an old church. But if you want to see how beautiful candles look, go to Evensong at Chislehampton near Oxford or at Tubney, if it is still being used.

But let us suppose you *must* have electric light, remember this first: the object of most electricians is to eliminate shadows; the whole point of an old church is that it must be *full* of shadows. That's what all those mouldings round the windows and arches and pillars are for. As soon as lights are hung or fixed at regular intervals along each wall or by every arch, the shadows are eliminated. Lights must be placed at irregular intervals so that you *will* have shadows. The electrician will think you are mad for suggesting such a thing. Next, the purpose of the light is not that you should see every crack in the wall and every bat hanging on a rafter but that you should be able to read your prayer book and hymn book; also that it should not dazzle you when you look up. That's why candles are best. But you can fit low-powered electric light bulbs (15–25 watts), which give plenty of light if there are enough of them and they are hung low. Few churches in any diocese have them.* Most electrically lit churches

---

* Originally: 'I know no church in the diocese which has them.'

have either pudding basins fixed in the roof or else regular rows of pendants with glass shades that remind one of a Government office or a bank.

The electrician will tell you that he will make your church at night look as though it were daylight. Even if he could accomplish this impossible feat, what would be the point – when you have two aspects of a church: a daytime one and a night-time one – to try and make them look the same at great expense? Artificial light can make even an ugly building beautiful. It can do wonders in the way of creating mystery and yet give plenty of light to read by in an old church.

These are the three best ways of lighting an old church with electricity:

(i) by having a great many lights of low power placed not at regular intervals but here and there where they are needed in the church. Fifteen-watt bulbs need not be shaded; they will look well hung above the pews in coronals of iron rings and they do not dazzle the eye.

(ii) by shading average-powered bulbs with a close-fitting opaque black shade, white inside, so that the light is cast downwards. In small churches and aisles, these can be hung from iron brackets on the walls.

(iii) by keeping the oil lamps intact and removing only the chimneys; and hanging bulbs in place of these chimneys. The light can be made less cold and bright by a thin coating of yellow paint on the bulb; watercolour and poster paint stick to most bulbs.

And the two general rules are:

(1) Get electric light of as low power as is practicable, hung as low down as possible.

(2) Call in an architect to direct the electrician. The architect will save you money in the end for he will want to do his best for the building; the electrician will want you to burn as much electricity as possible.

371

ELECTRIC LIGHT AND HEATING

Poems in the Porch
1954

. . .

Alternately the fogs and rains
Fill up the dim November lanes,
The church's year is nearly done
And waiting Advent not begun,
Our congregations shrink and shrink;
We sneeze so much we cannot think.
We blow our noses through the prayers,
And coughing takes us unawares;
We think of funerals and shrouds.
Our breath comes out in steamy clouds
Because the heating, we are told,
Will not be used until it's cold.
With aching limbs and throbbing head
We wish we were at home in bed.
　　Oh! brave November congregation
Accept these lines of commendation;
You are the Church's prop and wall,
You keep it standing for us all!
　　And now I'll turn to things more bright.
I'll talk about electric light.
Last year when Mr Sidney Groves
Said he'd no longer do the stoves
It gave the chance to Mrs Camps
To say she would not do the lamps,
And that gave everyone the chance

To cry, 'Well, let us have a dance!'
And so we did, we danced and danced
Until our funds were so advanced
That, helped by jumble sales and whist,
We felt that we could now insist
– So healthy was the cash position –
On calling in the electrician.
We called him in, and now, behold,
Our church is overlit and cold.
We have two hundred more to pay
Or go to gaol next Quarter Day.

Despite the most impressive prices
Of our electrical devices,
And though the Bishop blessed the switches
Which now deface two ancient niches,
We do not like the electric light,
It's far too hard and bare and bright.
As for the heat, the bills are hot.
Unluckily the heating's not.

They fell'd our elms to bring the wire,
They clamped their brackets on the spire
So that the church, one has to own,
Seems to be on the telephone.
Inside, they used our timbered roof,
Five centuries old and weather proof,
For part of their floodlighting scheme,
With surgical basins on each beam.
And if the bulbs in them should fuse
Or burst in fragments on the pews,
The longest ladder we possess
Would not reach up to mend the mess.
Talking of messes – you should see
The Electrician's artistry,
His Clapham-Junction-like creation
Of pipes and wires and insulation,
Of meters, boxes, tubes and all
Upon our ancient painted wall.

If Sidney Groves and Mrs Camps
Had only done the stoves and lamps
These shameful things we would not see
Which rob our church of mystery.

23

CLERGY

Dog Collars and Dogcarts

HOW DO THE CLERGY LIVE?

Evening Standard
13 November 1934

• • •

How well I remember staying at the rectory in the days of my youth. There was the journey on the branch line from the Junction, my friend the rector's dogcart in the quiet evening, the imposing front gate, the gravel drive between the rhododendrons, the large fire in the hall, the Morris wallpapers in the bedrooms, the long walk down carpeted passages to the bathroom, fourteen candles in silver sconces on the dinner table.

I went to that same rectory early this year. Another incumbent had taken the place of my friend. A hired taxi met me at the station, the front gate was broken and weeds covered the gravel drive. There was no fire in the hall; patches of damp showed through the wallpaper. I leapt from island to island of rush matting, trod barefooted in my bedroom to the brass can on the wash-hand stand. One lamp was on the dinner table and we had corned beef followed by tinned apricots. And it wasn't that the present incumbent of this vast Huntingdon rectory is inhospitable or mean. He has to keep up a house with eight bedrooms, a large garden, a wife and two children on £400 a year.

Nor is his the worst case. There are still eighty English livings worth less than £201 a year. Over a thousand are worth £300 a year and less. Over two thousand are worth between £300 and £350.

In some cases, outside grants or private means help the incumbents. I am not suggesting that the clergy should be rich: indeed, there has been a recent correspondence in the *Church Times* suggesting that the clergy should earn no more than the working man. But in that case they should be allowed to live as working men, in houses of reasonable size. At Corringham in Essex, the parsonage house has twenty bedrooms, no gas or electric light and the wages of a gardener and his assistant come to £2 15s a week. The living is worth £400 a year and is at present vacant. So, I should think, it will long remain. The parish of Wigan has a rectory with twenty-six bedrooms. It was once the pride of the town that the rector kept a coach and four and that there was always a horse waiting at the lodge gates for any of the curates who might be called off to distant parts of the parish. Even on £1,106 a year it was hard to keep up such state. Now, in a densely populated town requiring many curates, the income is totally inadequate.

These enormous parsonages are relics of the days when far more people had private means than have them now. They are relics of the days when the youngest son went into the Church as his brothers went into the Services. The 'fatter' the living and the less work, the better it was. In those days Settrington, in Yorkshire, was a living worth having, for it was worth £1,106 a year and there were only 600-odd inhabitants to minister to. Now, perhaps, the rector is not in such an enviable position. The parish is no bigger but the rectory is too big. It has twenty-one rooms, three staircases, a drawing-room 30 feet long and stabling for eleven horses.

Non-payment of tithes has not made things easier. Just over two months ago, in a South of England parish where there had been considerable tithe agitation, the Vicar dropped dead on his way back from church. Medical examination proved that he had died of exhaustion brought on through lack of food.

In 1933 after a hot debate on a subject that hardly seems debatable in a Christian collection of people, the Church Assembly appointed a Joint Committee to inquire into this question of unwieldy parsonages. Three people represented the Ecclesiastical Commission – rich landowners of church property – and three people represented the Governors of Queen Anne's Bounty, who have several hundred thousand pounds to play about with. The report of that committee has just been published. It says, in effect, that nothing can be done. Incumbents are allowed to sell their parsonages if they are too large for their incomes – but no one will buy them.

Some clergymen take in backward boys as pupils but in doing so they neglect their duty towards the parish.

The usual solution is for the incumbent to live in one or two rooms only but he is not allowed to let the rest of the house fall down. He tries to get money from the Dilapidations Board of his diocese to keep his house in repair. This is not always easy.

One solution has escaped the notice of the committee altogether. There are over fifty livings worth more than a thousand a year where the parishes have under a thousand inhabitants. The rector of Stainsby-with-Gunby, for instance, has £2,376 net income a year. The inhabitants of Stainsby-with-Gunby number 216. Two-thirds of the rector's income might help several starving clergy. The town of March, a decayed little place where one waits for hours if travelling by train in East Anglia, has about 10,000 inhabitants, many of them dissenters. The four churches in the town have livings worth, when added together, just under £5,000 a year net. Each living is worth over a thousand. Meanwhile the parish of Sparkhill in Birmingham has 24,000 inhabitants and the living is worth £600-odd a year.

There is certainly the money in the Church of England for helping in the upkeep and improvement, for selling purposes, of the many large parsonages that encumber poverty-stricken incumbents. But the money is unevenly distributed.

There are many comic anomalies in the Church of England like the rich Deans of Peculiars and the poor Dean of Arches. But the anomaly of large parsonages is hardly comic.

EXCHANGE OF LIVINGS

Continual Dew: A Little Book of Bourgeois Verse
1937

• • •

The church was locked, so I went to the incumbent –
   the incumbent enjoying a supine incumbency –
a tennis court, a summerhouse, deckchairs by the walnut tree
and only the hum of the bees in the rockery.
'May I have the keys of the church, your incumbency?'
'Yes, my dear sir, as a moderate churchman,
I am willing to exchange: light Sunday duty:
          nice district: pop 149: eight hundred per annum:
no extremes: A and M: bicyclist essential:
                  same income expected.'
'I think I'm the man that you want, your incumbency.
Here's my address when I'm not on my bicycle,
          poking about for recumbent stone effigies –
14, Mount Ephraim, Cheltenham, Glos:
Rector St George-in-the-Rolling Pins, Cripplegate:
non-resident pop in the City of London:
eight fifty per annum (but verger an asset):
willing to exchange (no extremes) for incumbency,
similar income, but closer to residence.'

TEN MEN TELL US WHAT TO SING

Daily Herald
31 March 1950

•   •   •

Parsons will look with dismay at the alterations in numbering in the new edition of *Hymns Ancient and Modern*, cut by 143, which will be published on Monday. So many famous hymns have different numbers in the new book that a church wishing to use it will probably have to buy copies for all the congregation as well as for the organist.

These famous hymns have been cut altogether: 'Sweet the Moment Rich in Blessing', 'The Roseate Hues of Early Dawn', 'There is a Blessed Home', 'O Paradise, O Paradise', 'I was a Wandering Sheep', 'The Voice that Breathed o'er Eden', 'Forward be our Watchword', 'We are Soldiers of Christ', 'Hushed was the Evening Hymn', 'Once to Every Man and Nation', 'On the Resurrection Morning', 'Praise to our God Whose Bounteous Hand', 'Saviour, Blessed Saviour', 'We are but Little Children Weak'.

The new editors seem to dislike too much mention of death and the following have also been omitted: 'A Few More Years Shall Roll', 'Days and Moments Quickly Flying', 'Safely, Safely Gathered In', 'When our Heads are Bowed in Woe'.

The gay vulgarity of mission services has been rationed and 'There was Joy in Heaven', 'Rescue the Perishing' and 'Beneath the Cross of Jesus' have gone.

Some simple teaching hymns have also disappeared, among them 'There is a Fountain Filled with Blood', 'I was Made a Christian' and 'I Lay my Sins on Jesus'. On the other hand Newman's famous statement of belief 'Firmly I Believe and Truly' is a newcomer.

Musical editors Mr Gerald Knight, organist at Canterbury, and Dr J. Dykes Bower, of St Paul's, who assisted Sir Sydney Nicholson until he died two years ago, have let in some famous Welsh tunes: 'All Through the Night', 'Hyfrydol', 'Cwm Rhondda' and 'Llanfair'. English words ('Guide me, O Thou Great Redeemer') are provided for 'Cwm Rhondda', which was composed in 1907 by John Hughes and 'God, that Madest Earth and Heaven' for 'All Through the Night'.

Other famous hymns admitted to the chosen 600 are Blake's 'Jerusalem' – now almost the second National Anthem – and Holst's settings of 'In the Bleak Midwinter' and 'I Vow to Thee my Country'.

Hymns Ancient and Modern, which is published by William Clowes, is administered by five trustees and the profits, after certain deductions, go to charity. It was first compiled in 1861. Exactly how the final inclusions and exclusions were made by the anonymous trustees and their five chosen assessors is not indicated – probably on a show of hands. But the final responsibility lay on the trustees and there is no appeal from their decision.

THE PERSECUTION OF COUNTRY CLERGY

Time and Tide
17 March 1951

• • •

Townspeople do not know of the persecution that the English country clergy endure, at any rate south of the Trent. And some villages may not be as uncharitable to their parsons as others. Most villages have one faithful family and perhaps two or three people of true humility, ready to put up with the parson. Yet I will be surprised if at least a few of the circumstances I am about to describe do not exist in every English village.

We hear much about how bad the worldly portion of country clergymen is, how vast their rectories, how inadequate their income to the social position expected of them. Their spiritual plight is often far worse.

Let us imagine a parson, young or old, coming with perfectly definite views, Catholic or Evangelical, to an English village. Let him be a man with a real love of souls, courageously uncompromising about Truth and not prepared to water it down to suit the consciences of his flock on the off-chance of filling an empty pew.

Let us imagine a village of the usual modern structure: the large house a ruin or a Government office, the late squire's unmarried daughter living in a cottage, two or three immensely prosperous farmers, a few weekenders, a few farm workers to drive tractors, a bus collecting most able-bodied people to a factory outside the nearest town, a bus collecting the men, women and children to the cinema once or twice a week in the evening. Other nights are occupied by dances and whist drives. The rulers of the village are the innkeeper at one end and the schoolteacher at the other. The farmers live their own lives among other farmers' families. Their womenfolk take only a sporadic interest in the Women's Institute, which is run by a schoolmistress or the squire's daughter (rarely by both) for the wives of the farm workers. The young men and the young girls think they are film stars and talk with American accents, go away on bicycles and buses every evening or else play together in the social club.

The wireless is on in every cottage as the remover's van arrives at the parsonage. Curtains are drawn aside, invalids peep with malevolent eyes from leaded windows, gossips lean on gates, young men and old happen to be casually walking by. What will the new parson be like?

On that first Sunday his church, for the first and last time of his incumbency, will be nearly full.

After the service the village will be agreed upon one point only – that his predecessor was much better. Some will think him too 'high', others too 'low'. What most of them will mean is that he is different from the man before. Villagers are notoriously ignorant of theology but conservative about ritual.

The people who may continue to go to church are the following. The late squire's daughter because of Church and State and her late father's views – but woe betide the parson if he tries to change anything or teach anything except vague morality. This will mean that no Labour people will go – that is to say, no farm workers because going to church means you are Conservative. The bell-ringers may continue because of the pleasure of ringing and because they admire Winston Churchill. The schoolmistress will not go, even if it is a church school she is teaching in, because, being semi-educated and class conscious, she has 'theories' about religion and regards the parson as too dogmatic. She will attempt to disaffect the children and their mothers. A young girl and her friend will go for a week or two because she has fallen in love with the new parson. The innkeeper will not go because if he is to please his employers the brewers, he must not seem to take sides. The farmers will not go except at Harvest Festival because the collections are for the Farmers' Benevolent, the only charity they allow themselves to notice. Everyone feels there is no need to please any landlord any more. The village is independent, materialistic and, like all villages, a bit out of date compared with the towns where people are coming back to church.

Except the 'prog' weekenders, now rather elderly, who take the *New Statesman*, all villagers will use the church, of course, for baptisms and burials; the Register Office is becoming increasingly popular for village weddings. The parson may think this use of the church is a sign that his people are Christian at heart. More probably it is a sign that they are superstitious, in the way we are about walking under a ladder.

If he is prepared to have a breezy word for everyone, give liberally of his small stipend to all funds and do a great many secretarial and transport and listening jobs for free, his fence will not be pulled down, the church may sometimes be cleaned (for a fee) and he and his family will be tolerated.

But if he teaches religion, if he attempts to be definite, if he admonishes and exhorts, if he really loves God and his neighbours fearlessly, he will be despised and rejected, when not actually mocked. Scandals will be spread about him and the witch-like malice of the self-righteous will fall upon him. The pride of the semi-educated, the anger of the greedy farmer, will flourish in village sloth. 'Many country people think there is something in all this religion,' as Samuel Gurney says, 'and they aren't going to have anything to do with it.' The country parson's cross is heavy with their apathy and sharp with their hate. He sees his failure round him every day. Only the very few help him to bear it. Small wonder if sometimes he falls.

BLAME THE VICAR

Poems in the Porch
1954

• • •

When things go wrong it's rather tame
To find we are ourselves to blame,
It gets the trouble over quicker
To go and blame things on the Vicar.
The Vicar, after all, is paid
To keep us bright and undismayed.
The Vicar is more virtuous too
Than lay folks such as me and you.
He never swears, he never drinks,
He never *should* say what he thinks.
His collar is the wrong way round,
And that is why he's simply bound
To be the sort of person who
Has nothing very much to do

But take the blame for what goes wrong
And sing in tune at Evensong.
   For what's a Vicar really for
Except to cheer us up? What's more,
He shouldn't ever, ever tell
If there is such a place as Hell,
For if there is it's certain he
Will go to it as well as we.
The Vicar should be all pretence
And never, ever give offence.
To preach on Sunday is his task
And lend his mower when we ask
And organise our village fêtes
And sing at Christmas with the waits
And in his car to give us lifts
And when we quarrel, heal the rifts.
To keep his family alive
He should industriously strive
In that enormous house he gets,
And he should always pay his debts,
For he has quite six pounds a week,
And when we're rude he should be meek
And always turn the other cheek.
He should be neat and nicely dressed
With polished shoes and trousers pressed,
For we look up to him as higher
Than anyone, except the Squire.

   Dear People, who have read so far,
I know how really kind you are,
I hope that you are always seeing
Your Vicar as a human being,
Making allowances when he
Does things with which you don't agree.
But there are lots of people who
Are not so kind to him as you.
So in conclusion you shall hear

About a parish somewhere near,
Perhaps your own or maybe not,
And of the Vicars that it got.
    One parson came and people said,
'Alas! Our former Vicar's dead!
And this new man is far more "Low"
Than dear old Reverend So-and-So,
And far too earnest in his preaching,
We do not really like his teaching,
He seems to think we're simply fools
Who've never been to Sunday Schools.'
That Vicar left, and by and by
A new one came. 'He's much too "High",'
The people said, 'too like a saint;
His incense makes our Mavis faint.'
So now he's left and they're alone
Without a Vicar of their own.
The living's been amalgamated
With one next door they've always hated.

    Dear readers, from this rhyme take warning,
And if you heard the bell this morning
Your Vicar went to pray for you,
A task the Prayer Book bids him do.
'Highness' and 'Lowness' do not matter,
You are the Church and must not scatter.
Cling to the Sacraments and pray
And God be with you every day.

24
POETRY
Wordsworth and Wordsongs

Rhyme and Rhythm (1947)
William Lisle Bowles (1946)
On 'A Few Late Chrysanthemums' (1954)

RHYME AND RHYTHM

From the series 'Time for Verse'

BBC Home Service
26 January 1947
Producer: Patric Dickinson

• • •

When I was first able to read, I preferred poetry to prose. I still enjoy it. The reason for that early enjoyment was the discovery of rhythm and rhyme. I did not know what the words meant and I did not care. But I would chant out poetry to whoever would listen. My mother remembers finding me sitting outside the pantry at home reading *Moore's Irish Melodies* to the cook who was occupied within.

I do not indulge in this autobiography to instance my early precocity. I mention it because the appeal of poetry to most of us, in childhood, is in its rhyme and rhythm. If it has not these, why not write the stuff in prose? For most of us, rhythm and rhyme are still the main appeal of poetry. Tonight I wish to instance a few examples of the wonderful flexibility of the English language, the amazing varieties of metre and sound, rhythm and rhyme, whatever you like to call them, that the poets of the past managed to fathom.

There is nothing technical or difficult about English rhythm and rhyme. All you have to do is listen. Anyone with an ear will be able to appreciate the extracts I will quote.

I think the popular English love of poetry was very largely due to its rhythm. That interest today has been diverted by the obscurity and lack of metre in most modern poetry to an interest in dance music. Take an obvious example of rhyme and metre: a verse from Poe's poem 'The Raven':

> Ah, distinctly I remember it was in the bleak December,
> And each separate dying ember wrought its ghost upon the floor.
>   Eagerly I wished the morrow; – vainly I had sought to borrow
>   From my books surcease of sorrow – sorrow for the lost Lenore –
> For the rare and radiant maiden whom the angels named Lenore –
>   Nameless here for evermore.

Notice that the strangeness is caught by the strange metre, the lonely hollowness by the long-sounding words

> wrought its ghost upon the floor

and the general dreariness is relieved by a line of alliteration and internal repetition of the sound 'ay':

> For the rare and radiant maiden whom the angels named Lenore.

You will find in that marvellous poem 'The Raven' no unusual adjectives, no startling sentences. The effect is all powered by rhyme, alliteration and rhythm.

But now let us go back to my early love Tom Moore. He was probably the first great metricist of our language. He infused into it strange rhythms that had never been heard before, some of which have never since been successfully copied. Take his poem 'At the Mid Hour of Night'. Remember these are words of a song designed for a harp accompaniment and the tinkling of an early piano in some late-Georgian drawing-room with candlelight shining on plasterwork and a wide ghost-haunted Irish park outside. These words seem to me to have a plucked sound like the swooping of a harp and they die away into the desolate Irish dark.

> At the mid hour of night, when stars are weeping, I fly
> To the lone vale we lov'd, when life shone warm in thine eye;
>   And I think oft, if spirits can steal from the regions of air
>   To revisit past scenes of delight, thou wilt come to me there,
> And tell me our love is remember'd, even in the sky.
>
> Then I sing the wild song 'twas once such rapture to hear!
> When our voices commingling breath'd, like one, on the ear;
>   And, as Echo far off through the vale my sad orison rolls,

I think, oh my love! 'tis thy voice from the Kingdom of Souls,
  Faintly answering still the notes that once were so dear.

Tom Moore is thought to have adapted ancient Irish metres. He did not. He invented his own. Gaelic poetry, like Anglo-Saxon, did not have rhymes at the end of the lines but internal repetition of sounds and alliteration. For instance, 'spacious' is a good enough rhyme for 'ancient'. The 'hedge-poetry' of late-Georgian Ireland is really Gaelic rhyme and rhythm in English. Here is a comic poem about the town of Passage near Cork, written in Gaelic style:

> Oh Passage Town
> Is of great renown
> For we go down
>   In our buggies there
> On a Sunday morning
> All danger scorning
> To get a corning
>   At sweet Passage fair . . .
>
> There's a patent slipping
> And dock for shipping
> And whale-boats skipping
>   Upon the tide
> There ships galore is
> And love before us
> With Carrigaloo
>   On the other side.
> 'Tis there's the hulk that's
> Well stored with convicts
> Who were never upon decks
>   Till they went to sea
> They'll ne'er touch dry land
> Nor rocky island
> Until they spy land
>   At sweet Botany Bay.
> Here's success to
> This foreign station

Where American ships
   Without horses ride
And Portugeses
From every nation
Comes in rotations
   Upon the tide.
But not forgetting
Haulbowline island
That was constructed
   By Mrs Deane
Herself's the lady
That has stowed the water
To supply the vessels
   Upon the main
And these bold sons of Neptune
I mean the boatmen
Will ferry you over
   From Cove to Spike
And outside the harbour
Are fishers sporting
Watching a nibble
   From a sprat or pike
While their wives and daughters
From no danger shrinking
All night and morning
   They rove about
The mud and sandbanks
For the periwinkle
The shrimp and winkle
   When the tide is out.

That poem is like a crude inn-sign board. Vivid and alive. It's a last relic of the poetic metre of the great Gaelic bards. You will see there is no resemblance between this and yet one more of Tom Moore's strange new metres that I will quote. It's called 'The Irish Peasant to his Mistress'.

Through grief and through danger thy smile hath cheer'd my way,
Till hope seem'd to bud from each thorn that round me lay;
The darker our fortune, the brighter our pure love burn'd,
Till shame into glory, till fear into zeal was turn'd;
Yes, slave as I was, in thy arms my spirit felt free,
And bless'd even the sorrows that made me more dear to thee.

Thy rival was honour'd, while thou wert wrong'd and scorn'd;
Thy crown was of briers, while gold her brows adorn'd;
She woo'd me to temples, whilst thou lay'st hid in caves;
Her friends were all masters, while thine, alas! were slaves;
Yet cold in the earth, at thy feet, I would rather be
Than wed what I loved not, or turn one thought from thee.

They slander thee sorely, who say thy vows are frail –
Hadst thou been a false one, thy cheek had look'd less pale!
They say, too, so long thou hast worn those lingering chains,
That deep in thy heart they have printed their servile stains:
O, foul is the slander! – no chain could that soul subdue –
Where shineth thy spirit, there Liberty shineth too!

One more example of this wailing Irish plaint poetry: it was
written by that unhappy man James Clarence Mangan, who died
comparatively young in 1849. It's called 'O'Hussey's Ode to the
Maguire' and purports to be a translation – a free one, I may add –
of a seventeenth-century Irish poet's lament for a chieftain who had
gone on a dangerous winter expedition. The metre is all Mangan's
own and it has in it something so un-English and suits a wail of bag-
pipes and rush of rain that one can hardly believe it was written in
the English language at all. Here are the opening stanzas:

Where is my chief, my master, this bleak night, mavrone?
    O cold, cold, miserably cold is this bleak night for Hugh!
    Its showery, arrowy, speary sleet pierceth one thro' and thro' –
Pierceth one to the very bone.

Rolls real thunder? Or was that red vivid light
    Only a meteor? I scarce know; but through the midnight dim
    The pitiless ice-wind streams. Except the hate that persecutes
                                                        him,

Nothing hath crueller venomy might.

An awful, a tremendous night is this, meseems!
   The flood-gates of the rivers of heaven, I think, have been
                                         burst wide;
   Down from the overcharged clouds, like to headlong ocean's
                                         tide,
Descends grey rain in roaring streams.

Tho' he were even a wolf ranging the round green woods,
   Tho' he were even a pleasant salmon in the unchainable sea,
   Tho' he were a wild mountain eagle, he could scarce bear, he,
This sharp sore sleet, these howling floods . . .

Do you see how, by the use of rhythm and alliteration, Mangan has turned the English language into Irish? Now hear how, by the same tokens, Thomas Hood can turn conversational cockney into poetry. He has used a bumpy long line like the raid patter of a music-hall comedian and he has breathed into it the spirit of semi-rural Middlesex and Essex a century ago when there were still little villages with goose-ponds, weather-boarded barns with red-tiled roofs, elms, oaks and dairy farms and the smoke of London rising round St Paul's dome three miles off in the valley below. It is called 'Our Village – by a Villager'.

Our village, that's to say not Miss Mitford's village, but our
                                village of Bullock Smithy,
Is come into by an avenue of trees, three oak pollards, two elders
                                and a withy;
And in the middle, there's a green of about not exceeding an acre
                                and a half;
It's common to all, and fed off by nineteen cows, six ponies,
                three horses, five asses, two foals, seven pigs, and a calf!
Besides a pond in the middle, as is held by a similar sort of
                          common law lease,
And contains twenty ducks, six drakes, three ganders, two dead
                dogs, four drown'd kittens, and twelve geese.
Of course the green's crept very close, and does famous for
             bowling when the little village boys play at cricket;

Only some horse, or pig, or cow, or great jackass, is sure to come
                              and stand right before the wicket.
There's fifty-five private houses, let alone barns and workshops,
                    and pigstyes, and poultry huts, and such-like sheds;
With plenty of public-houses – two Foxes, one Green Man, three
              Bunch of Grapes, one Crown, and six King's Heads . . .

Thus, simply by the use of rhythm, can English poetry sound like a banshee's wail or music-hall patter.

The greatest time for experiment in rhyming and metre in English poetry was the nineteenth century – greater even than the Elizabethan. William Barnes, a Dorset clergyman, was fascinated by rhyme and metre. He learned Persian, Anglo-Saxon and many more languages and was always trying to adapt the poetic tricks of the languages he learned to English verse. Barnes is a true poet, little read now because he usually chose to write his poetry in Dorset dialect (very correctly spelled out in phonetics) and we do not like dialect poetry today because we are all becoming so refined in our talk. So here is one of his poems in plain English. It's not his best but it has the most elaborate internal rhyming and alliteration of any poem I know – tricks he learned from Persia and Ireland. It is called 'Lowshot Light'.

As I went eastward ere the sun had set,
His yellow light on bough by bough was bright.

And then, by buttercups beside the hill,
Below the elm trees, cow by cow, was bright.

While, after heavy-headed horses' heels,
With slowly-rolling wheels, the plough was bright.

And up among the people, on the sides,
One lovely face, with sunny brow was bright.

And aye, for that one face, the bough and cow
And plough, in my sweet journey, now are bright.

That is what you can do with rhyme. There is also metre. Swinburne revelled in metre and he was never better than when describing a sparkling summer sea from the cliffs of Cornwall or the South Coast. Meaning does not matter so much in his poems. Here is a tumbling poem of his that by metre and alliteration suggests the sound of Homer: the breakers racing in on one another and the sun making sunbows in the spray blown back from roaring wave-crests.

Spray of song that springs in April, light of love that laughs
through May,
Live and die and live for ever: nought of all things far less fair
Keeps a surer life than these that seem to pass like fire away.
In the souls they live which are but all the brighter that they were;
In the hearts that kindle, thinking what delight of old was there.
Wind that shapes and lifts and shifts them bids perpetual memory
play
Over dreams and in and out of deeds and thoughts which seem to
wear
Light that leaps and runs and revels through the springing flames
of spray.

Dawn is wild upon the waters where we drink of dawn today:
Wide, from wave to wave rekindling in rebound through radiant
air,
Flash the fires unwoven and woven again of wind that works in
play,
Working wonders more than heart may note or sight may
wellnigh dare,
Wefts of rarer light than colours rain from heaven, though this be
rare,
Arch on arch unbuilt in building, reared and ruined ray by ray,
Breaks and brightens, laughs and lessens, even till eyes may hardly
bear
Light that leaps and runs and revels through the springing flames
of spray.

Year on year sheds light and music rolled and flashed from bay to
bay
Round the summer capes of time and winter headlands keen and
bare

Whence the soul keeps watch, and bids her vassal memory watch
                                     and pray,
If perchance the dawn may quicken, or perchance the midnight
                                     spare.
Silence quells not music, darkness takes not sunlight in her snare;
Shall not joys endure that perish? Yes, saith dawn, though night
                                     say nay:
Life on life goes out, but very life enkindles everywhere
Light that leaps and runs and revels through the springing flames
                                     of spray.

Friend, were life no more than this is, well would yet the living
                                     fare.
All aflower and all afire and all flung heavenward, who shall say
Such a flash of life were worthless? This is worth a world of care –
Light that leaps and runs and revels through the springing flames
                                     of spray.

Finally, there are the two great Victorian poets Browning and Tennyson. Tennyson said, fairly if rather cattily, of Browning, 'If the pronunciation of the English language were forgotten, Browning would be considered our greatest poet.' Certainly Browning wrote some hideous lines. Nothing quite as ugly as that with which the usually beautiful poet Matthew Arnold opens a sonnet –

     Who prop, thou ask'st, in these bad days, my mind?

'Thou ask'st'! I ask you! No, Browning was never as bad as that and sometimes his metre and rhythm are as lovely as they were original.

          Was the site once of a city great and gay
             (So they say)
          Of our country's very capital, its prince
             Ages since
          Held his court in, gathered councils, wielding far
             Peace or war.

The greatest Victorian poet and, for me, the greatest English poet who ever lived was Tennyson. He was a master craftsman. So delicate is his ear for words and rhythm that he can do anything he likes with our wonderful language – no straining after effect, no obscurity, never too sugary. My final selection is that lyric of Tennyson's from *The Princess* called 'Tears, Idle Tears'. It was the favourite poem of Edgar Allan Poe, himself a master of rhyme and metre. And what is so remarkable about this lyric is that if you look at it just as grammar and syllables, you'll see it's no more than simple ten-syllabled blank verse. Yet as you listen to it, I'll swear you think it rhymes and has some metre and collects into itself all the experiments in rhythm and alliteration you have heard in this talk. It is the simplicity of the perfect circle. Only a man who knows all rhythms could come back to such profound simplicity as this.

> Tears, idle tears, I know not what they mean,
> Tears from the depth of some divine despair
> Rise in the heart, and gather to the eyes,
> In looking on the happy Autumn-fields,
> And thinking of the days that are no more.
>
> Fresh as the first beam glittering on a sail,
> That brings our friends up from the underworld,
> Sad as the last which reddens over one
> That sinks with all we love below the verge;
> So sad, so fresh, the days that are no more.
>
> Ah, sad and strange as in dark summer dawns
> The earliest pipe of half-awaken'd birds
> To dying ears, when unto dying eyes
> The casement slowly grows a glimmering square;
> So sad, so strange, the days that are no more.
>
> Dear as remember'd kisses after death,
> And sweet as those by hopeless fancy feign'd
> On lips that are for others; deep as love,
> Deep as first love, and wild with all regret;
> O Death in Life, the days that are no more.

WILLIAM LISLE BOWLES

Eighth in the series 'Literature in the West'

BBC West of England Home Service
17 February 1946
Producer: Unknown

• • •

'My poetical style has been much *meliorated* by Bowles,' said Coleridge. The word 'meliorated' is strange enough but the thought that Coleridge's poetry can have been made better by someone called Bowles must seem stranger still. I wonder how many people who have heard of Coleridge have even heard of Bowles, let alone read him. I regard it as no merit in myself, rather I consider it a weakness that I have no difficulty in reading forgotten English poetry, so I have read all the volumes of Bowles's poetry including long epics about South America, the grave of the Last Saxon, St John of Patmos: they are as easy and pleasurable to me as are detective stories to the more balanced modern reader. I have even read his epic 'The Missionary'. So has Byron: he wrote, scathingly, of it

> I've read The Missionary,
> Pretty! Very!

But Bowles is no mean poet as I hope the quotations throughout this talk will show. It is my intention to trace his career from the cradle in King's Sutton, Northamptonshire, through his childhood at Uphill, Somerset, schooldays at Winchester, youth by Southampton Water, long pastoral life in Wiltshire to his death at the age of eighty-nine as an eccentric and pathetic canon of the green close of Salisbury. And as we take this placid, bee-haunted and elm-shadowed journey of his life, I shall intersperse it with quotations from his verse.

I shall not trouble you with which of his many compositions they come from, unless I think of it. Place yourself in my hands for a drowsy quarter of an hour and think yourself back to an England that hummed with bees and not with aeroplanes, where church bells called over elmy fields and the poor sat in the gallery of the church, the farmers in high pews in the nave, the squire in a great curtained oak box at the east end of the aisle or in the chancel.

This England of the end of the eighteenth century was one with the rich man in his castle and the poor man at his gate. That seemed the order of things appointed by God and none who lived in country villages questioned it:

> How false the charge, how foul the calumny
> On England's generous aristocracy,
> That, wrapped in sordid selfish apathy,
> They feel not for the poor!
>   Ask is it true?
> Lord of the whirling wheels, the charge is false!
> Ten thousand charities adorn the land,
> Beyond thy bold conception, from this source.
> What cottage child but has been neatly clad,
> And taught its earliest lesson from their care?
> Witness that schoolhouse, mantled with festoon
> Of various plants, which fancifully wreath
> Its mullion windows, and that rustic porch,
> Whence the low hum of infant voices blend
> With airs of spring, without. Now, all alive
> The greensward rings with play, among the shrubs –
> Hushed the long murmur of the morning's task,
> Before the pensive matron's desk!

He is describing the village school of his childhood at Uphill, Somerset, within sound of the Severn sea. And he goes on to picture old people, almsmen and almswomen, pensioned by private charities of the past. Years later, when Bowles was appointed Vicar of Bremhill, Wiltshire, he looked on Lord Lansdowne's vast estate of Bowood from his vicarage and thus, true child of his age, described himself:

When in thy sight another's vast domain
Spreads its long line of woods, dost thou complain?
Nay, rather thank the God that placed thy state
Above the lowly, but beneath the great!
And still his name with gratitude revere,
Who blessed the Sabbath of thy leisure here.

William Lisle Bowles was born in 1762 at King's Sutton, Northants. His father and his grandfather had been clergymen. He belongs to the great tradition of clergymen–poets and writers; in the quiet of their incumbencies, with sufficient income and an assured position in the village, they took to writing political descriptions of their parishes, often in the manner of William Cowper's *Task*. They had an interest too in antiquities, propounding all sorts of absurd and fanciful theories about little pieces of broken stone. They did watercolours of romantic views. Their books can still be found, tastefully bound in leather or cloth, in the second-hand shops – going up in price, alas, just now, for the merit of these loving and reverent delineations is beginning to be appreciated. They chronicled melodiously an England that has disappeared: in Bowles's Wiltshire alone there were several, such as the Reverend Charles Hoyle, Vicar of Overton, Wiltshire – the chief –

. . . nor on the themes
Of hallowed inspiration has his harp
Been silent, though ten thousand jangling strings
When all are poets in this land of song
And every field chinks with its grasshopper –
Have well nigh drowned the tones; but poetry
Mingles, at eventide, with many a mood
Of stirring fancy, on his silent heart
When o'er those bleak and barren downs, in rain
Or sunshine, when the giant Wansdyke sweeps,
Homewards he bends his solitary way.

Return to the picture of the young Bowles, a child of seven. He is riding in a coach from King's Sutton with his parents and sister and cook and nurse and five other children wedged in the hinder chaise and all space in both coaches not occupied by humanity is filled with cases of books that the father is bringing with him to his new living at Uphill, Somerset. A rustic lad, something between a footman and jockey, rides before on a scampering black pony. Young Billy Bowles, our poet-to-be, wears a new white hat with a strip of gold lace on the crown, a sky-blue jacket, and he can hardly stand up in a huge new pair of *Banbury Fair* boots. The cavalcade puts down at the Angel, Bristol. After a time they are ready to go on when

> a cry was heard – 'Where is Billy?'
>
> 'Merciful Heaven!' my mother exclaimed, as she afterwards told me. 'Where is that boy?'
>
> The servants were sent in every direction, cook, nursemaid and outrider. Every passenger was earnestly implored. 'Have you seen the little boy in blue jacket and boots?'
>
> 'He has strolled away! He is lost!' said my mother, half distracted. Now the truth must be told. As soon as the first chaise arrived at the Angel, Billy, attracted by the sound of the bells of Redcliffe Church, without a word said to anyone, very quietly wandered away, and was not missed in the hurry, till the party were just about to proceed on their journey. He was found at last, very peacefully seated, careless of the crowd around, in delight and wonder, listening to the peal from the old tower, on the ancient steps of this churchyard.

A significant story. Throughout his life, Bowles was to be the poet of church bells. One of his best sonnets on bells was written in 1787 – eighteen years later – when Billy was twenty-five and, mark you, ten years before Wordsworth published any sonnets – *ten years* before! – so no wonder the sonnets of Bowles impressed Coleridge. This describes hearing carillons on the beach of Ostend, very early in the morning. It also recalls the incident at Redcliffe tower:

> How sweet the tuneful bells' responsive peal!
> As when, at opening morn, the fragrant breeze
> Breathes on the trembling sense of pale disease,
> So piercing to my heart this force I feel!
> And hark! With lessening cadence now they fall!
> And now, along the white and level tide,

> They fling their melancholy music wide;
> Bidding me many a kinder thought recall
> Of summer days, and those delightful years
> When from an ancient tower, in life's fair prime,
> The mournful magic of their mingling chime
> First waked my wandering childhood into tears!
> But seeming now, when all those days are o'er,
> The sounds of joy once heard, are heard no more.

For those eighteen years between childhood and manhood, let us have a look at his poetical growth. There was Uphill, the little parsonage and the large family that he loved:

> Without a sigh, amidst those circling bowers,
> My stripling prime was pushed, and happiest hours
> . . . These woods, that whispering wave
> My father reared and nursed, now to the grave
> Gone down; he loved the peaceful shades, and said,
> Perhaps, as here he mused: Live, laurels green;
> Ye pines that shade the solitary scene,
> Live blooming and rejoice! When I am dead
> My son shall guard you, and amid your bowers,
> Like me, find shelter from life's beating showers.

But then he was forced to leave. There was Winchester, where when Bowles was a boy there, Dr Joseph Warton, one of three poetical brothers, was headmaster. It is often assumed, by those who get their knowledge of literature from textbooks rather than the originals, that Wordsworth wrote the first nature poetry after the 'artificial age' of Pope's eighteenth century. This is of course nonsense. The three Warton brothers, long before Wordsworth, wrote beautiful descriptive poetry and drew their inspiration from ancient Gothic architecture and natural scenery. We can see how greatly Joseph Warton influenced Bowles in all his poetry and hear the sensitive pupil pay tribute to his headmaster and see with his headmaster's eyes:

> . . . Thy cheering voice,
> O Warton! bade my silent heart rejoice,

And wake to love of nature; every breeze,
On Itchen's bank was melody; the trees
Waved in fresh beauty; and the wind and rain,
That shook the battlements of Wykeham's fane,
Not less delighted, when, with random pace,
I trod the cloister'd aisles; and witness thou,
Catherine, upon whose foss-encircled brow
We met the morning, how I loved to trace
The prospect spread around; the rills below,
That shone irriguous in the gleaming plain;
The river's bend, where the dark barge went slow,
And the pale light on yonder time-worn fane!

Bowles became Captain of the School at Winchester and then, that the Warton influence might continue, he chose to go to Trinity College, Oxford, where Joseph's brother Thomas was a fellow and tutor. It was the influence of the Warton brothers that later landed Bowles in one of the many violent literary quarrels of his later life. In 1807 Bowles published an edition of Pope and remarked that the best poetry was enlivened by description of nature and that Pope did not have enough of it. He also cast aspersions on Pope's personal character. Byron, Campbell and others attacked Bowles and nature poetry. Bowles replied in vigorous and amusing pamphlets. Hazlitt came down on Bowles's side and the battle was won. Meeting Bowles later, Byron found him a 'very gentlemanly fellow for a parson'. But this is a side issue. It is Bowles's poetical developments that mattered. When he left Oxford he fell on hard times, emotionally and financially. He was crossed in love. First he loved a girl who jilted him for someone richer and grander:

For one whom I had loved, whom I had pressed
With honest, ardent passion to my breast,
Was to another vowed, I heard the tale
And to the earth sank heartless, faint and pale
Till that sad hour when every hope had flown,
I thought she lived for me, and me alone . . .

Whether she was that girl he saw when he was

... visitor from Oxenford
Proud of Wintonian scholarship

on the sands near Southampton, I do not know. But he describes the
scenes so well, you had better hear it:

... The first ray shone
On the white seagull's wing, and gazing round,
I listen'd to the tide's advancing roar
When, for the old and booted fisherman,
Who silent dredg'd for shrimps, in the cold haze
Of sunrise, I beheld – or was it not
A momentary vision? – a fair form –
I looked that she would vanish! She had left
Like me, just left the abode of discipline
And came in the gay fulness of her heart,
When the pale light first glanced along the wave,
To play with the wild ocean like a child;
And though I knew him not, I vowed (oh hear,
Ye votaries of German sentiment),
Vowed an eternal love ... The vision smiled
And left the scene to solitude.

Wherever she was, Bowles was so depressed by his jilting that he
left England. On his return he became engaged to someone else. But
this lady died. The double grief produced a series of sonnets the best
of which were written in the months of April and May, 1793. Indeed,
some students of Bowles's say that the best poems he wrote were the
product of about this time, of one week's work in the whole eighty-
nine years of his life. I do not think I can quite subscribe to this
opinion for the middle distances of poetry are in their way as attractive to me as the heights. But here is an example of one of those many
melancholy sonnets of disappointed love that so delighted Coleridge
and influenced his own poetry and that of his great contemporaries:

O Time! who knowst a lenient hand to lay
Softest on sorrow's wound, and slowly thence
(Lulling to sad repose the weary sense)
The faint pang stealest unperceiv'd away;

On Thee I rest my only hope at last,
   And think, when thou hast dry'd the bitter tear
   That flows in vain o'er all my soul held dear,
I may look back on ev'ry sorrow past,
And meet life's peaceful evening with a smile —
   As some lone bird, at day's departing hour,
   Sings in the sunbeam of the transient show'r
Forgetful, though its wings are wet the while —
Yet ah! how much must that poor heart endure,
Which hopes from thee, and thee alone, the cure!

In the early 1790s, Bowles was Curate at Donhead, Wiltshire, on the edge of Wardour Castle. Later he was Vicar of Dumbleton, Gloucestershire, but he did not reside there. At this time, he had much popular acclamation as a poet but little money. It was still an age of patronage and Bowles went to London to solicit John Moore, the Archbishop of Canterbury, for a living. With characteristic absentmindedness, he forgot to leave his address with the Archbishop, so that it was some weeks before the fat and comfortable living of Bremhill in Wiltshire was presented to him, in 1804.

Bowles was delighted. He had married by now. We do not hear much about his wife but this may well be her:

How many blessings silent and unheard,
The mistress of the lonely parsonage
Dispenses, when she takes her daily round
Among the aged and the sick, whose prayers
And blessings are her only recompense.

And Vicar of Bremhill Bowles remained until his death in 1850. I have not visited that lovely village and parsonage for many years but it stands very vividly in my memory still: the elm-shaded eminence on which the thatched cottages are scattered; the large stone church, restored by Victorians in 1850; the dark churchyard where we looked about among the old headstones for inscriptions that Bowles might have written; the peculiar column to Maud Heath, high on a hill looking towards Chippenham where her stone causeway winds across the vale to keep Bremhill people walking to market safe from flood.

This column we saw: it was erected by Henry, Marquess of Lansdowne, Lord of the Manor, and W. L. Bowles, Vicar of the Parish of Bremhill, 1837:

> Thou, who dost pause on this aerial height
> Where Maud Heath's Pavement winds thro' shade and light;
> Oh! Christian Pilgrim, in a world of strife
> Look round, and ponder on the Path of Life.

And on the grassy slopes below were Wiltshire cottages with still blue smoke rising into the elms – cottages and elms, I have no doubt, cleared away today by modern 'progress'. The ghost of Bowles seemed to be with us and the vicarage was Bowles himself: *there* were the Gothic battlements and gables he had given it to make his house 'in keeping with the church'; the terraced garden looking for miles across elms and blue meadows to the smooth outlines of the downs and Westbury's White Horse. And in this garden were the remains of the hermitage and the seats and fountains with which Bowles had adorned it.

His neighbour Tom Moore lived at Sloperton Cottage a few miles away. In his diary, that delicate and sweet poet records with some humour old Bowles's parsonage where 'he has frittered away its beauty with grottoes, hermitages and Shenstonian inscriptions: when company is coming, he cries "Here, John, run with the crucifix and missal to the hermitage and set the fountain going." His sheep bells are tuned in thirds and fifths. But he is an excellent fellow notwithstanding.'

I think Moore was jealous, for, beside Bremhill, Sloperton Cottage is not much of a place. When Southey visited Bowles he described the 'Two swans, who answer to the names of Snowdrop and Lily, have a pond to themselves, and if not daily fed, they march to Mrs Bowles's window.' And many stories of Bowles's timidity and absentmindedness survive. How when he was dining at Bowood with Lord Lansdowne, he could not find his stocking and had to come down to dinner with one leg bare; Mrs Bowles then discovered he had put both stockings on the same leg. How he started for Chippenham from Bremhill on horseback, dismounted to walk down a steep hill, leading the horse by the bridle slung across his arm, and continued to the turnpiking gate where he offered his toll, to be told, 'We don't charge nothing for your honour, as you beant on osback.' On turning round he saw the bridle hanging on his arm but no horse attached to it.

Forgetful of himself he may have been, but not of his parishioners. He composed for them his *Villager's Verse Book*, which was designed to illustrate scriptural truths by way of simple country images. Among the best is 'The Glow Worm':

> Oh, what is this which shines so bright
> And in the lonely place
> Hangs out his small green lamp at night
> The dewy bank to grace?
>
> It is a glow worm, still and pale
> It shines the whole night long
> When only stars, O Nightingale,
> Seem listening to thy song.
>
> And so amid the world's cold night,
> Through good report and ill,
> Shines out the humble Christian's light,
> As lonely and as still.

Notice those two lovely lines –

> When only stars, O Nightingale,
> Seem listening to thy song.

They have the quality of pure poetry; they are more than mere descriptive verse, however good that can be.

The contemplative nature of Bowles's poetry endeared him to the Lake poets, more than many clergyman poets whose descriptive writing may have been more graphic. Thoughts such as these, for instance, at a waterfall in Coombe Ellen, Wales:

> . . . As now its roar
> Comes hollow from below, methinks we hear
> The noise of generations as they pass
> O'er the frail arch of earthly vanity

To silence and oblivion . . .
So ever to the ear of Heaven ascends
The long, loud-murmur of the rolling globe . . .

Or again, there are his great phrases such as that on Hannah Moore's death, where she

Waits meekly at the gate of paradise
Smiling at time.

Though the Lake poets and the literary critics may have admired his sentiments, it was Wiltshire villagers who loved the man. And it was Wiltshire that he loved and described so truly: here in the *Villager's Verse Book* (and I have seen a tiny edition bound in watered silks, suitable for presentation in honeysuckle-hung village schools) we see the lovely downs above the Bath Road, in a poem on a shepherd and his dog:

The gray stone circlet is below
The village smoke is at our feet;
We nothing hear but the sailing crow,
And wandering flocks, that roam and bleat.

Far-off, the early horsemen hies
In shower or sunshine rushing on.
Yonder the dusty whirlwind flies;
The distant coach is seen and gone.

For Bowles was a poet of downs, elms, thatched cottages, gypsy encampments and church bells. Sometimes he tried his hand at describing jungle or the gorgeous East and he sent great goddesses and angels, vague personifications of moral qualities, creaking across his familiar skies. When he introduced machinery like this, he spoiled his poems. People seem to have remembered the bad in Bowles and forgotten the good, so that now he is nearly forgotten altogether.

When he was seventy-three, he grew deaf. This must have been a grief to him for he played the fiddle and delighted in oratorios and cathedral music – rather like Prebendary Harding. We have a more cheerful picture of his deafness when we find him visiting Tom Moore with a new ear trumpet that Miss Martineau, the political economist, had recommended to him. He stood at one end of Moore's room and got Moore to play to him at the other. It worked.

'Now,' said Bowles, 'I will tell you what I have done. Southey told me that with this trumpet I should be able to hear the bees hum, the birds sing and the oxen low. So the other day I saw a bee flying about, so I got near him and put my trumpet down; indeed I heard him quite plain – buzz – I then went through the Barton, and what do you think – the very first thing I heard was – cock-a-doodle-doo. I then went out past the cowhouse, and there I heard – the oxen lowing! There, what you think of that?'

Moore, who was splitting with laughter and scarcely able to keep his countenance, replied in a moment. 'Why, I will tell you what, Bowles; if you had told this to anybody else, they would have said that it was a very Cock and Bull story.'

In 1828, the Dean and Chapter of Salisbury made Bowles a canon, partly for his literary distinction and partly because his churchman-ship must have been acceptable. At this time, the diocese was on the whole High Church in the pre-Tractarian sense of 'high and dry'. Bowles was an old-fashioned High-Churchman. He did not hold with dissent and revivals. He admired Bishop Ken and King Charles the Martyr and Laudian divines. He administered the Sacraments about four times a year and read morning and evening prayers every Sunday from his three-decker in Bremhill church.

In 1844, Mrs Bowles, that practical self-effacing lady, died and the poet was disconsolate. They had already settled in Salisbury for most of the year, putting a curate into Bremhill. From now until his death in 1850, Bowles existed rather than lived. We have a picture of the old canon, fine looking, with long grey locks fringing a bald head, wearing breeches and buckled shoes, a relic of the eighteenth century surviving into the railway age. He is seen performing a characteris-tically timorous rite in the close. He has ascertained the height of Salisbury spire and is pacing the ground between the cathedral and his house to see whether, should the spire fall, it will damage his residence.

Bowles had the greatest pity and respect for old age. It is sad that his own should have been so lonely and pathetic with his faculties almost all gone. Well might his words to William Sommers, one of his old parishioners at Bremhill, be applied to his own last years:

> Like a scathed oak; of all its boughs bereft,
> God and the grave are thy best refuge left.
> . . . the murmured prayer alone
> Rose from the trembling lips towards the Throne
>   Of mercy; that ere Spring return'd again
> And the long Winter blew its dreary blast,
>   To sweep the verdure from the fading plain,
> Thy burden would be dropped, thy sorrows past!
> O blind and aged man, bowed down with cares,
> When will the grave shelter thy few gray hairs!

Bowles was buried beside his wife in 1850. Their old bones are under Salisbury Cathedral. But the spirit of his love of Wiltshire people still hangs over Bremhill and I hope it will pardon this all-too-public attempt to shed some of its influence over more distant parts of the West of England.

ON 'A FEW LATE CHRYSANTHEMUMS'*

Spectator
8 October 1954

• • •

As I do not belong to a press-cutting agency nor listen to the wireless, I have only been half aware of what sort of reception my latest book of verses, *A Few Late Chrysanthemums*, has had. This

---

* Published under the title 'John Betjeman Replies'.

escapism is partly deliberate. I have come to dread all but unstinted praise or friendly and constructive criticism from people who write poetry themselves. Perhaps an experience I had when a boy of about fifteen at school may partly account for this morbid fear. I was in a set taught by Mr H. L. O. Flecker, the present headmaster of Christ's Hospital, a brother of the poet, and I showed him a poem I had written about a City church. It was very bad and, for motives no doubt kindly meant, he read out my verses to the boys, making fun of each line as he went along. Most boys who write verse must have had a similar ragging, if not from masters at least from contemporaries.

But most boys who write poetry do not intend to be poets all their lives. That had always been my intention. As early as I can remember I have read and written verse. I have always preferred it to prose, known that its composition was my vocation and anything else I have written has been primarily a means of earning money in order to buy the free time in which to write poetry.

My verses are my children, sometimes too private to be shown in public. They are part of me and attacks on them I take as personal and feel inclined to answer in terms of personal abuse. When they are published my verses have generally grown up into comparative strangers. But they are still mine. Some I would gladly disown, notably three that seem to have stuck to me, try to get rid of them as I may: 'In Westminster Abbey', 'Come friendly bombs and fall on Slough' and, in my latest volume, 'Phone for the fishknives, Norman'. These now seem to me merely comic verse and competent magazine writing, topical and tiresome.

Verse-writers will know the lengthy and painful business of giving birth to a poem. First there is the thrilling or terrifying recollection of a place, a person or a mood that hammers inside the head saying, 'Go on! Go on! It is your duty to make a poem out of it.' Then a line or phrase suggests itself. Next comes the selection of a metre. I am a traditionalist in metres and have made few experiments. The rhythms of Tennyson, Crabbe, Hawker, Dowson, Hardy, James Elroy Flecker, Moore and *Hymns Ancient and Modern* are generally buzzing about in my brain and I choose one from these that seems to me to suit the theme. On the backs of cigarette packets and old letters I write down my lines, crossing out and changing. When I reach home I transfer the

whole to foolscap and cross out and change again. Then I start recit-
ing the lines aloud, either driving a car or on solitary walks, until the
sound of the words satisfies me. Then I try reading the poem out to a
patient friend whose criticisms I gladly accept, provided they are detail
only. After that I may have the courage to send it to a magazine.

This may explain why verses are the children of their creator and
so deeply personal. Reactions of readers to a man's verses are personal reactions to him. And here I must express gratitude for the
enormous amount of notice my poems seem to have attracted. The
thick pile of press cuttings that my gentlemanly publisher and friend
Major John Grey Murray has lent to me is an unexpected tribute. So
is his news of the sales of the book. I feel humbled, too, for this week
I have been reading the new *PEN Anthology* and found in it poems
by comparatively unestablished poets whose work often seems better
to me than my own and who deserve the publicity and sales with
which I have been honoured.

Poems are personal and that means that they must be sincere.
What I was when I published my first volume of verse in about 1930,
I am not today. Nor, I hope, are you. In those days my purest pleasure was the exploration of the suburbs and provincial towns and my
impurest pleasure the pursuit of the brawny athletic girl. When most
of the poems in my latest book were written I was the self-pitying
victim of remorse, guilt and terror of death. Much as I dislike trying
to conform to Christian morality (which makes Peter Quennell
detect a note of Martin Tupper* in my verse), the only practical way
to face the dreaded lonely journey into Eternity seems to me the
Christian one. I therefore try to believe that Christ was God, made
Man, and gives Eternal Life and that I may be confirmed in this belief

---

* Martin Tupper (1810–89) was a quintessential Victorian moralist. He wrote uplifting proverbs ('It is sure to be dark if you shut your eyes') which, first collected under
the title *Proverbial Philosophy* in 1838, became a popular gift and made his reputation,
not least in America. Betjeman admired him for his Victorian pieties and his interest in archaeology (in the late 1830s Tupper opposed the closure of a Saxon church
in Albury, Surrey), though Karl Marx singled him out in 1865 as his primary aver-
sion. By then, however, Tupper's popularity was also waning in Britain, after he had
been passed over for poet laureate on the death of Wordsworth in 1850 in favour of
Tennyson.

by clinging to the Sacraments and by prayer. This is sometimes implicit in my poems. An anonymous friendly critic in *The Times* certainly knows a thing or two when he says, 'He suffers agonising twinges of guilt, but bravely incurs the reproaches of a delicate conscience by going on exactly as before.' That means that he recognises my verses at least as sincere. For there is no doubt that fear of death (a manifestation of the lack of the faith I deeply desire), remorse and a sense of man's short time on earth and an impatience with so-called 'progress' did inform many of the poems in my latest volume. Since then I have grown a little more cheerful and thankful and hope to produce some poems expressing the joys of being alive.

It has pleased me to find long and understanding notices·in Christian papers from the *Methodist Recorder* to the *Tablet* and the *Church Times* and the *Church of Ireland Gazette* and to find avowed Christians like Tom Driberg, Evelyn Waugh and Frank Singleton and G. B. Stern and John Arlott appreciating the reasons for the gloom of some of my verse. It is doubly pleasing when this change of mood is recognised and accepted by critics who may not subscribe to my religious beliefs. That fine poet and critic Geoffrey Taylor expresses his reaction neatly when he says in *Time and Tide*, 'It is rather as though something friendly, familiar and furry and easily frightened had turned at bay and bitten one in the bathroom.' I do not know what are the beliefs of another good poet and critic, G. S. Fraser, but I am grateful to him for his defence of my point of view in the *New Statesman* and I quite agree with him that I am not at my best in 'Joyce Grenfell or *New Statesman* Competition mood'. Indeed to summarise the helpful criticism I have received from so many papers and journals, not forgetting the provincial press, which employs today as intelligent writers as one can find anywhere, I would say they advise me to keep off satire and anger. This is sound advice.

The criticism of poetry can only be really useful if it is written by poets, even if they be not popular poets. They know the meaning of words like 'technique' and 'rhythm' as applied to poetry. And criticism of poetry is useless and stultifying if the critic does not recognise the change of mind and outlook in an author he is criticising. A bad critic is like the sort of schoolmaster who sets himself up as perfection, remains static in that ridiculous position and regards any deviation from his own norm as a step in the wrong direction. Inevitably there were a few people like this who wrote or spoke about my verses. They blamed them for not containing qualities that they were never intended to have. I can only reply that I was not addressing myself to the *vieux jeu avant garde* – if I may string four French words together – which still lingers on in the *Critics* programmes of the BBC. Yet even to them I can express gratitude. A reaction was achieved and that by no means negative.

25

HERITAGE

Homes and Hearths

English Cottages (1982)

ENGLISH COTTAGES

Introduction to *English Cottages*
By Tony Evans and Candida Lycett Green
Weidenfeld & Nicolson, 1982

• • •

England is a constant delight because of its rapid change of scene; almost within a few hundred yards the character of a place changes. That is why building materials tell us where we are.

Looking at buildings can still be a pleasure provided we disregard the classifying of them into categories and dates but just look at them for themselves and their setting. Whether it is a half-timbered cottage built in the thirteenth century at Alfriston in Sussex or a half-timbered cottage built in 1906 at Godalming in Surrey does not really matter.

Although this book covers only England, far more architectural influence in the eighteenth and nineteenth centuries than most people imagine came from Scotland (from men like the Adam brothers, Lorimer and Mackintosh) and from Wales (from men such as John Nash, whose practice began at Carmarthen and continued into the twentieth century, and later, the innovating architects North and Padmore). There is no doubt that their influence reached cottage architecture. Neither must the Isle of Man be forgotten where, from the Georgian front of Douglas to the Arts and Crafts cottages by Baillie Scott, there is no lack of variety. (Baillie Scott in fact was so sea-sick on his journey over to the Island that he remained there for a long time summoning up the courage to go back. He is said to have held an exhibition of his drawings there and some of the pictures he hung upside down because he thought they looked nicer that way.)

My daughter is quite right when she says that people think their cottages are far older than they are but the first cottages were no more than shelters for human bodies against the elements and architecture did not come in until the eighteenth century, and then not consciously. I have seen the sole black house in these islands on the island of Foula beyond the outer Hebrides: it had no windows and the place was full of smoke from a fire lighted in the middle of the room. This was what early cottages were like before people improved themselves. From solidified tents to the village street and on to the pre-fab, the process is continuous. The great houses remain aloof and alone but this book contains the ordinary houses – the cottages that we all dream of having.

In stone districts, human beings and cattle were housed under one roof and two storeys were a rarity. Many a past village has been discovered through aerial photography showing up field patterns. In 1349 the Black Death wiped out a third of England's population and whole villages disappeared. Labour became in great demand, villagers moved further afield to offer their services or set themselves up independently and a new class of successful farmers, merchants and tradesmen was born. As noblemen were building great houses all over the South-East and gradually spreading north (and noblewomen too, like Bess of Hardwick who built 'Hardwick Hall, more glass than wall' in Elizabethan times), so the new 'yeoman' classes were building smaller houses, now referred to as cottages, and it is these that, together with the church, form the hearts of many of our villages today.

The years between 1550 and 1660 are sometimes described as the 'Golden Age' of cottage building but the ones built in that period were the homes of men of relative means who could afford to use lasting materials. In the past two centuries cottages were built at an ever-increasing rate. Though they look cosy and homely enough now, in his *How the Poor Live*, written in the 1880s, George R. Sims painted a terrible picture of the filth and poverty many of them witnessed:

> The room was no better and no worse than hundreds of its class. It was dirty and dilapidated, with the usual bulging blackened ceiling and the usual crumbling greasy walls. Its furniture was a dilapidated

four-post bedstead, a chair and a deal table. On the bed lay a woman, young, and with features that, before hourly anguish contorted them, had been comely. The woman was dying slowly of heart disease. Death was 'writ large' upon her face. At her breast she held her child, a poor little mite of a baby that was drawing the last drain of life from its mother's breast. The day was a bitterly cold one; through the broken casement the wind came ever and anon in icy gusts, blowing the hanging end of the ragged coverlet upon the bed to and fro like a flag in a breeze.

The cottages of model villages were built with the best intentions and were a conscious effort to provide better living conditions. Some of the most successful were those built by free churchmen, especially the Quakers. The Cadburys, for example, built the wonderful village of Bournville near Birmingham, which was designed by Alexander Harvey to house workers in the chocolate factory. The shoe-making Clarks of Street in Somerset also built many cottages for their workers and Jordans, near Gerrards Cross in Buckinghamshire, was a settlement built by the Quakers. Their outlook on life went with temperance and alcohol was not encouraged.

Swindon railway village, with its church and drying ground for clothes lines, has proved itself today by being ahead of its time and keeping human scale, in marked contrast to the factories and offices that dwarf it. William Owen, Lever's company architect, did a good job at the village of Port Sunlight in Cheshire too as did Lockwood and Mawson at Saltaire in Yorkshire, one of the first industrial model villages. I think my favourite model village of the lot is Whiteley near Cobham in Surrey, built by William Whiteley, the founder of Whiteley's stores in Bayswater, to house retired tradesmen. The village is carefully landscaped and provides seemingly casual vistas, churches, chapels, communal halls and comfortable homes. (William Whiteley was shot by his illegitimate son.) Of the private estate villages, I think the most beautiful is the most famous: Milton Abbas in Dorset. It was designed in the 1770s, possibly by Sir William Chambers, and blends naturally with the landscape.

Garden suburbs are quite distinct from garden cities. Garden suburbs came first and the pioneer Arts and Crafts garden suburb was

Norman Shaw's Bedford Park, Middlesex. A ballad of the time said of these houses:

> With red and blue and sagest green
>   Were walls and dado dyed,
> Friezes of Morris' there were seen
>   And oaken wainscot wide.
> Now he who loves aesthetic cheer
>   And does not mind the damp
> May come and read Rossetti here
>   By a Japanese-y lamp.

Dame Henrietta Barnett was the daughter of a clergyman. She lived first in Whitechapel and then moved with her husband to Hampstead where she founded one of the first garden suburbs. She wanted to bring sunlight and nature into the lives of the poor. Every home in the Suburb is so arranged that it can be seen to be as good at the back as it is at the front. In fact it was the reverse of façadism. Towns had grown straight and packed along streets but the garden suburb brought nature in-between, fresh air from the Hampstead hills and a village atmosphere. Letchworth and Welwyn garden cities were thought of as communities with a life of their own.

As state rooms in the great houses of England were designed for walking in and the furniture was to be seen in three dimensions, so Picturesque cottages were to be seen as three-dimensional pictures from a window across the park. They were also built to be walked round and gazed at. Perhaps the best example of all is Blaise Hamlet for it is not only a pleasure to walk round but provides a new view with every step you take. Harford's old retainers who moved in to its cottages in 1812 were actually comfortable; many former inhabitants of Picturesque cottages had been living in the pitch dark under exaggerated eaves and behind windows of heavily leaded lights. In the park of Alton Towers, Uttoxeter, in Nottinghamshire, Loudon created perhaps the oddest Picturesque folly of all which looked like Stonehenge built in two storeys and near it there was a pagoda that alternately spurted out gaslight and water.

Arts and Crafts cottages were the last rumble of a farm cart in an uneven country lane. The estate cottages at Buscot and Eaton

Hastings in Berkshire built by the Butler-Henderson family are a perfect example. The Butler-Hendersons financed a railway company, the beginning of which was the Manchester, Sheffield and Lincolnshire line, soon known as the 'MS and L' ('Money Sunk and Lost'); it then became the Great Central Railway or 'GC' ('Gone Completely'). Despite losing a lot of money they built numerous stone cottages designed by Sir Ernest George. During the last war they were inhabited by Basque refugees at the invitation of Lord Faringdon and became known as the Basque Cottages. They are a lasting tribute to the influence of William Morris, lying across the Thames in Kelmscott churchyard under a stone designed by Philip Webb, whom Norman Shaw described as 'a very interesting man with a strong liking for the ugly'.

Ugly the cottages in this book certainly are not. Is this why we love them so? I do not think it is for their beauty alone. People much prefer things hand done. For the last two centuries people who did not have to live in cottages have been irresistibly attracted by them, sometimes to the point of obsession. In 1906 G. L. Morris and E. Wood wrote, in their book *The Country Cottage*, something that is as apt today as it would have been at the end of the eighteenth century:

The increasing demand for 'a cottage in the country' is not confined to any one class of people, nor is it any longer significant of a humble mode of life. In olden days the dwellers in cottages were presumably the poor. Poets hymned the cottager as the man of toil, to whom the kindly parson ministered at his family festivals and for whom the joy of living must depend largely on his relations with the squire. The cottage lass went barefoot from poverty rather than from choice, and her kindred accepted the hewing of wood and the drawing of water as the chief of the inevitable duties of life . . . Cottages are wanted to suit almost every kind of domestic life that can be found in English society. The home of one of our younger princesses of the royal blood is a cottage of much smaller dimensions than the house of many a prosperous tradesman. Its elegance lies in what it fulfils of that simplicity and frugality of life – so much easier to conceive than to live up to – which seem to be the last word of a true civilisation.

The last sentence is, I think, what we are after – 'the simplicity and frugality of life'; but how uncomfortable and sometimes how pretentious some of us have been in that search.

As early as the 1780s people who *certainly* did not need to do so were already living in cottages. Richard Payne Knight, a well-known theorist of the Picturesque movement, relinquished his large and fanciful Downton Castle in Shropshire with its marble dining-room inspired by the Pantheon and its army of servants and retired to a small cottage on his estate. He referred to it as 'my little domestic dell' and scorned his peers for spending their time 'pent up in a bed or a dining room or . . . toiling through turnip fields and stubble in pursuit of partridges'. He went on in a letter to his friend, Lord Aberdeen, 'They really do not know what a delightful planet this is, or what a delicious portion of it has fallen to the lot of us grumbling Englishmen.'

There was a certain smugness about those Picturesque theorists who, though they eulogised the glories of cottage life, did not know true poverty or anything near it and I wonder if they spent most of their time writing of sublimity from the comfort of their libraries? The writers, however, were probably the most genuine 'new' cottage dwellers of that period. In the early 1800s William and Dorothy Wordsworth, and later Mary, found true happiness in their Lakeland home Dove Cottage.

> Yes, Mary, to some lowly door
> In that delicious spot obscure
> Our happy feet shall tend.

Thomas De Quincey took on Dove Cottage after the Wordsworths and remained in it for twenty-six years, living, it seems, in comfort:

> Candles at 4 o'clock, warm hearth rugs, tea, a fair tea-maker, shutters closed, curtains flowing in ample draperies on the floor whilst the wind and the rain are raging without.

Eventually the number of his children and books became so many that he was obliged to leave for a larger house.

The vogue for the 'simple life' took off and flourished over the first few decades of the nineteenth century. The rich began to settle in the country, especially beside the sea, in elegant cottages. In his *Life in the English Country House* (1978), Mark Girouard writes:

> The strong element of artificiality in the whole back-to-nature movement came into the open in one of its most engaging but also ridiculous products, the *cottage orné* – the simple life, lived in simple luxury in a simple cottage with – quite often – fifteen simple bedrooms, all hung with French wallpapers.

Though Regency society took the idea of the cottage far beyond its limits, the desire for a little place in the country burned fervently and more genuinely through the second half of the nineteenth century. The English fondness for the rustic was epitomised by Helen Allingham and Birket Foster's watercolours of idyllic rose-covered cottages, many of which were in Surrey and Sussex. Surrey had been the least populated of the Home Counties, being wild and difficult to get to, but in the 1850s the railway opened its glories to the cottage builder and dweller. Once again, it was the artistically inclined who led the way into the gay gardens of the Home Counties.

> Bring orchids, bring the foxglove spire,
> The little speedwell's darling blue,
> Deep tulips dash'd with fiery dew
> Laburnums, dropping-wells of fire

wrote Tennyson who lived for over twenty years in a house on Leith Hill called Aldworth, in Sussex, just over the Surrey borders.

William Morris, poet, craftsman and socialist, revived the simple life in many a middle-class heart. Colonies of 'new' cottagers began to spring up all over the place and gained momentum by the 1900s. Artists and artisans like the group at Sapperton in Gloucestershire set other shining examples. Writers, poets and film-makers clustered round Clough Williams-Ellis's Portmeirion in North Wales in whitewashed cottages on verdant mountainsides.

In the 1920s it became very much 'the thing' to have a cottage in the country; actors and actresses had them tucked away in Kent. People put up with any discomfort provided it was the country. You could buy cottages for £200–£300 then. Nowadays the desire for a thatched half-timbered cottage dripping with honeysuckle is almost universal. Estate agents echo the advertisements in the pattern books of the 1800s:

> Perfectly restored and modernised period cottage affording much charm and character and many exposed timbers, within easy reach of Etchingham Station.

(How amazed Cobbett would have been to see the hovels he visited bedecked with bathrooms and with a Jaguar parked outside.)

I would like to say how grateful I am to my daughter for sharing my pleasure in looking at buildings. The great thing is not to bore and 'one good illustration is better than ten pages of text', F. E. Howard used to say. Tony Evans has followed the moods of the book with his excellent photographs.

26

FAITH

Hope and Charity

THE CHRISTIAN'S WAY
Letter to Roy Harrod

25 March 1939

• • •

Ivery much like to think of you, you dear old thing, giving a daily thought to the mysteries of mind and body. No one is less of a philosopher than I am, and they still remain mysteries and I would be the last person to attempt an intellectual defence of Christianity as practised by Catholics. Father D'Arcy can do that or C. S. Lewis.

But your letter, despite this, leaves me puzzled. 'What I feel about theists is that on the whole in modern times they are bores, throw no light on the situation, tell us nothing of interest' . . . 'The inspiration has not been handed down to the modern world' . . . 'Revealed religion, even if one could accept it, leaves most of the great problems unsorted.' What are the great problems? For you, economic ones? That someone is worse off than someone else? That

> After two thousand years of mass
> We've got as far as poison gas?

That people are tortured and unhappy mentally and physically? That time and space are so inexplicable? That one new dimension leads to another? You put your attitude clearest when you say that revealed religion leaves most of the great problems *unsolved. Unsolved.* What is the solution of any 'problem'? I suppose it is knowing how it is done, with one's mind and being able to solve future problems of a like nature for other people, if they cannot solve them themselves.

Now I quite agree with you that the church is imperfect, that many problems can be solved and aren't solved because of human slackness and weakness. For instance, there should be no slums, bullying should be curbed, armaments should be abolished, hysterical people should be psychoanalysed, prisons should be reformed. Those are some of the thousands of problems which could be solved by the human mind. But the problem behind it all, and the one I expect you are referring to is 'Why aren't these reforms made?' And that brings everything down to the fundamental 'Why aren't we perfect?' and that goes down to 'What is perfection?' and that goes back to theism and theories of good and evil. And as soon as one talks of good and evil, one is bound to set up a criterion and then comes the time for one to choose a way of life.

I choose the Christian's way (and completely fail to live up to it) because I believe it true and because I believe – for possibly a split second in six months, but that's enough – that Christ is really the incarnate son of God and that Sacraments are a means of grace and that grace alone gives one the power to do what one ought to do. And once I have accepted that, the questions of atonement, the Trinity, Heaven and Hell become logical and correct. Of course my attitude to them is different from that of an Italian peasant but that is because words can never explain mysteries; [but] my *knowledge* of them is the same as that of the peasant. By knowledge I mean knowing with more than the intellect. You would not hold this possible. You believe that the intellect is our highest faculty and that mind and body are all we have. If you throw in spirit, then even a thing like positive, almost tangible, evil becomes possible. Then one's spiritual life becomes the activist of one and we are racing in an arena of witnesses living, dead and unborn into the world.

I feel this will shock you, you dear Liberal intellectual old thing. And for every book you can produce which disproves the existence of the spirit, I can produce one which proves it. It boils down to the alternative: materialist or Christian. For intellectuals the materialist standpoint is the obvious one and the easiest. The second is harder, but I hold that it is the most satisfactory, especially when one comes up against injustice, birth and death. But there is no argument. The intellectual is too proud to surrender to the seemingly ridiculous story when viewed from outside. But there are comparatively few intellectuals. A course of Von Hügel will show you, though, that there is plenty of room for the intellect in Christianity.

I fear this letter sounds arrogant, proselytising and smug. It is bound to do that, because it is written from one point of view, whereas your kind letter was tolerant of everything. As I know that you are intolerant of unreality, avarice and indeed the Seven Deadly Sins (New Inn Hall Street),★ I know that you are an Agnostic Christian. So am I for most of the time. But I know that Christianity is not a negative force but may even do some service by immunising people against worse creeds, such as Fascism. I believe it's positive and can alone save the world, not from Fascism, or Nazism, but from evil. If I did not believe that I should live in the present and squeal at death all the time, instead of most of the time.

God is not mentioned in Eliot's new play *Family Reunion*. But do go and see it and regard the Eumenides as Christianity and then see the variety of planes we live in. It puts what I mean far more clearly than I can.

THE CONVERSION OF ST PAUL

The Listener
10 February 1955

● ● ●

Now is the time when we recall
The sharp Conversion of St Paul.
Converted! Turned the wrong way round –
A man who seemed till then quite sound,
Keen on religion – very keen –

★ St Peter's Hall, later St Peter's College, had been founded in New Inn Hall Street, Oxford, by the Bishop of Liverpool in 1929 to educate poorer students.

No one, it seems, had ever been
So keen on persecuting those
Who said that Christ was God and chose
To die for this absurd belief
As Christ had died beside the thief.
Then in a sudden blinding light
Paul knew that Christ was God all right –
And very promptly lost his sight.
Poor Paul! They led him by the hand
He who had been so high and grand
A helpless blunderer, fasting, waiting,
Three days inside himself debating
In physical blindness: 'As it's true
That Christ is God and died for you,
Remember all the things you did
To keep His gospel message hid.
Remember how you helped them even
To throw the stones that murdered Stephen.
And do you think that you are strong
Enough to own that you were wrong?'
They must have been an awful time,
Those three long days repenting crime
Till Ananias came and Paul
Received his sight, and more than all
His former strength, and was baptised.
St Paul is often criticised
By modern people who're annoyed
At his conversion, saying Freud
Explains it all. But they omit
The really vital point of it,
Which isn't *how* it was achieved
But what it was that Paul believed.
He knew as certainly as we
Know you are you and I am me
That Christ was all He claimed to be.
What is Conversion? Turning round
From chaos to a love profound.

And chaos too is an abyss
In which the only life is this.
Such a belief is quite all right
If you are sure like Mrs Knight★
And think morality will do
For all the ills we're subject to.
But raise your eyes and see with Paul
An explanation of it all.
Injustice, cancer's cruel pain,
All suffering that seems in vain,
The vastness of the universe,
Creatures like centipedes and worse –
All part of an enormous plan
Which mortal eyes can never scan
And out of it came God to man.
Jesus is God and came to show
The world we live in here below
Is just an antechamber where
We for His Father's house prepare.
What is conversion? Not at all
For me the experience of St Paul,
No blinding light, a fitful glow
Is all the light of faith I know
Which sometimes goes completely out
And leaves me plunging round in doubt
Until I will myself to go
And worship in God's house below –
My parish Church – and even there
I find distractions everywhere.

What is Conversion? Turning round
To gaze upon a love profound.
For some of us see Jesus plain

★ In January 1955 the psychologist and humanist Margaret Knight argued in two
BBC radio talks that moral education should be uncoupled from religious education.
This poem is Betjeman's reply.

And never once look back again,
And some of us have seen and known
And turned and gone away alone,
But most of us turn slow to see
The figure hanging on a tree
And stumble on and blindly grope
Upheld by intermittent hope.
God grant before we die we all
May see the light as did St Paul.

CHRISTIAN VALUES

Letter to Evelyn Waugh

27 May 1945

• • •

I am reading for a second time *Brideshead Revisited* since it has come to me for review in the bloody old *Daily Herald*. It will get a spanking good notice. To me it is a great treat to read a book with a standard of values behind it – Christian values, what is more. I shall have somehow to hint this fact to readers without letting it be apparent to the Editors, since I recently had a letter from them to say that I was using this paper for *Roman Catholic propaganda* and that 'The *Daily Herald* finds itself in conflict with the Catholic Church on several points.' I was also accused of 'Jesuitry'. This made me rather proud. Of course, I have not altered my tactics. I find that there is no longer any left or right but merely those who want to run a Slave State (your phrase, which I now always use) and those of us who don't want to be run.

CHRISTMAS

Harper's Bazaar
December 1947

• • •

The bells of waiting Advent ring,
    The Tortoise stove is lit again
And lamp-oil light across the night
    Has caught the streaks of winter rain
In many a stained glass window sheen
From Crimson Lake to Hooker's Green.

The holly in the windy hedge
    And round the Manor House the yew
Will soon be stripped to deck the ledge,
    The altar, font and arch and pew,
So that the villagers can say
'The church looks nice' on Christmas Day.

Provincial public houses blaze
    And Corporation tramcars clang,
On lighted tenements I gaze
    Where paper decorations hang,
And bunting in the red Town Hall
Says 'Merry Christmas to you all.'

And London shops on Christmas Eve
    Are strung with silver bells and flowers
As hurrying clerks the City leave
    To pigeon-haunted classic towers,
And marbled clouds go scudding by
The many-steepled London sky.

And girls in slacks remember Dad,
   And oafish louts remember Mum,
And sleepless children's hearts are glad,
   And Christmas-morning bells say 'Come!'
Even to shining ones who dwell
Safe in the Dorchester Hotel.

And is it true? And is it true,
   This most tremendous tale of all,
Seen in a stained-glass window's hue,
   A Baby in an ox's stall?
The Maker of the stars and sea
Become a Child on earth for me?

And is it true? For if it is,
   No loving fingers tying strings
Around those tissued fripperies,
   The sweet and silly Christmas things,
Bath salts and inexpensive scent
And hideous tie so kindly meant,

No love that in a family dwells
   No carolling in frosty air,
Nor all the steeple-shaking bells
   Can with this single Truth compare –
That God was Man in Palestine
And lives today in Bread and Wine.

THIS I BELIEVE

Contribution to a series hosted by Ed Murrow

CBS
Recording date 21 September 1953; broadcast date unknown
Producers: J. K. (Keith) Kyle and Barbara Halpern (BBC)

• • •

About five hundred words – it is very difficult to tell you in so few words why I was born, what I am meant to do on this earth and why I am a member of the Church of England which is the same as the Episcopalian Church of America and part of the great Anglican branch of the Catholic Church throughout the world.

'I believe in God the Father Almighty, Maker of Heaven and Earth, and in Jesus Christ His only begotten Son Our Lord,' as we say in the Creeds and I don't mind saying that I find this very hard to believe. I often ask myself, 'Can it really be true that the force that created these fingers of mine, which are holding the bit of paper from which I am reading to you, and also made the stars and the universe, cares in the least for me or what I say, let alone for the few remaining hairs on my bald head?' Yet if it isn't true and if we are all the result of a blind accident then I think I would want to cut my throat or rush off and indulge myself in every physical excess of which my body is capable. But then I am asked to believe something much more difficult and that is that God the Son, two thousand years ago, became Man in the womb of a Jewish virgin in Palestine. Eternity became part of time in this simple way. If it is true then everything in the world, whether you believe in Evolution or whether you don't, led up to that supreme moment of the birth of Christ and everything since that date leads away from it. How right are we to date everything before Christ BC and everything after him AD. I *want* to believe that Christ was God become Man. If that is so, then the Resurrection, the Sacraments of the Church, prayer and the Scriptures are comprehensible. If it is not true there is no point in everything; my own prayers that I have found answered, my own sins that have found me out, grace that comes to me in the Sacraments and particularly when I receive Holy Communion, are all delusions: the huge cathedrals, the many priests and ministers and millions of Anglicans, our Anglican monks and nuns as well as priests and ministers of other Churches and Chapels are all deluded.

But of course it is true. I have seen people die secure and believing that they are cared for and loved by God become Man, I have sat by deathbeds and I know that the Christian religion is true. I know that there is a world beyond this one that is all round us, that good and evil spirits are fighting here among us and that here we are born into this battle between good and evil – which is another way of saying that we were born in Original Sin. And I hope that when I die I shall understand more of the purpose of God. He hides much from me now because my finite brain would not be able to understand it.

I do not believe that human nature is capable of perfection on this earth, I do not believe that bigger is better, nor that doctors will ever be able to take death away from us. I believe that love and not atomic energy is the most powerful thing on earth. I know that my own Church is full of love – or charity as we call it – and I believe that it is the true Church. I know that Christ, who was Perfect Love, lives in it. I force my will to make me believe that God became Man nearly two thousand years ago. Lord, I believe. Help Thou mine unbelief.

INDEX

NOTE: Works by John Betjeman (JB) appear directly under title; works by others under author's name

John Betjeman titles available from John Murray

Collected Poems

Collected Poems made publishing history when it first appeared, and has now sold more than two million copies. This newly expanded edition incorporates all Betjeman's poems and, with a new introduction by Poet Laureate Andrew Motion, it is the definitive Betjeman companion.

9780719568503 | Paperback | £12.99

Tennis Whites and Teacakes

A treasure trove of Betjeman's poetry, journalism, radio and television programmes and private letters, revealing his lifetime love affair with England – a place of freckle-faced girls and Oxford toffs, steam trains and country churchyards.

9780719569043 | Paperback | £8.99

Trains and Buttered Toast

Broadcasting in the golden age of wireless, Betjeman was a national treasure for millions of devoted listeners. Here his eccentric, whimsical and homespun radio talks are collected in book form for the first time. From trains and buttered toast to hymn writing vicars and Regency terraces, he teaches us how to appreciate our heritage.

9780719561276 | Paperback | £7.99

'Betjeman was an original and a star' Daily Mail

The Best Loved Poems of John Betjeman

With a new foreword by Barry Humphries, this selection is a cherished reminder for those who already know Betjeman's poetry, and the perfect gift for those who still have in store the pleasure of discovery.

9780719568343 | Hardback | £9.99

Summoned by Bells

With a new foreword by Griff Rhys Jones, Betjeman's verse autobiography tells the story of his growth to early manhood: seaside holidays; meddling aunts; school bullies; an unexpected moment of religious awakening; then Oxford, and sparkling pen-portraits of the literary greats he met there. His unabashedly musical verse is poignant, comic, reverent, defiant, devoted and – always – full of feeling.

9780719522208 | Hardback | £10

Sweet Songs of Zion

John Betjeman's radio broadcasts on the subject of hymns and hymn writers were his swansong as a broadcaster. 'Hymns are the poems of the people,' Betjeman observes in his first talk, and he shows how this insight has been borne out over generations. Rich in anecdote, these timeless talks will inspire anyone who has a fondness for hymns and delights in Betjeman's unique voice.

9780340963883 | Paperback | £8.99

Order your copies now by calling Bookpoint on 01235 827720 or by visiting your local bookshop